# Mastering
## Management Skills

# Palgrave Master Series

Accounting
Accounting Skills
Advanced English Language
Advanced English Literature
Advanced Pure Mathematics
Arabic
Basic Management
Biology
British Politics
Business Administration
Business Communication
Business Environment
C Programming
C++ Programming
Chemistry
COBOL Programming
Communication
Computing
Counselling Skills
Customer Relations
Database Design
Delphi Programming
Desktop Publishing
Economic and Social History
Economics
Electrical Engineering
Electronic and Electrical
  Calculations
Electronics
English Grammar
English Language
English Literature
Fashion Buying and
  Merchandising Management
Fashion Styling
French

Geography
German
Global Information Systems
Human Resource Management
Information Technology
Internet
Italian
Java
Management Skills
Marketing
Mathematics
Microsoft Office
Microsoft Windows, Novell
  NetWare and UNIX
Modern British History
Modern European History
Modern US History
Modern World History
Networks
Organisational Behaviour
Pascal and Delphi Programming
Philosophy
Photography
Physics
Practical Criticism
Psychology
Shakespeare
Social Welfare
Sociology
Spanish
Statistics
Systems Analysis and Design
Theology
Visual Basic
World Religions

**Palgrave Master Series**
**Series Standing Order ISBN 0–333–69343–4**
*(outside North America only)*

You can receive future titles in this series as they are published by placing a standing order. Please contact your bookseller or, in case of difficulty, write to us at the address below with your name and address, the title of the series and the ISBN quoted above.

Customer Services Department. Macmillan Distribution Ltd
Houndmills, Basingstoke, Hampshire RG21 6XS, England

# **Mastering**
## Management Skills

Richard Pettinger

palgrave

First published 2001 by
PALGRAVE
Houndmills, Basingstoke, Hampshire RG21 6XS and
175 Fifth Avenue, New York, N.Y. 10010
Companies and representatives throughout the world

PALGRAVE is the new global academic imprint of
St. Martin's Press LLC Scholarly and Reference Division and
Palgrave Publishers Ltd (formerly Macmillan Press Ltd).

ISBN 0–333–92938–1

This book is printed on paper suitable for recycling and made from
fully managed and sustained forest sources.

A catalogue record for this book is available from the British Library.

10  9  8  7  6  5  4  3  2  1
10  09 08 07 06 05 04 03 02 01

Printed in Great Britain by Creative Print
and Design (Wales), Ebbw Vale

# ◪ Contents

# ▼ Preface

To this day many organisations are not quite sure what management is. Is it a necessary expense? An investment? In whose interests is it supposed to act? The shareholders? The staff? The customers? Even the usual answers to these questions – that management exists in order to achieve things through people, to cope with change and uncertainty, and to combine resources for profitable and successful activities: and that it has to act in everyone's interests and reconcile conflict of interests – bypass the core of all this, which is what managers and supervisors actually do, and how they do it.

There are no blueprints. These are neither available nor appropriate for managerial activity. Indeed, they are neither available nor appropriate for any trade or profession. Carpenters following precise plans still have to decide how best to execute these, and then choose the appropriate tools. Chefs following precise plans – menus – still have to decide which ingredients to use, and how to combine these to best effect. Doctors are faced with precise and definable sets of symptoms, but they still have to decide how best to treat these.

So it is with managers and supervisors in their own situations. The broad area of activity is more or less defined, whether it is marketing, medical support, diplomatic services or the dot.com revolution. However, in these and every other case, managers still have to pick, choose and use effectively the skills that they have. The approach taken in this book, therefore, has been to follow this line of reasoning – identifying more or less precise and universal contexts and activities required of managers and supervisors. The skills and expertise required are then analysed and identified, and the ways in which these are to be combined and implemented so that they are used to best effect are indicated and identified.

Chapter 1, the introduction, forms the basis on which the rest of the book is developed, identifying the fundamental skills required in order to be effective. Chapters 2 to 13 then deal, in turn, with the main management and supervisory issues: integrity; communication; presentation and advocacy; motivation; measuring performance; planning; decision making; problem solving; negotiating; health and safety; groups; and leadership.

The approach taken is to identify the nature and level of the skills required in each set of circumstances, and to illustrate with examples some of the ways in which these are applied, and the opportunities and consequences of using or not using them. Three key areas of management practice are identified – achieving things through people, coping with uncertainty and change, and establishing required and desired levels of performance. Each chapter ends with a summary based on these three areas. Except where indicated, the examples are all drawn from direct experience.

The book will have especial value to those on NEBSM, CMS, DMS and general 'Skills of Management' in-house organisation-directed management courses, including 'Graduates into Management Programmes'; those following professional studies courses – in particular, those of the Institute of Personnel and Development, the Institute of Management, and the Institute of Administrative Management; and chartered accountancy, secretarial and marketing foundation and professional studies programmes.

It will also be of value to those on HND/HNC courses in business and management studies, and in technical studies where there is a management element; and for those following undergraduate degree courses in engineering, technical and technological disciplines. Furthermore, it is a useful background reader for those following in-house NVQ programmes at Levels 3 or 4 that have a general management skills and applications element.

RICHARD PETTINGER

# ■ ∇ ▌ Introduction: managing in a changing environment

## Introduction

At a time when ever greater demands are placed on organisations to produce better results in an environment dominated by increased competition and technological change and advance, it is easy to lose sight of the key central issues and concerns of management that have to be implemented by all organisations, managers and supervisors in whatever sphere they operate. These are:

- achieving things through people
- coping with uncertainty and change
- the ability to identify, establish and develop required and desired levels of performance.

These areas are represented diagrammatically in Figure 1.1. This model is used as a form of summary at the end of each chapter in this book.

The skills required in order to be successful in each of these areas form the basis on which all effective managerial activity is built. Their precise application is driven in each set of circumstances by:

- organisational and environmental pressures
- the specific demands of the particular industrial, commercial or public-service sector in which individual managers and supervisors find themselves
- developing and improving products and services in terms of quality, volume and output; and organising, developing and improving overall resource utilisation
- working within resource constraints; optimising and maximising resource utilisation
- the demands of specific and universally required managerial and supervisory skills and activities in their particular context – integrity, leadership, communication, motivation, decision making, the ability to plan, working with groups, appraising and measuring performance, managing health and safety, negotiating and solving problems.

## Achieving things through people

All managers and supervisors deal with people – staff, peers, subordinates, customers, clients and suppliers. Some also have to deal with the media, shareholders and other organisational stakeholders (see Box 1.1).

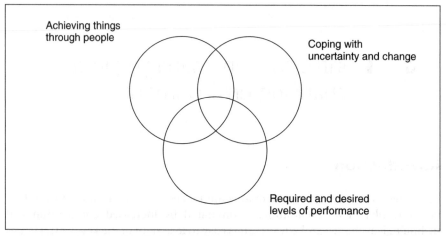

*Figure 1.1*   The interrelationship between the key areas of managerial skills, practice and expertise.

## Box 1.1   Stakeholders

A stakeholder is anyone who has a legitimate interest or concern in the success, effectiveness and performance of an organisation:

- *Staff:* who depend on the organisation for their livelihood; and on whom customers and clients depend for quality products and services.
- *Customers:* on whom the organisation depends for necessary and required levels of business.
- *Shareholders and backers:* those who invest resources – especially money – in the organisation, and who require a return on this investment.
- *Suppliers:* dependent on the organisation taking particular volumes (whether this supply is product, services, raw materials, components or information) for their own continuing existence.
- *Communities:* dependent on the organisation for product and service outputs; bringing prosperity to the communities; employment; and contribution to the community.
- *Media:* especially a concern to high-profile public and national institutions (national media); and high-profile local institutions (local media).
- *Competitors:* their concern as a stakeholder is when an organisation leaves the sector altogether (which may cause destabilisation); or when a new – especially large or dominant – player comes into the sector, which may change the entire set of rules by which it operates.

It is usual to identify:

- *the dominant stakeholder:* overwhelmingly the financial interest
- *the key stakeholders:* staff and customers

and to recognise the conflict inherent between the two – the drive for short-term share price rises (shareholders), that has to be reconciled with the need for long-term secure levels of business and activity (the concern of staff and customers).

The range of skills required as a prerequisite for this part of the managerial task are speaking, listening, hearing, reading and writing.

There is nothing remotely contentious in this – everyone has these skills to a greater or lesser extent. However, they do have to be developed so that they can be applied effectively to meet any set of circumstances that may arise in the manager's or supervisor's particular domain.

To this list may be added, therefore, the skills of sympathy, empathy and understanding; and the setting of basic standards of attitude, behaviour and performance.

## Sympathy, empathy and understanding

In managerial terms at least, sympathy, empathy and understanding are closely related. Skills in these areas include:

- Genuine recognition of the strength and validity of other people's points of view, priorities, aims and objectives, whether work-related or not.
- Genuine awareness and understanding of the strength of feelings of other people and the reasons (including prejudices) why they have them.
- Genuine awareness and understanding of the effects on others of particular organisational, managerial and individual actions – especially when these are negative (e.g., redundancies).
- Genuine awareness and understanding of the effects of work issues that are certain to cause personal hardship and non-work-related problems and stresses.

## Attitudes, behaviour and performance

In managerial terms, the setting of standards in these areas means har-monising the relationship between what is done and how it is done. This is so that:

- work is carried out; aims, objectives and deadlines are set and met; priorities are established and achieved
- a fundamental humanity is achieved, based on equality, respect, value and common decency so that the place of work is pleasant and harmonious as well as productive
- standards of attitude, behaviour and performance can either be *designed* or *emergent* (see Box 1.2).

# Box 1.2 Designed and emergent standards

*Designed*

This is where the manager or supervisor decides what standards are to be and then insists that they are followed. If this is to be truly effective in the long term these have to be:

- positive not negative
- capable of acceptance (or at least acquiescence) by all
- ethical and 'correct', with the principle of equality very strong.

*Emergent*

This is where the staff are allowed to set their own standards or where these are allowed to gradually emerge and develop informally. Invariably this is dangerous and divisive. For this to stand any chance of success, each of the conditions outlined above for designed standards must be present. Otherwise, managers and supervisors must nip any decline in standards in the bud and, if necessary, discipline those who would impose alternative ways of doing things. In general, emergent standards are invariably lower than what the situation actually demands, and are not therefore to be entertained.

---

— EXAMPLE —

During a quiet period in one of Boot's stores, a shop assistant, a girl of twenty, took a packet of sweets off one of the counters, broke it open, took out a sweet and put it in her mouth. She put the packet back on the counter. However, she was seen by a supervisor and marched off to the manager's office. The store personnel officer became involved and an investigation took place. The company rules were clear — anyone taking or using products off the store shelves was liable to dismissal. The case was proven, the girl admitted what she had done and she was dismissed.

Speaking afterwards of the case, the store manager said: To this day, I cannot understand why she didn't say that she had picked the sweet up off the floor, or that she had taken it out of her pocket. It would still have been serious — eating while in the customer area is strictly forbidden. But at the end of the day, we had no choice but to dismiss her, really for just being silly.

This is a useful example because it immediately raises the points:

- What standards are and what they are for. The clear implication here is that these rules were designed to reduce or eliminate pilfering by staff and to preserve the desired form of staff presentation to customers.
- 'We had no choice'. This is a constant refrain of managers and supervisors, and in many cases, it is fully justified. By this company's own rules and standards it was fully justified in this case. However, this example ought at least to begin to make people think, and to make them aware that there is a very fine balance to be struck between setting and maintaining high standards, and rigidity and intolerance.

## Managing by walking about

The required standards are best maintained through constant and continued interaction between staff, supervisors and managers. Everything else is reinforced in this way also – the rate of progress can be observed, real and potential problems can be observed or inferred early and remedial steps taken. It is also the cornerstone on which is built:

- staff, group, departmental and organisation identity
- real and perceived mutuality of interest
- positive, professional, organisational occupational relations.

Preaching perfection, all managers and supervisors ought to set aside enough time every day in order to walk the job, to talk and to listen. They should carry a notebook with them to record particular issues – and then to return to whoever raised them with feedback. This way also, managers and supervisors get to know their staff as people, and to understand their hopes, fears, ambitions and aspirations.

---

**EXAMPLE**

Liberace was a virtuoso pianist and popular entertainer. Between 1954 and his death in 1981, he worked constantly with large numbers of people – musicians, orchestras, dancers and other entertainers.

Speaking in May 2000, the comedian Bob Monkhouse said of him: 'Liberace made a point of getting to know everyone he worked with, asking about their family, wives, husbands and children. And whenever they met again – if it was years later – he would remember the person's name, and would ask after the husband, wife and children by name also. The effect on the morale of the company, the orchestra, the dancers, was fantastic. He never had a minute's trouble with anyone who worked either with him or for him.'

Source: *Reputations*, BBC2 (23 May 2000).

---

## Knowing and understanding people at work

Organisations and managers have tried for years to simplify the complexities involved in knowing and understanding people at work. On the one hand, this is fair enough – every individual is extremely complex. On the other, homespun wisdom, preconceived ideas, halo and horns effects are no substitute for identifying the skills, knowledge, attitudes and behaviour that are required to carry out work, and those that are brought by individuals into organisations (see Box 1.3).

There are no easy answers. Whether staff are required as recruits or for promotion, they have to be approached from the point of view that:

- provided that they are treated well and with value and respect, they will tend to respond positively
- if they are not treated well, with value and respect, they will respond primarily and overwhelmingly in their own self-interest.

## Box 1.3    Halo effects and homespun wisdom

*Higher education:* the principal of a higher education establishment in south-east England stated: 'I never smile at job candidates. I am always rude and abrupt with them. This puts them under pressure, and I can tell how they will react under pressure in the future'. (All it actually demonstrates is rudeness, ignorance and a lack of understanding.)

*Politics:* Margaret Thatcher stated: 'I usually make up my mind about someone in thirty seconds and rarely change it after that'. (She actually had 23 Cabinet reshuffles in her eleven years as Prime Minister.)

*Oil:* the human resource director of a UK oil company stated: 'After we have met candidates for promotion, we take them to a bar. We pay for all the drinks. Then we observe whether they can hold their drink or not. From this, we can tell their character'. (Analysis of the account produced after the November 1999 promotion exercise revealed that 92% of the expenditure had been on soft drinks.)

*Football:* Peter Swales, Chairman of Manchester City Football Club from 1970–1992, stated: 'When I'm choosing a manager, I always go for a top name, a media star or an ex-international player. That way, you are sure of getting the best'. (The Club had 19 managers in his 22 years in charge, and fell from being one of the UK's top football clubs into the second division.)

The onus is on the organisation, its managers and supervisors to create positive conditions. Beyond that, it is the responsibility of individual managers and supervisors to identify the skills, knowledge, attitudes, behaviour, quality and expertise that they require. Then – possibly in conjunction with human resource management specialists – selection processes can be set up that:

● test what can be tested
● prove what can be proven
● infer what can be inferred (see Box 1.4).

Such are the problems and pitfalls with a mechanistic approach to understanding people, that many organisations now tackle the issue from the reverse point of view. This involves organisational, departmental, divisional and functional approaches designed with the purpose of removing most of the factors that cause bad attitudes, behaviour and morale. This involves:

● Creating, maintaining and developing an open, visible and egalitarian style of management and strong corporate and group identity, underpinned by simple direct procedures applicable to everyone.

## Box 1.4  Testing people for work

Testing people for work is a multi-edged sword for the following reasons:

- Psychometric and other personality tests suffer from the fact that they reveal present personality characteristics and traits, not present and future work performance. At least twice, they have been described by the Institute of Personnel and Development as 'useless' for predicting performance. This does not prevent their being used in approximately 80% of managerial promotions and appointments.
- Skills and aptitude tests demonstrate capability, not willingness or commitment. However, at least if capability is present, attention can be concentrated on attitudes.
- Attitudes are impossible to prove. They can only be inferred from extensive observation, analysis and evaluation of the demeanour of the particular individual.

- Engaging in extensive and continuing induction; orientation; job, occupational and career training programmes, including reference to people's personal ambitions and aspirations; and giving full flexibility and variety of work in the situation.
- Paying and rewarding people well on the fundamental basis of equality not division.
- Avoiding quick-fix solutions to problems, especially large-scale redundancies.
- Concentrating everything, as far as possible, on demonstrably productive efforts; and making sure that 'the lousy jobs' – cleaning, tidying, photocopying, filing – are shared out as far as possible.

In return for all this, staff are required and expected to work as the company directs. It also means:

- early formation of positive attitudes, behaviour and identity which can then be developed and built on
- that extensive job, occupational and professional training are in place, the initial concentration is on attitudes and willingness to work
- problems with attitudes and willingness to work can be identified and remedied early, if necessary by asking people to leave.

This approach was first introduced into the UK by the Japanese companies Nissan, Honda, Sony, Sharp and Toyota, and they cite it as a major foundation stone of their high enduring product, quality, output values, and long-term commercial success. Similar approaches are also in place at EasyJet, Ryan Air, Body Shop, Virgin and some private schools and hospitals (see Box 1.5).

## Box 1.5  Knowing and understanding why people dislike and leave jobs

Knowing and understanding why people dislike and leave jobs is also a key managerial quality. It is the reverse of the coin indicated in the main text. The reasons may be positive or negative.

*Positive*

- Increased wages or salaries; better opportunities; more variety; entry into a new field; career change and development. If these opportunities are genuinely not available, organisations and their managers and supervisors have relatively little ability to influence them.
- Greater convenience, closeness to home, less trouble getting to work. Again, managers and organisations have little influence over these.

*Negative*

- Dishonesty and duplicity in dealings with the organisation and its managers and supervisors; bullying, victimisation and harassment.
- Bad or declining interpersonal, inter-professional and inter-occupational relationships.
- Scapegoating and blame.
- Boredom and lack of opportunities.

Organisations, managers and supervisors have overwhelming influence in all this. The negative conditions start with them. Losing staff for these reasons is also extremely expensive in terms of the costs involved in:

- the management and supervision of departure; and then the recruitment, selection, induction and orientation of the new starter
- lost production or service output during the leaving–starting period.


# Change

All managers and supervisors work in a constantly changing environment. This is driven by:

- *Stakeholder demands:* especially customers requiring ever-improving quality and standards of products and services, and shareholders and backers requiring ever-increasing returns on their investment.
- *Technological development:* affecting all social, economic and business activities, rendering many occupations obsolete and creating new ones.
- *Social change:* the changing of people's lives, bringing about ever-greater expectations and anticipations.

- *Expectational change:* in which changes may be expressed as from stability to a state of change itself, a state of flux, changes in occupation, training and profession, changes in markets and activities.

The importance of understanding, managing and directing this process is fundamental to its success. Rather than passive acceptance or allowing it to happen, managers and supervisors must assume responsibility for, and direction of, the process of change and the activities required to make it effective and successful.

It is first necessary to identify the barriers to effective change.

## Operational barriers

These include the following:

- *Location:* this is a barrier when, for whatever reason, it becomes impossible for the organisation to continue to operate in its current premises. Relocation has consequences for the resettlement of families, retraining and organisational development.
- *Tradition:* this is a problem where there has been a long history of overtly successful work in specific, well-understood and widely accepted ways.
- *Success (and perceived success):* if the organisation is known to be, or perceived to be, successful in current ways of doing things, then there is a resistance based on 'why change something that works?' This is especially true if there is a long history of stability and prosperity.
- *Failure:* this is a barrier to change where a given state of affairs has been allowed to persist for some time. The view is often taken by both the organisation and the staff concerned that this is 'one of those things', a necessary part of being involved in a given set of activities.
- *Technology:* this is a barrier for many reasons. It is often the driving force behind jobs, tasks, occupations and activities. Technological change causes trauma to those affected by the consequent need for job and occupation change, retraining, redeployment – and often redundancy. Technological changes may also themselves cause relocation. Technological changes cause changes to work patterns, expertise and methods.
- *Vested interests:* the needs for organisational change are resisted by those who are, or perceive themselves to be, at risk. Vested interests are found in all areas. They include senior managers threatened with the loss of functional authority; operational staff faced with occupational obsolescence; people in support functions; and those on promotional and career paths for whom the current order represents a clear and guaranteed passage to increased prosperity and influence.
- *Managerial:* the managerial barrier occurs where there is a divergence between the organisation's best interests, and the needs of individuals and groups of managers to preserve their own positions.
- *Bureaucracy:* this barrier occurs where patterns of order and control have grown up over long periods and is now no longer suitable to the proposed future direction.

- *Redundancy and redeployment:* this is a barrier in its own right because, in the current context, any proposed change carries redundancy and redeployment as possibilities, and because it has so often been the consequence of other changes.

## Behavioural barriers

The main behavioural barriers are as follows:

- *'It cannot be done' and 'there is no alternative':* these attitudes are barriers to confidence and understanding, based on a lack of true, full and accurate information, briefing, counselling and support concerning the matters that the organisation is proposing. These barriers may be used and manipulated by vested interests, occupational and managerial groups, and trade unions, in trying to defend the status quo. *'There is no alternative to the ways in which we do things now'* is a very popular defensive position.
- *Lack of clarity:* if organisations have not sorted out the basis of the changes that are proposed, neither staff nor customers will go along with them with any degree of confidence or understanding. Aims and objectives must be clearly stated and understood as the prerequisite to successful and effective change.
- *Fear and anxiety:* these are human responses to situations that are unknown or uncertain. They are a part of the initial response to any change that is proposed; if allowed to get out of hand, they can become an exercise in the devising and promulgation of hypothetical scenarios that could, in certain circumstances, become problems.
- *Perfection:* at the point at which change is proposed, suddenly everything concerning the status quo becomes 'perfect'. Anything that is proposed as an alternative has therefore to address this barrier.

It follows from this that all change requires individual and group briefing, consultation, counselling and support mechanisms to be put in place. These are for the purpose of reassurance, the continued addressing of lingering or persistent uncertainties, and providing the means of tackling individual problems and issues. Moreover, they provide behavioural messages that, in themselves, reflect the organisation's concern for, and commitment to, individuals and groups. The extent to which this approach is used reflects the importance attached by the organisation to basic stability, permanence and long-term continuity. It is also especially important from a 'humanitarian' point of view because so much change in the recent past has led to large-scale redundancies, and people are conditioned to think that every time changes are proposed they are in danger of losing their job.

## Production and service volume and quality

Achieving the required levels of product and service volume and quality is the primary concern of all managers and supervisors. This has to be carried out:

- through people
- in a changing environment.

There are two extreme views of this.

- *Theory X:* stating that people have to be bribed, bullied, cajoled and threatened into work; that they will avoid work and responsibility.
- *Theory Y:* that people seek responsibility, satisfaction, achievement, enhancement and development from their work; that they seek self-respect, self-worth and the respect, value and esteem of others in their work.

Supporters of Theory X cite banking, insurance, manufacturing, transport infrastructure and public services as examples of organisations that have a long-term history of success – or at least of non-failure – and that have been built up through largely coercive and confrontational management styles. It must be noted, however, that, without exception, all of these are sectors in which performance is declining.

Proponents of Theory Y argue that because this theory offers much closer alignment between work demands and human demands, long-term sustainable and profitable enterprise is much more likely to occur (though this is not guaranteed).

Managers and supervisors influence the workings of their department in the pursuit of productive output in one direction or the other. It is important to note that:

- any coercive approach must be underpinned by equality, fairness, openness and honesty if it is to stand any chance at all of success
- any humanitarian approach must also deliver the results required.

There are many ways in which the results of management influence can be measured and assessed.

## Production

Production may be measured as follows:

- Output per production line; output per production shift; output per location; output per piece of equipment/technical unit/item of technology; output per member of staff.
- Frequency/density of machine usage; operations as a percentage of total capacity/potential.
- Time taken for components to be assembled into finished products; assembly time for given operations; product to market time; speed of product turnover; speed of components turnover.
- Volume of supplier complaints; nature of supplier complaints; volume of customer complaints; nature of customer complaints.

## Sales

Sales performance is measured as follows:

- Total sales as a percentage of prospects, leads, calls, website hits; sales by location; sales by outlet.

- Sales per product; sales per product cluster; effect on total sales of introduction of new products/withdrawal of some products.
- Speed, frequency and density of sales – per product; per product cluster; per outlet; per location.
- Sales by format – retail; wholesale; mail order and catalogue; newspaper and magazine; website.
- Inter-relationship of sales formats – e.g., are people attracted to buy from shops because of the availability of catalogues, websites and newspaper outlets?
- Income per customer; income per location; income per region; nature of customer expenditure – cash, cheque, credit card, standing order, hire purchase, finance plans.
- Attraction/expenditure: the frequency and density with which window shoppers or website browsers become customers.

Initial and continuing identification of these measures indicate the following:

- the effectiveness and potential of the particular product or service
- efficiency and effectiveness of resource combination and utilisation
- where improvements might be made
- whether actual output and sales income measure up to required or desired output and sales income.

## Administration

Administration and support functions should also be assessed. This is carried out as follows:

- Length and purpose of administrative procedures; the extent to which procedures meet their stated purpose.
- Volume of administration and support functions as a percentage of total workload and activity.
- Numbers of staff in support functions; percentage of staff in support functions.
- Proportion of fixed costs allocated to administration; proportion of premises allocated to administration; levels of business required to cover administration.
- Cost of administration per member of staff; total cost of administration; total cost of administration as a proportion of total organisational cost.

## Human resource management

The points of inquiry here are:

- general staffing information: by occupation, age, gender, disability, ethnic origin, department, division, function, location.
- Balance of staff numbers in primary and support functions.
- Balance of managerial and non-managerial staff.
- Rates of absenteeism, sickness, labour turnover by occupation, department, division, location and function.

- Rates of accidents, illnesses and injuries by occupation, department, division, location and function.
- Rates of disputes, grievances, strikes by occupation, department, division, location and function.
- Rates of disciplinary activity – above all, the use of disciplinary procedures – by occupation, department, division, location and function (see Boxes 1.6 and 1.7).

## Box 1.6   Measuring production, quality, volume and output

Managers and supervisors must have the capability to choose appropriate measurement tools for their particular situation. These have then to be used in ways appropriate to the situation. This can only occur as the result of full situational knowledge and understanding, together with an assessment of the particular pressures present.

Levels of performance are therefore clearly a matter of managerial or supervisory judgement. There are no absolute right or wrong answers. However, it is always useful to bear the following in mind.

- Equipment, staff and technology standing idle are expensive.
- A relationship has to be drawn between production capability and sales potential.
- Costs and consequences of breakdowns and blockages in production and output (including computer crashes and information management problems) can be measured in terms of lost sales.
- The costs of managing and resolving customer and supplier complaints can be calculated.

In the particular matter of the management of people, the following can be calculated.

- Every percentage point of absenteeism effectively adds one person per hundred to the payroll.
- It is possible to isolate the cost of recruiting particular members of staff and set this against the costs of retention and motivation.
- It is possible to calculate the costs of disputes, grievances, accidents and injuries, and to relate this to the cost of prevention.
- It is possible to cost the number of staff required for, and the total staff cost of one unit of production, one unit sold, total production output and total sales volume.

Each of these measures can also be adapted to fit the requirements of, for example, retail activities, commercial services (e.g., travel insurance), e-commerce and telecommunications technology.

## Box 1.7 Induction

Many organisations still fail to carry out adequate and effective induction processes. This is because:

- managers and supervisors do not have the time
- managers and supervisors do not see the value
- the organisation does not insist that it is done.

Yet, both in terms of ensuring that the new starter or promoted individual understands the full operational demands of the situation and also that they have the desired attitudes and behavioural standards (see above), proper induction is essential.

The purpose of induction is to get the new or promoted member of staff as productive as possible, as quickly as possible.

An effective induction process consists of:

1. Setting the attitudes and standards of behaviour required, ensuring that all employees know what is expected of them, and that they conform to these expectations and requirements; it is most important that organisations, managers and supervisors assume absolute responsibility for this.
2. Job training and familiarisation, mainly to do with the ways of working required by the organisation, and including any technological, customer, supplier or colleague familiarisation necessary.
3. Establishing the required standards and methods of work, where to go for supplies and inputs (if required or desired), how to deal with customers and clients.
4. Introductions to the team, work colleagues and other key contacts as part of the process of gaining confidence, understanding and mutuality of interest, and for the development of effective enduring working relationships.
5. Familiarisation with the environment, premises, ways of working and particular obligations on the part of the employer; familiarisation and understanding of emergency procedures and other written rules and regulations.

Commitment to induction is vital. Taking time and trouble at the start of a new or promoted individual's period of employment reduces the opportunity for future misunderstandings and mistakes in product or service delivery. Many organisations go to much trouble to ensure that this is adequately and effectively completed – it is a key feature of the success of both Japanese and indigenous companies referred to above (page ••) that they spend extensive periods of time on induction and orientation before a new member of staff is allowed to work. Once they are allowed to work, however, the companies have complete confidence that the induction process has made them fully commercially productive.

## Financial aspects

Managerial and supervisory performance must also be understood in terms of the financial aspects present.

## Costs

The following costs must be distinguished:

- *Fixed Costs (FC):* these are the costs incurred whether or not any profitable or effective business is conducted. FC consist of capital charges, premises costs, staff costs and administrative, managerial and support function overheads.
- *Variable Costs (VC):* these are the costs incurred as the result of engaging in activities. They consist of raw materials, packaging, distribution costs, and telephone and information systems usage. The amount of each varies according to levels of activity.
- *Marginal Cost (MC):* this is the cost incurred by the production of one extra item of output. This reflects the extent to which the production or output capacity of the organisation may be extended without incurring additional fixed costs in the forms of investment in new plant, staff, equipment and technology.

    There comes a point at which the production of an extra item pushes the organisation to its total current capacity; and when the production of one more item requires this additional level of investment.
- *Opportunity Costs (OC):* this is what is foregone as the result of engaging in a given set of activities – by doing one thing, an organisation is not able to do other things.

### Specific points of inquiry

The following should be understood:

- Cost and income per employee: including all the employees of the particular organisation, department, division or function, not just those engaged in frontline or sharp-end operations.
- Income per customer: by which the total income over a period is measured against the number of customers; average income per customer.
- Income per product/service: either on an individual, product mix, or product range basis (see Figure 1.2).
- Income per outlet: by whatever terms the outlet is defined – the office, sales person, the department store, the catalogue, the airliner, the restaurant, the website.
- Income per square foot, per square metre, per product stack, per website, per website page: this can also be developed to cover individual premises and the total premises owned.
- Income per location: having regard to relative levels of prosperity, disposable income and propensity to spend at the local client base served; and again, this includes websites.

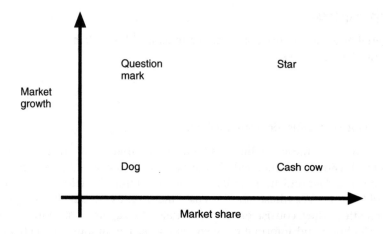

This is a convenient and simple way of parcelling up products and services to demonstrate where and how they are performing. The definitions are: *Cash cows:* high share of low growth market; today's breadwinners; the main source of income; *Stars:* high share of high growth market; today's and tomorrow's breadwinners from which future cash cows will come; normally need high investment and support to maintain position; *Question marks:* low share of high growth market; tomorrow's potential breadwinners; not all will succeed; *Dog:* low share of low growth market; normally only kept if they have some distinctive positive feature.

*Figure 1.2*   The 'Boston Group' matrix.

Each of these items may also be represented as profit (profit per employee, per customer, per outlet, per offering, per square metre).

Financial aspects should also be understood in the following terms:

- Volume sales: per product, per product cluster, per product range; volume sales per square foot, per outlet; volume sales per member of staff.
- Density/frequency of usage: this especially applies to sport; health care; hotel facilities; public transport; bank cash points; websites; commercial durables such as photocopiers.
- Longevity of usage: this can usefully be applied to private transport; public transport; consumer durables; clothing; white goods.
- Speed of turnover: which reflects the level of finance necessary to support the requirement to keep everything adequately stocked.

## Budgets

Budgets are most effective when they are concentrated on the allocation and use of variable costs – above all, materials and other resource usage in departments and functions that change according to the level of activities.

A budget is a plan (with sub-plans) constituting part of a process of knowing and controlling levels of expenditure in departments, divisions and functions, and on projects and initiatives. The purpose is to provide an accurate picture of where and how resources are being used, the speed and frequency of this, and to create the basis for making future judgements on the levels of finance required to remain effective.

A budget enables specific analysis and evaluation of the accuracy of the resource allocation process and variances from it, and the explanation of why particular resource targets and projections have not been met. Budgets provide definable and quantifiable bases for corrective action – whether this is to do with eliminating profligacy, or whether it relates to identifying parts of an organisation and particular activities that are being starved of resources essential for effective operations.

It is also essential to be able to reconcile control with flexibility and this, in turn, requires a measure of leeway so that, for example, productive initiatives that need small extra amounts of resource in order for them to be fully effective can be accommodated without, at the same time, calling into question the whole credibility of the budgeting process. All budgeting systems must be specifically designed to support the organisation's initiatives, operations, projects, staff and facilities.

---

┌─ EXAMPLE ─────────────────────────────────────────────────────────

When I took over Semco from my father it was a traditional company in every respect with a pyramid structure and a rule for every contingency. Today, our factory workers sometimes set their own production quota and even come in in their own time to meet them without prodding from management or overtime pay. They help pre-design the products, they make and formulate the marketing plans. Their bosses, for their part, can run our business units with extraordinary freedom, determining business strategy without interference from the top brass. They even set their own salaries with no strings. Then again, everyone will know what they are since all financial information at Semco is openly discussed. Our workers have unlimited access to our books (and we only keep one set). To show we are serious about this, Semco, with the labour unions that represent our workers, developed a course to teach everyone including messengers and cleaning people to read balance sheets and cashflow statements.

We don't have receptionists. We don't think they are necessary. We don't have secretaries either or personal assistants. We don't believe in cluttering the payroll with ungratifying dead-end jobs. Everyone at Semco, even top managers, fetch guests, stand over photocopiers, send faxes, type letters and use the phone. We have stripped away the unnecessary perks and privileges that feed the ego but hurt the balance sheet and distract everyone from the crucial corporate tasks of making, selling, billing and collecting.

We are not the only company to experiment with participative management. It's become a fad. But so many efforts of workplace democracy are just so much hot air.

The rewards have already been substantial. We have taken a company that was moribund and made it thrive, chiefly by refusing to squander our greatest resource, our people. Semco has grown six-fold despite withering recessions, staggering inflation and chaotic national economic policy. And we have had periods of up to 14 months in which not one worker has left us. We have a backlog of more than 2,000 job applications, hundreds from people who say that they would take any job just to be at Semco. In a poll of recent college graduates conducted by a leading Brazilian magazine, 25% of the men and 13% of the women said Semco was the company at which they most wanted to work.

Not long ago, the wife of one of our workers came to see a member of our human resources staff. She was puzzled about her husband's behaviour. He was not his usual grumpy autocratic self. The woman was worried. What, she wondered, were we doing to her husband?

We realised that as Semco had changed for the better, he had, too.

Source: Ricardo Semler (1993) *Maverick*, Free Press.

# Conclusions

This chapter has indicated the basic range of skills required by all managers and supervisors in every set of circumstances. To these must be added the ability to judge, analyse and evaluate, so that both the hard elements of performance, related to production, sales, income and output volumes, and the soft elements of performance, referring to the effectiveness of the human aspects of management, may be developed.

The key skills, therefore, lie in using communication, knowledge and information as carpenters use their tools – they have a range at their disposal, but which is used on a particular occasion, depends on the nature of the specific job in hand, whether delicate and intricate, large and overwhelming, or anything in between.

Managers have therefore to be able to choose and use these skills in accordance with the particular demands of the situation. The demands common to all managerial and supervisory situations form the basis of the rest of the chapters in this book.

QUESTIONS

1. Discuss the pros and cons of the Theory X and Theory Y approaches to the management of people and performance.
2. What are the lessons to be learned from Semco (Example, pages 17–18)? Which of these lessons could be most usefully learned by your organisation and why?
3. Construct and apply a set of production and financial measures to your own department. Why have you chosen these? What do they show? What do they not show?
4. Produce a one-week job training and organisational familiarisation plan (and induction programme) for your organisation or department with the specific aims of:
   a) achieving things through people
   b) establishing required levels of performance
   c) identifying and assessing any boundaries or barriers to progress and change.
   How does this differ from what you organisation does at present, and why?

# ⌄ 2 Integrity

## Introduction

At first sight, it may seem strange that 'integrity' is raised as an issue at all, let alone as a management skill that needs to be practised. However, to consider the opposite point of view, a lack of integrity in working relationships, whether with staff, customers, suppliers, or between departments, divisions and groups within organisations leads to:

- an overriding presumption of dishonesty rather than honesty in all dealings and relationships
- assumptions by staff that they are not being told the truth, or at least the full truth
- a general loss of morale and commitment – nobody likes to be in any situation, work-related or otherwise, that they know to be dishonest or unwholesome
- avoidance of responsibility or decision making – one of the main outputs of a fundamentally unwholesome working environment is the search for scapegoats and people to blame when mistakes are known, believed or perceived to have been made
- a broader mutual loss of confidence between the particular organisation, its customers, suppliers and communities, as the nature of internal relationships becomes apparent
- the development of siege mentalities among particular groups of staff (see Box 2.1).

## Box 2.1   Lack of integrity

The issue of integrity is not always clear cut. There are plenty of honest people working in dishonest organisations; and plenty of dishonest people working in overtly honest organisations. The following points should be noted:

- Very few of those working in the frontline of public services – teachers, nurses, social workers – believe politicians or senior managers when they say that new resources, technology or equipment are to be made available. This, however, does not prevent most teachers, nurses and social workers doing the best possible job under extremely difficult and limiting circumstances.

- Those working directly on production or sales in the private sector fully understand that it is they who will lose their jobs if those responsible for the policy, direction and long-term well-being of their organisations make mistakes. This also does not prevent them from committing themselves to the needs of the task or job in hand, or the needs of particular customers and clients.
- Those who work on information, construction or engineering projects know that once the work is completed, they will not necessarily have any further work to go on to with the same organisation – whatever the contractor or client may say. This again, does not prevent the great majority from committing themselves to the job in hand; though those that receive fresh job offers during the course of project work increasingly view these prospects from their own partial points of view, rather than a commitment to see the existing job through.
- Many people, especially small companies and sole traders, find themselves carrying out work at prices that barely cover costs. This is done in the anticipation – or hope – that their customers and clients will be prepared to pay more for future work. In these situations, the customer or client is both willing and able to take advantage of the supplier's perceived or actual need to drop prices just in order to gain work. These small companies fully understand what is happening – yet it does not prevent them doing an excellent job anyway.

In each of these examples, a fundamental lack of integrity is acknowledged. However, the following points require understanding:

- In public services, the shortage of frontline staff is acute and certain to get worse.
- In commercial services and industry, there are serious problems of retention and loyalty, and companies are consequently having to increase commitment and expenditure on recruitment, selection, induction and training, and also on the use of agency staff.
- In project work, those with scarce or desirable skills can command high fees and salaries; while those with general skills are able to change employers at will.
- Smaller companies are becoming increasingly wary of working at non-commercial rates as customers and clients show no reciprocal loyalty or interest, but simply shop around anyway.

For each of these cases, there is a clear common lesson: that both the work and the working relationship would be much more effective if a greater measure of integrity was present.

Each of these factors is avoided only if the organisation overall, and its managers and supervisors, commit themselves to a fundamental honesty in all aspects of the working relationship. Where organisations are not prepared to do this, managers and supervisors can at least take steps to ensure that their own part of the house is in order. They do this through a personal and professional commitment to dealing with their own people in an honest and straightforward way. The skills required to do this are:

- managing loyalty, including managing conflicting and divided loyalties
- creating a good quality of working life, including the rewards available
- personal and professional visibility and accessibility
- having, and showing, commitment, enthusiasm and energy
- having the ability to deal with sensitive issues.

## Loyalty

Those occupying managerial and supervisory positions must recognise the following range of loyalties:

- loyalty to oneself
- loyalty to staff
- loyalty to the organisation
- loyalty to superiors
- loyalty to department, division or functional output
- loyalty to customers
- loyalty to suppliers
- loyalty to colleagues.

They must recognise that the following loyalties are also legitimate; and that, from time to time, they bring legitimate pressures into the workplace:

- loyalty to family and home
- loyalty to outside interests, non-work groups, clubs and societies; and also to personal outside interests and friends.

This is further compounded by the following legitimate loyalties:

- organisational and occupational loyalties to the past, to the present, and to the future
- personal and professional loyalties to the present and the future
- loyalty based on group, occupational, and organisational integrity, culture and ethos.

These are the critical foundation stones on which successful professional, occupational and personal relations are built. The more that these are present, the greater the inherent quality of the working and operational relationship. Where they are not all present, or where they are not capable of being reconciled, it is essential:

- to recognise the fact
- to recognise that, from time to time, problems are certain to arise as the result
- to take steps to build loyalty on each front so far as this is possible (see Box 2.2).

## Box 2.2 Loyalty

Building loyalty is not always possible, at least not on all the counts indicated above. For example, it is entirely unreasonable to expect loyalty to an organisation when there have been rounds of redundancies, or when top managers have been awarded pay rises at the expense of frontline staff. Often, the best that managers and supervisors can hope for in these situations, is a personal, professional and occupational loyalty from their staff within the confines of the particular department or group.

In some cases, even this is not possible. Even when particular managers or supervisors are known to be honest and trustworthy, they nevertheless are identified as being a part of 'the management', and therefore not to be taken seriously or believed regarding anything to do with the organisation or its works.

At this point, it is tempting to say: 'Well, why bother then?' There are three reasons:

- loyalty has to be earned and this is only possible if it is first given out by those in authority
- removal of loyalty and trustworthiness only makes even a bad situation worse
- individual managers and supervisors who are disloyal or dishonest gain an individual, as well as an organisational and collective, reputation for this.

Loyalty is built on value, trust, respect, a positive identity and delivery.

In order to gain trust, managers and supervisors have to be trustworthy and to demonstrate this. In order to gain respect, respect must be shown. This especially applies in dealings with subordinate and junior staff. It is demonstrated in all aspects of the management or supervisory task – dealings with people, allocation of work, setting and managing deadlines, acceptable volumes and quality of work.

A positive identity is generated through recognising and accepting the strengths and weaknesses of the working situation, and working with a positive attitude within them – operating as far as possible to the strengths and minimising, as far as possible, the weaknesses or negative aspects. For example, the best managers and supervisors in the situations referred to in Box 2.1 get good enduring work out of their people by doing just this.

Delivery concerns results – the ability to achieve that which was ordered or requested, in the right volume and quality, to the required time scale, in the correct ways, and within resource and other constraints. Staff respond to this.

They also respond where praise and rewards for achievements are shared equally. When mistakes are made, or deadlines are not met, loyalty is nevertheless enhanced if a full and open inquiry is held. The point at which mistakes were made can be identified and rectified without blame being apportioned.

This again reinforces the point (see Chapter 1) that praise is shared and blame accepted as part of the managerial task.

## Divided loyalties

As stated above, in addition to the workplace, people have legitimate loyalties to family, friends, clubs, societies, interests and their life outside work. Orders of priority become apparent, and these vary between individuals. For example, a single person at the beginning of a career path is likely to place work a lot higher on the list than someone who has a partner and children; especially when the partner or child is taken ill. Part of the manager's role is to know their staff well enough to understand exactly where the priorities of each member lie.

Divided loyalties become a problem when staff loyalties are 'illegitimate' – when they subscribe, for example, to counterproductive group pressures or 'canteen cultures'. These have to be tackled, first by recognising their existence; and secondly, by identifying the specific standards, attitudes and behaviour that are not acceptable, and tackling each in turn. Such problems invariably arise when the staff have no reason to show any loyalty to the organisation, or manager or supervisor.

If there is nothing that can be done, then the manager or supervisor has to be able to remove the main outputs of this form of unacceptable divided loyalty – the self-regulating, self-serving bonds of loyalty and activity that have been superimposed by the 'canteen culture'. Where present, it is high on the operational and managerial priority list, and requires constant attention if the damage that it can cause is to be minimised.

# Quality of working life and environment

The quality of working life and environment is a major reflection of the integrity of working relationships. Paying attention to this takes the form of:

- a full assessment of the working environment, its strengths, weaknesses and shortcomings
- a full assessment of the expectations of individuals and groups and what the require to do their jobs properly and effectively
- prioritising those areas that require attention
- identifying those factors inside and outside the control of those involved.

If people are required to work in untidy, dirty, damp or drafty conditions, then there needs to be a good, honest and acceptable reason for this. People will not otherwise respect such an environment, and it is likely to deteriorate further. This always has an adverse effect on the quality of performance. The manager's role here lies in:

- assessing what can be done immediately, and organising people to do it
- scheduling any small works that need to be carried out

- recognising and acting upon the extent of their authority (e.g., in budgeting or authorising expenditure or activity to improve the quality of the working environment)
- lobbying for additional resources and activities for those matters outside their direct remit (see Chapter 7).

If none of this is possible, then managers need to recognise that they will have to deal with problems of absenteeism, turnover, inadequate performance and proliferation of disputes and grievances as a direct consequence. Whatever is possible should therefore clearly be undertaken as a priority. Nobody likes working in bad conditions.

## Extremes of heat, noise and cold

Extremes of heat, noise and cold are a separate issue as there are invariably overwhelming operational reasons why such conditions exist. In these cases, problems are overcome through providing the necessary protective clothing and equipment, and scheduling breaks away from the extremes. These situations are, in any case, tightly regulated. The main managerial and supervisory skill here is to ensure that protective clothing and equipment are worn and used at all times, and that anyone who does not comply is made to do so. In this way, the conditions are addressed and the integrity of the working relationship is maintained.

## Dirty working

Dirty working exists in most sectors to a greater or lesser extent; and this extent is not always obvious. For example, those handling cash, printed material, clothing and plastics always get dirty; as do people working in health, education and social services.

Whatever the situation, the role of the manager is to recognise the extent to which 'dirty working' exists, and to take steps to minimise its effects. People are entitled to basic standards of cleanliness and hygiene. If, for any reason, that is not possible (e.g., they do not have the authority, or the senior management fail to address the issue) then it is essential to recognise that this will bring other problems (see Box 2.3).

## Box 2.3   Dirty working

The following examples all came to light in the first three months of the year 2000 in the town of Folkestone, Kent:

- The town branch of one of the High Street banks has had great difficulty in retaining junior staff because the washing facilities are not adequate.
- A contract printer on the outskirts of the same town has lost two members of staff, whom it refused to compensate for having their own clothes ruined by ink and chemical spills.

- A medium-sized building contractor lost staff to a competitor, because the latter firm provided better on-site toilet, washing and restroom facilities.
- A department store in the town caused a wave of staff unrest because it started to ration the amount of soap available in the staff washrooms.

These situation are clearly plain silly. So long as adequate provision – whether uniforms, washing facilities, overalls, barrier creams – is present, there is nothing to worry about. Yet each of these companies – that otherwise pay extremely good wages and offer otherwise good working conditions – have incurred recruitment, induction and familiarisation costs. This is, in part, because they failed to recognise the value of these parts of the working environment, their effect on the perceived integrity of the working relationship, and the respect and value accorded to the staff.

## Functional comfort

Good quality of working life and environment is based on functional comfort. Functional comfort involves the provision of the correct equipment and clothing as stated above. It requires attention to health and safety (see Chapter 11). It further requires attention to individual's and group's preferred and required ways of working, though clearly this must never become an excuse for organisational, managerial or staff indulgence. Both organisations and individuals who overspend on their trappings and furnishings come to be treated with contempt similar to that where insufficient attention is paid.

Basic human needs do, however, need to be addressed. Again, there is a problem where this does not occur. Again, it goes to the core of the integrity of the working relationship.

Problems also occur where:

- functional staff are accommodated in bad working conditions when senior staff are accommodated in luxury
- senior staff are known, believed or perceived to overspend on their own office furnishings, expenses, personal assistants and advisors, consultants; and also on cars, travel and other expenses
- there are different standards of discipline and grievance for different categories of staff; and again, this invariably favours senior and other non-frontline staff at the expense of those who make, produce and sell
- other benefits – e.g., pension scheme, holidays, flexitime – are available to some categories of staff but not to others (see Box 2.4)
- senior staff and strong personalities are known, believed or perceived to be able to get away with personal dominance; in the worst cases this leads to bullying, victimisation, discrimination and harassment.

## Box 2.4   Inequalities, integrity, morale: the consequences

Each of the following occurred in 1999 and 2000:

- A large oil company flew 33 senior managers to luxury accommodation in the Seychelles where they spent a week discussing job cuts, staff reorganisations, and pay freezes for those working in the oil fields. Similarly, senior officials of a UK government department booked themselves into 5-star accommodation on the outskirts of London to discuss cuts in frontline services.
- A higher education college in south-east England undertook extensive refurbishing work on senior management offices; the college already had a budget deficit of £2 million; having spent a further £750,000 on the refurbishment, it was required to announce 33 redundancies and the closure of two departments.
- A telesales company operating out of a city to the north of London monitors all incoming and outgoing calls. It announced that because of static or declining productivity on the part of the telesales staff, there would be no pay rise for any of them for a period of 18 months at least. The company's top 73 managers then awarded themselves performance-related bonuses of 25% of salary each.

---

┌─ EXAMPLE ─────────────────────────────────────────────

The Dagenham plant of Ford UK achieves an output of 55 cars per worker per annum. While great strides in productivity have been taken over the past decade (in 1990 the output was 38 cars per worker per annum), this is described by the parent company in the USA as 'unacceptable'.

To remedy this, staff have been threatened with redundancy and even the closure of the plant. It has also become apparent that there is a strong culture of bullying and racism within the plant. This came to light in 1999 when a group of production workers from the Asian community took their grievances to the company head office in the USA. Ford UK responded by stating that the problem had only recently come to light. This was contradicted by statements from both individual workers and their trade unions that racism had been institutionalised for many years. One trade union official stated that the matter reached back as far as the mid 1970s, when increases in employment from the local Asian community first took place. The problem was exacerbated by a survey of the ethnic mix of senior and middle management at the Dagenham plant. This demonstrated that those in positions of authority came overwhelmingly from the white community.

The company's present attitudes are unlikely to resolve the productivity problems. This contrasts strongly with Nissan UK, which is located in Washington, Tyne-and-Wear. The company produces 105 cars per worker per annum. Because it has taken steps to avoid a management style that might call into question the whole integrity of the working relationship, and because problems of both racism and output are identified early and addressed immediately they become apparent, such problems do not, in fact, exist. The basic integrity of the working relationship and general quality of working life are also enhanced. Viewed from this standpoint, integrity is extremely cost effective and profitable.

## Rewards

It is next necessary to recognise the importance of reward packages in creating loyalty and integrity. These are destroyed where those at the top of the organisation are known, believed or perceived to benefit at the expense of those at the bottom.

The greater the transparency in the design and implementation of pay scales and other payments (e.g., bonuses, commissions and performance-related pay) and benefits (e.g., holiday allowances, expenses, pensions), the greater the reinforcement of the principle of integrity. Where this transparency is not present, again it calls into question the whole integrity of the working relationship.

Problems also arise with underpayment and overpayment.

### Underpayment

Underpayment is not only a problem because it causes economic hardship, but also because it represents a lack of value and respect. In many cases – the financial industry, management consultancy, direct sales, industrial purchasing and supply – both frontline and support or back office staff are well paid in volume terms, but the level of pay nevertheless does not reflect the full contribution made.

### Overpayment

Overpayment, where people are paid in excess of their contribution, comes in the following main forms:

- in-built overtime, in which those involved do little or no effective work during normal hours in order to preserve the certainty of premium-rate payment.
- skimming, in which results are predictable with a fair degree of certainty, at least in the short- to medium-term, and rewards in-built. This occurs in many parts of financial services where operations, and therefore results, are largely generated by computer programmes. It also occurs in some point-of-sale activities where the representative or salesperson effectively acts as accounts servicer or client liaison operator, rather than as a business developer.
- top salaries, in which shareholder-appointed chairmen, chief executive officers, directors and senior managers receive payments in excess of their contribution to the organisation's performance. This occurs in all sectors; however, it does not apply to self-started international companies (e.g., Richard Branson at Virgin, Gordon and Anita Roddick at Body Shop, Martha Lane Fox at Lastminute.com) (see Box 2.5).

- paying high salaries, wages or fees because of a known, believed or perceived reputation or expertise in particular individuals. The most high-profile examples are sports, film, entertainment and media stars; it is also prevalent in the areas of management consultancy, stockbroking, e-business and project management services. It causes great resentment among 'those who also serve'. When they feel able, it leads to lobbying by other staff for steps to be taken to bring them into line with the new 'star'.

The problem again for managers and supervisors is to recognise the extent to which each of these aspects is present. They then need to be able to assess their own ability to do something about it; or if they have no influence in the matter, they need to recognise that problems are certain to occur.

## Box 2.5 The top–bottom divide

Another way of looking at under- and overpayment is through the top–bottom divide or top–bottom differential.

The genesis for this was studies carried out by Richard Wilkinson in 1998. These studies were concerned primarily with health care. The hypothesis was that health care problems were at their greatest in those parts of the world where the differences in income between rich and poor were also at their greatest.

This led business researchers to adapt the hypothesis to try and establish whether a similar connection could be made between company profitability and effectiveness, and the extent of disparity between top and bottom salaries. The work was carried out in 1995 and 1996 at the University of Indiana, USA. The main conclusions were that:

- In the developed world, long-term profitability, product performance, customer service, creativity and innovation, were at their greatest where the salaries of those at the top of the organisation were no more than eight times the size of the salaries of those at the bottom of the organisation.
- Companies that sustained a salary differential of between 30 and 50 were able to do so only because there was some in-built factor in their product or service that meant that the market was largely captive. Overwhelmingly, this was found to occur in the gas, electricity, water, telecommunications and transport sectors.
- The overwhelming majority of companies that had increased their salary differentials had seen profits, reputation and customer numbers fall exactly at the time that the differential was being increased.

Source: R. Wilkinson (1998) *Unhealthy Societies*, Routledge.

# Honesty, visibility and accessibility

Everybody requires – and likes to have – access to their boss. It is a human, as well as an occupational or professional need. Managers and supervisors, therefore, need to make themselves physically available to their people. It is essential to commit to at least one of the following.

- *Total open access:* a genuine open-door policy, meaning that staff can reach the manager or supervisor for any reason, at any time.
- *Stated times of open access:* at which the manager or supervisor is available; and that are blocked out of the working week and are not available for anything else except crises and emergencies.
- *Managing by walking about (MBWA):* in which operational managers or supervisors physically walk the department, meeting their staff, identifying problems and issues; and also identifying and reinforcing areas where things are going particularly well.
- *Staff meetings and gatherings:* at least once a week, even if only for ten minutes or so; many companies have staff clusters at the beginning or end of every day on this basis. More formalised gatherings are also required at least once a month (see Box 2.6).

## Box 2.6    Staff meetings and gatherings: examples

The frequency and value of these meetings – and indeed of any approach to visibility – reinforces the openness, and therefore integrity, of the working relationship. Different organisations have different approaches; however, the output is always the same. For example:

- A high-prestige ladies fashion shop in the west end of London requires its entire staff to attend a 20-minute meeting every morning. These meetings take place without fail, and if there is nothing specific to discuss, staff are required to remain in the room and chat socially with each other. The store manager is quite adamant of the value of the meetings. She says: 'In fact, there is very seldom any occasion on which no operational or commercial matters are raised. They may also become apparent during the course of social chit-chat. Moreover, it gives us the opportunity to identify and, where possible, support domestic problems and issues that may affect people's availability or commitment for work. And, we never have any problems scheduling or prioritising people's holidays!'
- An advertising agency, also in the west end of London, depends heavily on meetings for its commercial success. Staff cluster groups, creativity groups, brainstorming, and meetings with clients that take place on the premises are always carried out standing up. No refreshments are made available. The agency's senior partner again is quite clear of the value: 'If we sat everybody down for meetings and provided refreshments, nothing would ever get done. By doing things this way, everyone

concentrates on the matter in hand. I trust them to raise points that are important. If we do need to sit down and discuss things, we go off site. And our monthly staff meetings are always conducted off site.'

Conversely, the development of flexible working increasingly means that many people are now working in isolation from the organisations that employ them. This has always been a problem for field sales staff. It is now, however, becoming an increasing issue for administrative staff and those in specialist functions who, because of the availability of technology, can now work from home or from business centres. It is necessary from time to time to gather people together who work in this way. When this happens, time should be built-in to discuss general problems and issues, and also to ensure that the staff are able to get to know each other on a social and personal, as well as professional, level.

Where these do not, or for whatever reason cannot, take place, managers have to recognise that:

- people will work as they themselves see fit
- people will assume that whatever they do is at least satisfactory
- people will tend to pursue their own agenda, often at the expense of that of the department or organisation
- groups will set their own standards and norms, that may, or may not, be compatible with those of the organisation.

Most insidiously, it creates an environment in which 'canteen cultures', bullying, victimisation and harassment flourish.

## Variations on the theme

Senior and regional managers and those with more diverse responsibilities will not be able to 'walk the job' on a regular basis. They must ensure that their deputies do so; and when they visit outlying parts of their empire, they need to make sure that time is set aside for social, as well as professional and occupational, meetings with their people.

- Mark McCormack of IMG, the public relations and representation company, practices managing by ringing around. His view is that even though his people work far from home for weeks or months at a time, they still need to hear from the person in charge. He therefore makes a point of telephoning each of his staff at least once a week.
- E-mail has revolutionised the ease by which people working in remote and inaccessible locations can keep in touch, and in these cases, it is a great bonus. It is also an excellent means of promulgating the same information extremely quickly and accurately. Integrity is compromised, however when it is used as a substitute for, rather than complementary to, face-to-face communication. Indeed, it simply becomes the very latest means of circulating memoranda and other official documents.

# Commitment, enthusiasm and energy

Positive expressions of commitment, enthusiasm and energy exude integrity. Nobody can expect these qualities, from their people if they are not prepared to demonstrate them themselves.

Commitment, enthusiasm and energy are required for every aspect of the manager's sphere of influence and activity, not just in terms of the end results. It is always apparent when a manager's heart is not in the work or part of the work.

---

EXAMPLE

Danny Murphy opened *The Prince of Wales* nightclub in Charlottetown, Prince Edward Island, Canada, in 1986. Though the provincial capital, Charlottetown is a small town (population 20,000) and there was a lot of local opposition. The community believed that the club would bring the worst forms of behaviour associated with nightclubs elsewhere in the world – especially drunkenness, fighting, drugs and prostitution. The town prided itself on having none of these problems.

Danny Murphy gave an undertaking that none of these would occur. The club opened, and continues to open, five afternoons and five evenings per week. Whenever it is open, either Danny Murphy or one of his managers is always on the public floor helping to handle customer needs and identifying early potential problems.

The club was one of the first in Canada to subsidise the 'driver's soft drinks' scheme. Sponsored by Pepsi Cola, this enabled one member of a nightclub party to receive free soft drinks for the evening on the grounds that he or she then drives their friends home.

Attention to this, and to every detail, is seen as critical to ensuring the continued high standards of the club, and its acceptability in the community. Murphy himself has become a successful and respected member of the community; and of the 22 people employed at the club when it first opened, 17 are still there 15 years later. Murphy himself says: 'If there is nothing else for me to do, I collect empty cups, glasses and plates, clean the toilets, empty the ashtrays, pick things up, and sweep the floors. I love doing this. It keeps me in touch with the customers and it shows that we all care about the general state of the club. We have something special here and we do not want to lose it.'

He might also have added that he therefore never puts himself in the position of asking people to do things that he himself is not prepared to do.

---

Those parts of the organisation or work that the manager neglects, the staff invariably also neglect. Those tasks given a low profile or priority by managers are given the same treatment by staff – or else carried out by perceived inferior or lower status staff. Moreover, the work is carried out without commitment, enthusiasm or energy. This is detrimental to total performance. If allowed to persist over the medium- to long-term, a pedestrian or sedate attitude and approach to work leads to those involved slipping into a sedate and complacent working life. It is not their fault – they have been shown this way of doing things and it has been endorsed by the failure of the manager to do anything about it. It is also always traumatic to those involved when someone requires swift or sudden changes, or otherwise breaks up this complacent state of affairs.

## Sensitivity

Showing sensitivity to the needs of others is a mark of respect and value, and therefore integrity. It is neither soft nor submissive; rather the opposite, it means treating each person, problem, crisis or issue on its own merits and resolving each in a clear and direct way.

The starting point for the manager has to be that if someone raises a point then they have considered it important enough to bring it to the manager's attention – it is therefore deserving of a considered answer (see Box 2.7).

### Box 2.7  Trivia

The stock responses to the issue of management 'sensitivity' are as follows:

- managers are not nursemaids or nannies
- the staff do not want wrapping in cotton wool
- they will be demanding flowers on the drinks machine next
- this is a place of work, not a doctor's surgery.

Each of these is a defensive response based on ignorance, a lack of capability in the area, or willingness to tackle the issues raised. For example:

- *Nursemaids and nannies:* this precise phrase was used by the Townsend Thoresen car ferry company operating out of Dover, France and Belgium in December 1986 in response to requests from ships' officers for greater attention to on-board safety. Three months later, the company's ship, *The Herald of Free Enterprise*, set sail from Zeebrugge with its bow doors open, and capsized with the loss of 192 lives.
- *Cotton wool:* this phrase was used at the Redcar plant of British Steel in 1996, again in response to complaints from staff that they were not being fully protected from extremes of heat when they were working in the furnace cooling towers. In February 1997, a member of staff suffered 70% scalding burns to his skin, in spite of his protective clothing, when the locomotive he was driving stalled in a cloud of boiling steam.
- *Flowers on the drinks machine:* this is a double-edged approach. If staff genuinely had nothing else to request, then this should cause managers and supervisors to ensure that they carry on what they are doing as clearly they are doing it well. Conversely, it may be that the staff have much deeper issues to raise. The only way that they can see of breaking into other problem areas, is to raise something as overtly frivolous or non-contentious as this.

- *The doctor's surgery:* counselling is a key part of the manager's job and it is raised in more detail and different contexts in later chapters (Chapters 5, 8, 10, 11, 13, 14). The manager's role as counsellor is fourfold: listening to, and resolving, work-related issues; insisting that people are referred on for specialist treatment in specific cases (e.g., for stress, drink, drugs problems); supporting (but not carrying) people through personal difficulties and tragedies (e.g., divorce, bereavement); and arbitrating in cases of personality, professional or occupational clash within the department. To do this effectively, it is essential that managers know the extent of their capability and authority, the actions that they can and cannot take, and the consequences of those actions.

On the rare occasions when someone is genuinely making frivolous requests or wasting the manager's time, they need to be told so, directly and assertively.

Sensitivity also means respecting confidences and preserving confidentiality. Something that is told in confidence must remain in confidence. Even where serious offences – e.g., bullying, theft, fraud, assault – have been notified by a member of staff who wishes to remain anonymous, there is nothing to prevent managers investigating the matter as if they themselves had discovered it. And once the matter is out in the open, people can normally be persuaded to put their names to statements.

Again, it is necessary to recognise the effects of the converse of having and using sensitivity. Nobody likes, trusts or respects anyone who breaks confidences, or who becomes known for not treating on their own merits legitimate requests or issues raised by staff.

# Conclusions

The purpose of this chapter has been to identify some universal aspects of management and supervision, and consider them from the point of view of their effects, both positive and negative, on working relationships, and therefore output. When viewed in this way, it becomes clear that integrity, loyalty, respect and trust are absolute qualities. They are also, therefore, skills of management in that:

- when present, no working situation is ever completely negative, whatever the pressures
- when absent, no working relationship is ever completely positive or fully developed, whatever the rewards
- when absent, managers and supervisors are certain to face increased absenteeism, turnover, discipline problems, grievance and dispute problems, as well as declining productivity and output.

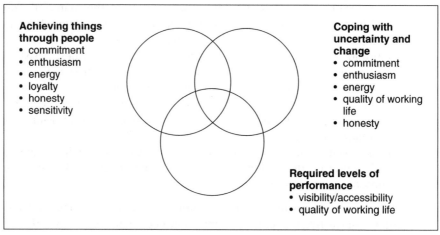

*Figure 2.1* Chapter and model summary.

The demonstration of integrity in these ways therefore becomes a set of skills that all those in managerial and supervisory positions must accept and develop. Whatever the state of the integrity of the rest of the organisation, at least all those involved in the particular team or department always know where they stand. Moreover, any stresses or strains can be dealt with on an open basis.

Finally, it is important to note that managers and supervisors do not necessarily receive credit or recognition for committing themselves to a management style based on integrity. Once it is apparent, staff accept it as an act of fundamental humanity, of ordinary common decency. However, if it is ever called into question or destroyed, serious problems always occur, and it takes a very long time to rebuild broken trust, loyalty and integrity.

Using the Model referred to at the start of Chapter 1, the material in this chapter is summarised in Figure 2.1.

QUESTIONS

1. How can issues of bonuses and rewards be resolved to the satisfaction of all concerned without affecting integrity?

2. Identify those barriers to trust that exist in your department, place of work, or place of study. What actions should be taken by those responsible to overcome these? How soon would you expect to see results; and what form would you expect these results to take?

3. How should Ford UK deal with the problems of productivity and racism outlined on page 26?

4. 'I get excellent results out of my team; but I am a bully and I don't care who knows it.' Discuss this statement (made recently by a senior manager in the financial services industry). What, in your view, could, and should, be done to make him change his attitude?

5. The manager of a call centre asks you to resolve a problem. His staff are paid £5 per hour. They work in rows of cubicles. Every call is monitored by a supervisory

telephone listening system and the workplace is under constant scrutiny from security cameras. The manager has been told that he faces losing a lot of staff if he does not quickly pay attention to the 'quality of working life'.

Identify the actions that you would take to help him resolve this problem. On the basis of what you have been told, which aspects of the quality of the working environment need immediate attention and why?

# ⓜ **3** Communication

## Introduction

Effective communication is vital for the successful functioning of any organisation. All organisations normally establish:

- formal methods, mechanisms and processes; vertical and lateral lines and channels of communication to provide the means by which facts, ideas, proposals, emotions, feelings, opinions and problems can be exchanged;
- informal mechanisms, based on the desired and adopted management style, and giving greater scope for all round discussion, which is more likely to give early indications of potential problems, crises, and more generally, people's hopes, aspirations and fears.

Effective communication is dependent on the volume, quality and accessibility of information; the means and media by which it is transmitted and received; the use to which it is put; its integrity; and the level of integrity of the wider situation.

Communication and information affect the quality of all human and professional relations within organisations. Good communications underline effective relations and enhance the general quality of working life, motivation, morale and, therefore, output. Bad and inadequate communications lead to frustration and enhance feelings of alienation, lack of identity and disunity, invariably leading to increases in customer complaints and loss of productivity and effectiveness, as well as an internal proliferation of disputes and grievances.

## The communication process

Communication takes place in writing, orally or verbally, and through the other senses – sight, touch, taste, smell, and hearing. It is clear, therefore, that it is not just the words stated or written that are important, but also:

- the ways in which they are spoken or written
- the context in which they are spoken or written
- the relationship between those giving and those receiving
- what is not stated or written
- what is precise
- what is imprecise or, worse, deliberately vague.

Every communication is dependent on a mixture of these elements; clearly, therefore, the greater the precision, clarity, openness and completeness of what is stated or written, the greater the chance of it being accepted and understood by those on the receiving end.

Communication may be:

- *one-way:* where edicts are issued by organisations to their employees without the opportunity for response
- *two-way (or multi-way):* engaging in a communication-and-response process (or dialogue), the results of which, when positive, are understanding, enlightenment, effective action and agreement
- *downward:* the use of organisational and managerial hierarchies and structures for communication purposes
- *upward:* using formalised channels such as joint consultative committees and informal contacts in which views and suggestions are invited from staff
- *lateral:* communication between departments, divisions and functions; communication between peers, superiors and subordinates on a basis of human and occupational egalitarianism, a key feature in breaking down organisational and occupational barriers
- *chains of communication:* in which messages are handed on from one person to the next, to the next, and so on. It is important to note that the more filters through which a message has to pass, the longer the chain of communication and, therefore, the greater the chance of distortion. This weakness is especially inherent in the 'cascade' effect (see Figure 3.1). The 'cascade' effect is attractive to the top managers of sophisticated and complex organisations because it is simple and visual and therefore easy to understand. It is almost universally inappropriate as a means of effective communication, at least without substantial reinforcement through other means and channels.

## Elements necessary for effective communication

The elements necessary for effective communication are:

- *Clarity of purpose on the part of the sender or initiator:* this means addressing the questions of what the message is, and why it is being sent; the receivers and their likely reactions and responses; the possible range of reactions and responses; what is to be achieved as the result of the communication; and what the barriers to this achievement might be (see page 41 below). This is the basis of 'saying what is meant and meaning what is said'.
- *Integrity of purpose:* this is the relationship between what is said, what is not said, what is meant, and what is intended. At its best, this means using clear, concise and unambiguous terms so that there is no doubt about the impact on the receiver.
- *Integrity in communications:* tends to reinforce the general ways of working of the organisation and also the wider state of mutual trust, respect and esteem held by all concerned for each other (see Chapter 2).

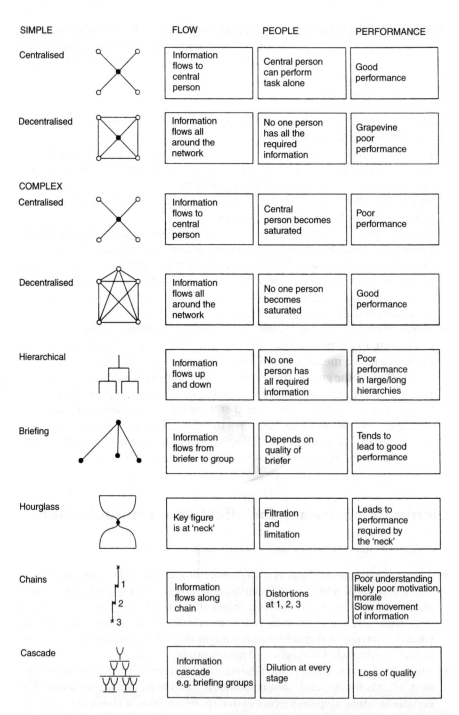

| SIMPLE | | FLOW | PEOPLE | PERFORMANCE |
|---|---|---|---|---|
| Centralised | | Information flows to central person | Central person can perform task alone | Good performance |
| Decentralised | | Information flows all around the network | No one person has all the required information | Grapevine poor performance |
| **COMPLEX** | | | | |
| Centralised | | Information flows to central person | Central person becomes saturated | Poor performance |
| Decentralised | | Information flows all around the network | No one person becomes saturated | Good performance |
| Hierarchical | | Information flows up and down | No one person has all required information | Poor performance in large/long hierarchies |
| Briefing | | Information flows from briefer to group | Depends on quality of briefer | Tends to lead to good performance |
| Hourglass | | Key figure is at 'neck' | Filtration and limitation | Leads to performance required by the 'neck' |
| Chains | | Information flows along chain | Distortions at 1, 2, 3 | Poor understanding likely poor motivation, morale Slow movement of information |
| Cascade | | Information cascade e.g. briefing groups | Dilution at every stage | Loss of quality |

Note the comments in the right-hand column – and especially the fact that very few of the methods used lead to good communication performance.

*Figure 3.1* Channels of communication.

- *Integrity of relationships involved:* at the core of this is the mutual trust and honesty of the particular relationship or relationships. It is underpinned by the practices and processes of the organisation, and its reactions to those who breach this integrity (whether this is indifference, whether it is punishment, or whether it is reward).
- *Use of language and media:* the basic rule is simple – say what needs to be said, write what needs to be written, make best uses of all the senses of those affected. The simpler and more direct the language and media used, the greater the initial levels of familiarity or information gained on the part of the receiver, and the quicker and more effectively things can be moved on. It is important to note that the selection of the correct media is essential, and many communications go wrong simply because the wrong choice is made.
- *Volume and quality of communications:* it is essential to balance the volume of information with delivering it so that it is understandable and acceptable, capable of response and use. The purpose is not to limit access to information, but rather to ensure that everything received is seen to be of value.
- *Visibility:* people respond much more positively if they know and respect the person or group initiating the communication.
- *Unity of overall purpose and direction:* the greater the commitment to this, the greater the likelihood of effective communications. In contrast, where this is not present, and where people tend to pursue their own interests, the more likely it is that the nature and quality of communications is diluted. This leads to the issuing of material for the glorification of particular departments or individuals, self-promotion, and, sometimes, the denigration of others.
- *Ordinary common decency:* including matters of common courtesy, manners, the extent of genuine and general respect and value held between members of an organisation or group.
- *Being positive:* a positive approach to communications reinforces general positive attitudes, values and feelings on the part of all concerned. Language and messages should therefore reflect all the associated elements of encouragement, enhancement, clarity, enrichment, satisfaction and achievement.

## Non-verbal communication

The elements of non-verbal communication give an impression of people to others before anything is said or written. They also reinforce what is being said or written. They also tend to give the real message – the non-verbal message is invariably much stronger than what is stated. The main components that must be understood are:

- *Appearance:* including age, gender, hair, face, body shape and size, height, bearing, national and racial characteristics, clothing and accessories.
- *Manner:* indicating behaviour, emotion, stress, comfort, formality/informality, acceptability/unacceptability, respect/disrespect.

- *Expression:* expression, especially facial expression, becomes the focus of attention in verbal communication, and that is where people concentrate most of their attention.
- *Eye contact:* regular eye contact demonstrates interest, trust, concern, affection, sympathy and honesty. Depth of expression in the eyes generates people's perception of feelings (anger, sorrow, love, hatred, joy). Lack of eye contact is normally seen as an indicator of dishonesty (though it may also occur when two people are not familiar with each other).
- *Pose:* either static or active, relaxed, calm, agitated, nervous or stressed. Pose reinforces the overall impression conveyed. Different parts of the body (especially arms and legs) are used for expression, emphasis, protection and as a shield.
- *Clothing:* in work situations, clothing provides an instant summary of people. Technicians are instantly recognised by their overalls, the police by their distinctive uniforms, and so on. Many organisations whose staff deal regularly and consistently with the public insist either on a dress code, or the wearing of a uniform, as it helps to reinforce organisational image, and the general confidence of the public.
- *Touch:* touch reinforces a wide range of perceptions, especially first impressions.
- *Body movement:* reinforces and conveys messages of anger, high emotion, comfort, or forcefulness and emphasis (e.g., the person banging their fist on the table).
- *Position, props and settings:* each is used to reinforce impressions of luxury or formality; or dominance and dependency; or to give one person an advantage over others in a particular situation (e.g., the superior sitting behind a large desk, on a high chair, conveying a difficult message to subordinates sitting on low chairs at the other side of the desk).
- *The senses:* these include the use of scent and fragrance, the use of colour, or the design and use of materials, each of which reinforces particular impressions.
- *Social factors:* people are conditioned into having preconceived ideas and general expectations of particular situations and individuals. For example, people do not generally attend promotion panels or job interviews unshaven or dressed informally. There is no rationale for this other than the expectations of society, and a general need and requirement to conform.
- *Listening:* listening is both active and passive. Passive listening may be no more than an awareness of background noise, or may be limited to a general awareness of what is going on. Active listening requires the listener to take a dynamic interest in what is being received. While the message is received through the ears, it is reinforced through eye contact, body movement, the other senses, and through the reception of any other non-verbal signals that are given by the speaker.
- *Reinforcement:* non-verbal communication always reinforces relative and absolute measures of status, value, importance and achievement (both positively and negatively), as well as relative and absolute measures of authority, power and influence.

# Communication barriers and blockages

Barriers and blockages exist either by accident, negligence or design.

- *Accident:* this is where the choice of language used, the timing or the method of communication is unintentionally wrong. In such cases, those involved normally simply step back from the situation and rectify it as quickly as possible. The worst thing that can (and frequently does) happen is that the organisation takes on a defensive position; a simple misunderstanding therefore quickly becomes a major dispute.
- *Negligence:* this is where barriers and blockages are allowed to arise by default. The organisation and its managers perceive that things are at least 'not too bad' or 'going along pretty well'. In such cases, communication malfunction is seen as 'one of those things'. Specific problems are ignored or treated with a corporate shrug of the shoulders. If allowed to develop, communication negligence is perceived by the staff as a sign that the organisation does not care for them, or what happens to them.
- *Design:* this is where the barriers and blockages in communication are both created and also manipulated by those within the organisation for their own ends. In these cases, information becomes a commodity to be bought and sold, to be corrupted, skewed, and filtered in the pursuit of narrow sectoral interests. This is endemic throughout the mid to upper echelons of the military, civil and public service institutions, multinational companies, and other multi-site organisations with large and complex head office functions.

We now move on to consider some specific barriers to communication. These are simplest to remove when they exist by accident; it is essential that they are addressed and removed when they have been allowed to arise through negligence or design.

## Distance

Distance in communications is both physical and psychological. The physical barrier also carries psychological overtones, as physical distance acts as a barrier to visibility. This can lead to feelings of isolation and alienation. It can also lead to feelings of autonomy and, when this becomes corrupted, of arrogance.

Psychological distance is compounded or reduced by the presence or absence of trappings such as offices, secretaries, forms of address, and titles.

## Trappings

Trappings are a barrier when they exude fear. For example, the person who has a car parking space, two personal assistants, a personal washroom, and an office suite puts up barriers to communication with other staff. The others are, in turn, psychologically discouraged from approaching that individual. Moreover, when that individual approaches them, their chances of engaging in productive communication are reduced.

## Interest

The subject of communication must contain something of value to the receiver. Positive steps must be taken to engage a positive interest, whatever the message being transmitted. This reinforces the need for the issues of clarity, language, media, use, and timing, to be effectively addressed.

## 'The need to know'

Barriers occurs where organisations decide that information is to be issued in different ways, or different information is to be issued to different groups and individuals. This is a process of limiting the availability of information and, overtly, there might appear to be some sense in this: most organisations have far too much information to issue for any one person to understand, analyse and internalise. However, the barrier arises from the reasoning behind 'the need to know'. The message invariably given is one of:

- an implied lack of capability of subordinates to understand what is being said, and especially that the organisation (or an individual superior) does not think or believe that the subordinates have this capability
- a real or perceived lack of value placed on different groups of staff, especially those who are excluded from the 'need to know' list
- inequality of access – in order to be privy to certain information, it is necessary to have reached a particular level or status within the organisation
- general disrespect – this approach shows an overall lack of respect to those affected
- psychological distance – this form of filtering information emphasises the differences and divisions that exist in organisations, and between its functions, departments, ranks and individuals.

## Confidentiality

Confidentiality becomes a barrier when it is used as a means of attracting or acquiring status, rather than for operational effectiveness, or for ethical reasons. While some matters clearly are operationally sensitive (e.g., personnel files, inventions, marketing initiatives), others are not, and putting a 'confidentiality' barrier around such matters reinforces feelings of disregard and disrespect.

## Arrogance

People who are treated with arrogance by others always feel slighted. In many cases, these feelings are much deeper, and again, include lack of respect, even contempt. Arrogance in communications is found in forms of words that include: 'Do this because I say so', 'Do this because I know best', 'You are only the receptionist/computer operator/personnel manager'.

## Negativity

Use of negative language is always disruptive. The balance of negative and positive language is critical to effective communication. Where the balance is overwhelmingly positive, people react quickly and positively, and any negative is overcome. Where the balance is overwhelmingly negative, the positive gets lost altogether.

## Jargon

Jargon is a barrier where the message receivers are not a party to the phrases or acronyms used. Using 'department-speak' out of its normal context is part of the negativity barrier. This can also lead to serious misunderstandings at a later date.

---
**EXAMPLE**

Two senior members of one of the country's leading universities had an overtly productive conversation leading to a commitment to proceed with a substantial research project. This project became known as the W.I.R.S. project.

The project had to be cancelled and then re-commissioned when it became clear that one member of staff was talking about the *whole-industry research study* (relating to the construction and civil engineering industries), while the other was talking about the *workplace industrial relations survey*.

---

Barriers to effective communication are clearly widespread. They exist in all organisations to a greater or lesser extent. It is important to realise, therefore, that there is a great potential for even the simplest and most positive of communications to go wrong.

This is compounded when the wider organisation culture and ethos has, for whatever reason, become toxic.

## Organisational toxicity and communications

The problems indicated above are greatly compounded when the wider organisational context is deemed to be toxic, i.e., where standards, quality of working life, and overall integrity have become greatly compromised. In these situations, many communications take the following forms:

- *Blame and scapegoat:* in which organisations find individuals to carry the can for corporate failings. Accusation, counteraccusation and back-stabbing prevail. Individuals may either be 'named and shamed' officially or, more insidiously, they may not be named officially, but 'through the grapevine'.
- *Departmental feuding:* some organisations actively encourage this in the always mistaken belief that by putting departments at loggerheads with each other, improved performance and output will occur.
- *Meddling:* where persons or departments meddle outside their legitimate areas of concern or activity. One of the most extreme forms of this is where top and powerful individuals promise favoured customers or staff that special activities and deals can be done on their behalf.

- *Secrets:* in a toxic situation, information becomes a commodity to be used as a source of influence and as a bargaining chip; communication is therefore most concerned with control, editing, filtering and presentation of information, rather than its absolute quality.
- *Toxic communicators:* toxic communicators issue toxic communications. These may be general, and may be no worse than putting negative or pessimistic constructs or gossip on any form of information. More insidiously, some individuals introduce toxicity. They do this in the knowledge that how the information is presented will have particular effects. Toxic communicators misrepresent, lie, and cheat; they also manipulate information to their own partial point of view.

---

┌─ EXAMPLE ─

In March 2000, the UK Government promised an extra £22 billion of spending on the national health service over the following three years. This received widespread positive media coverage and medical professionals and their clients looked forward to enhanced quality of treatment.

It subsequently became apparent that the £22 billion promised was not this figure at all, but rather £10 billion. The figure was presented thus:

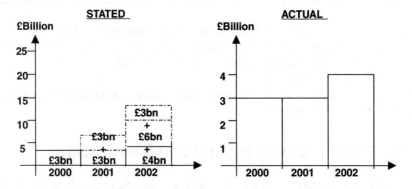

The government was in fact writing the previous two years expenditure (which had already been spent) as part of its present spending proposals.

When the Government was first called to account for this by the *Panorama* television programme, it refused to comment. It subsequently had to retract the figure. In going some way towards apologising for the presentation of these figures, a government spokesman was able to give no better explanation than that this was 'normal government practice'.

Source: BBC Television, *Panorama*, 13 March 2000.

---

# Rules and principles of communication

Having established the boundaries of the communication process, and having identified the great range of things that can go wrong in communication, a set of rules and guiding principles can now be drawn up. All managers and supervisors should know these, and be able to apply them:

- The simpler the language used, the greater the chance of the message being accepted, understood, valued and believed.
- The more complex the language used, the less the chance of the message being accepted, understood, believed and valued.
- The best way to ensure that a message is received is to tell people face to face, and then to reinforce with a written transcript or summary.
- If there is any discrepancy between what is stated, what is implied, and what is written, people will believe the worst aspects of each.
- If there is any discrepancy between the stated message and the non-verbal message or body language, people will believe the body language (see Box 3.1).
- The use of general phrases, such as 'We are doing all we can', 'We always comply with the law', always gives the impression that a minimum effort is being put in.
- The use of bland phrases, such as 'hitting the ground running', 'high achiever', 'cutting the mustard', are never taken seriously by receivers, because they do not understand what is meant.
- The use of toxic phrases, such as 'There are no plans for redundancies at present', are always treated with suspicion, mistrust, even contempt, by the receivers.
- The inability or refusal to answer direct questions is always assumed to be a mark of dishonesty.
- The use of positive language always engages a greater active interest on the part of the receivers; the use of negative language is always generally demoralising (except when it is used on such rare occasions as to make people sit up and take notice).
- Threatening communications have an instantaneous effect, and this is always negative.

## Box 3.1 Mixed messages

- In the 1980s, Mikhail Gorbachev, the last First Secretary of the USSR, was extremely adept and controlled in using words. However, he was unable to control his body language (the non-verbal aspects). In particular, he was unable to prevent himself from going red when either angry or under stress, and when he was being asked questions that he did not wish to answer.
- Ronald Reagan, President of the USA at the same time, was an actor by trade. Because of his training, he was able to control both his presentation of words, and also, to an extent, his body language. However, his advisors always made him stand behind a screen that obscured the lower half of his body, because even he was unable to prevent himself shifting from foot to foot when faced with difficult or contentious questions, or those that he felt unable to answer fully.

A company based in London owned a frozen food factory in north west England. Over a period of years, the factory developed a reputation for poor industrial relations and low productivity. Whenever production deadlines were not met, or whenever there was a collective dispute or grievance, the head office in London always responded by threatening to close the factory down.

This process went on for a period of twelve years. The first time the threats were made, they were taken seriously, and productivity improved for a period of several years. However, as the problems escalated, and the company's response remained the same, people no longer took the threats seriously. The collective view of the workforce was along the lines of: *'One day you'll probably close us down anyway, because that is clearly your attitude towards us; the threat therefore has no potency. In the meantime, it is clear that you are treating us with disrespect and contempt'.*

Until the announcement of the factory closure was made, nobody from the head office with any authority went up to see the problem for themselves. No meaningful communication took place. Everything was carried out by telephone, fax or memorandum. This all took place at a time when the frozen food industry was growing at a rate of 11% per annum.

## Empathy

For these rules to be applied effectively, empathy must be applied. In communication, empathy means understanding the ranges of likely responses and issues on the part of the receivers once they have read or heard the message. The key skills lie in being able to answer accurately and honestly:

- What would I be thinking if I had just been told this?
- What would I now want to know?
- What would I now be most concerned about and why?

It is a skill that is not presently given sufficient importance, nor practised often enough. Especially in the upper echelons of organisations, it is hardly applied at all.

The Chief Executive of a major London clearing bank was required to announce several thousand redundancies from among the company's junior- and middle-management staff. When asked to consider the effects of redundancy on the lives of these members of staff, he refused. He put the case against empathy as follows: *'I understand what you are saying, but I don't agree. Of course, I understand the effects of my actions on people's lives. But if I allowed myself to think about them too deeply, I'd go mad. I simply would not be able to do my job.'*

This is spurious – a self-absolution of responsibility. It is also very close to the statement made by General Colin Powell, former USA Chief of Staff, which was: *'I always understand what I'm asking my people to do. If I thought too long about the ruined*

*and shredded bodies, the burns, the dead and the bereaved, I'd go mad. But I think about*
*them anyway. Then I give the orders anyway.'*

The view of General Powell is much more wholesome in that those within armies do at least understand that the time is likely to come when they have to fight and perhaps get injured, wounded or even die.

Source: T. Peters and N. Austin (1985) *A Passion for Excellence*, Harper & Row.

More generally, the ability to apply empathy in communications should engage managers and supervisors in a process of thought that may be summarised as:

- What have I got to say? What is the best way of saying it?
- Am I being completely honest – or as honest as I am genuinely allowed?
- Having thought of the likely responses, how am I going to handle these?

Managers can then order their thoughts, information and presentation much more effectively.

The rules and principles outlined here apply in all communications. It is essential that they are learned and followed if communication is to be effective.

It is now necessary to consider their application in circumstances common to all organisations. These are:

- managing meetings
- giving references
- producing and presenting reports
- using e-mail and the Internet.

## Managing meetings

Managers and supervisors have to be able to lead their own meetings and contribute to others. It is, therefore, necessary to have available and accessible, usable substantial information and, where necessary, the expertise to reinforce it.

Meetings that managers must be able to lead are: staff meetings, team briefings, team meetings, subgroup meetings, ad hoc meetings, crisis meetings and, where applicable, daily, weekly and monthly general meetings.

Where the managers have the authority or influence, the following rules should always be applied:

- Issue the agenda in advance.
- Begin on time.
- End on time; and if the business finishes early, end early.
- Design and operate the agenda in descending, not ascending, order of importance.
- Avoid lengthy presentations; ask for key summary points, and make sure that the full supporting information reports and schedules are available to all concerned to refer to if they need.
- Allow time for questions on each matter from everyone, and draw everyone into the meetings.

- Record and circulate minutes, summaries, action points, responsibilities and deadlines for progress.

Managers are also required to attend organisation meetings where they will be required to contribute and to hold their own with peers and superiors. This again requires command of the information supporting the matters in hand. Managers may also be required to take part in project groups, quality circles or quality assurance groups, and these also need the same high level of commitment.

Problems with meetings arise when:

- too many points are packed into too little time
- the meeting is dominated by one or two powerful personalities or vested interests and everyone is not given the opportunity to contribute
- the agenda is nobbled, normally through having the most important or contentious point slipped in at the end. Anyone who does this, should be aware that those involved will always eventually work this out for themselves, or else be told that this has happened
- the recording of the meeting is not the same as that which actually occurred
- the meeting is too large and unwieldy
- the meeting is badly chaired or led
- the meeting becomes known, believed or perceived as a useful group to be a member of, a networking rather than operational facility, the opportunity to shine in front of senior or powerful people
- the meeting becomes known, believed or perceived to be a cosy, and, therefore, expensive, leisure facility, a period of time away from operational priorities.

### A note on team briefings

For team briefings to be effective, the rules concerning quality and availability of information must be followed, and those responsible must be able to structure the briefings to provide effective information. Where team briefings are used as part of a 'cascade effect', the message is always diluted by the time it reaches the last levels of the organisation to receive the message (see page 37). If the team briefing approach is used, it is essential that managers are aware of their limitations and, where possible, have quality printed material available in support of what is being stated.

## Giving references

At some time, all managers have to give references; and they also have to read them.

Rationally, all references are useless for the following reasons:

- Past excellent performance is no guarantee of future excellent performance.
- Past poor performance is no guarantee of future poor performance.
- Past excellent attitude and high level of commitment is no guarantee of future excellent attitude and high commitment.
- Past poor attitude is no guarantee of future poor attitude.

In spite of this, they are regularly asked for.

There is a legal obligation to confirm that the person named held a particular job for a particular period of employment. Otherwise, there is no obligation to say anything else at all. If anything else is to be said, it must by law, always be positive unless negative comments (e.g. on timekeeping, performance, attitude and demeanour) can be substantiated and supported from existing organisational records (see Box 3.2).

## Box 3.2   References

Some organisations try to get over the problem by issuing pro forma questionnaires. Some of these require boxes to be ticked, for example:

- 'Has the subject's performance been . . . ?'
- 'Is the subject always punctual?'
- 'What is the subject's attitude to co-workers?'

These also all require subjective responses. Again, anything that gives any form of negative impression must be capable of being sustained and supported. It also assumes that both the questionnaire issuer and reference giver, having probably never met before, are going to put exactly the same construct on what constitutes good, medium and poor performance.

One of the most insidious of questions asked in this way is: 'Would you re-employ?' It was used in the 1970s by the building trade as a coded weeder-out of perceived militants and troublemakers. (The only acceptable answer to the question was 'Yes'. Anyone who put 'Probably', or 'If there was a job for the subject', was believed or perceived to be putting up a warning signal.) In practice, it is impossible to give a wholesome answer. There is a world of difference between 'Would you?', the general favourable response, and 'Will you?' There may be no vacancy for the person. The person may not wish to come back. The organisation may change its culture, values, technology or structure – each of which may better or worse accommodate the subject of the reference.

## Producing and presenting reports

The requirements for producing and presenting reports vary between organisations, and between departments and divisions within organisations. It is, therefore, impossible to produce a blueprint. However, there are principles:

- The remit or request must be met in full.
- Information capable of supporting or sustaining arguments must be available even if it is not required by the report's commissioner.
- Any recommendations must always be prioritised, time scaled, scheduled and include resourcing implications.
- A full evaluation of opportunities and consequences must always be made clear.

## Report production

Whatever is required, and by whom, the process is one of:

- agreeing the remit, terms of reference and reporting deadline (including any reference to progress monitoring, production of initial and interim findings)
- establishing a methodology, which simply means determining what is to be done, how it is to be done, why, when and where
- carrying out research, making investigations, gathering information, including piloting and testing any questionnaires that may be necessary
- analysing, evaluating and summarising the information gathered
- producing conclusions and, if requested, producing recommendations.

As stated above, what is actually presented is limited by what the report's commissioner requests. For example, some people ask for a summary on a single sheet of paper, others ask for fully referenced substantial write-ups. In each case, and for any in between, the process is always the same.

The job is also limited by the amount of time available. For example, something required later the same day physically limits both the quality and volume of research possible. On the other hand, something with a six month deadline may require substantial revision along the way as circumstances and the commercial, economic and organisational environments change.

## Report presentation

As stated above, this is to be in the form requested. If the final presentation is to be very short, the substance and the information on which it was based must always be produced anyway, and available in case points of debate or inquiry come up. Beyond this again, there are principles of presentation:

- Reports produced for senior managers must always include cost and financial implications.
- Reports produced for staff or subordinates are likely to produce questions about redundancy, redeployment, quality of working life, quality of work, pay and performance requirements, or changes in ways of working.
- Reports produced for customers or clients are likely to produce questions about quality of product and service.
- Reports on technological feasibility always have operational implications and implications for training, development and reorganisation.
- Reports on strategy, policy and operational direction always have operational and staffing implications.
- Reports may not give the answer required; they may also, if the work has been carried out in support of a particular proposal, arrive at the conclusion that the particular issue is not viable (see Box 3.3).

## BOX 3.3  Unwholesome use of reports

The following are common examples.

- Consultants are employed by organisations to produce particular slants on policy or direction; at the point of subsequent implementation, top managers of the organisation can say that they are simply following the recommendations of the consultants and it is not their responsibility. This is in widespread use as a tactic for the introduction of radical change, redundancies, new management styles and structures. It is also a complete abdication of managerial responsibility.
- Research groups and think-tanks are engaged to come up with information and background material in support of something that has already been decided. This is especially a problem in public services where many initiatives are overtly politically desirable but unworkable in practice.
- Fully considered reports are produced that prove or strongly indicate that a particular venture is certain not to work; because of other drives, the report is ignored, or bypassed, or suppressed.
- Reports are produced that come up with 'the wrong answer'; the report writer is then told to go away and rewrite it to come up with the 'right answer'.


## Using e-mail and the Internet

E-mail is an operationally efficient and cost effective way of communicating with people. To those working in remote locations, for example, in oil and civil engineering or on overseas postings or regional offices, it is a lifeline. It also has great value to those working away from the organisation, for example field sales staff, and those working non-standard hours.

Problems arise when e-mail is used as a substitute for face-to-face encounters and so these are removed from managers' schedules. Off-site staff and those working in remote locations require social, as well as professional, interaction on the rare occasions that they do come into the office.

Problems also arise when some staff have e-mail access and others do not. Remedies for this are:

- to ensure that information is promulgated manually as well as by e-mail
- to ensure that everyone is given e-mail access as soon as possible and that they are trained in how to use it.

The most insidious problems arise when there is e-mail 'apartheid' – where particular categories and groups of staff are singled out to be given e-mail access, while others are not. This is at its worst when it is based on status, seniority and proximity to head office, because it is used as a tool to exclude people from parts of the communication process, rather than to enhance the process itself.

## A note on the Internet

There are vast quantities of information available on the Internet. Used properly, it is a quick and effective means of gathering information together without having to leave the location. However, unless people are adequately trained in its usage, it is extremely expensive. This expense is incurred in two ways:

- the telephone charges that accrue as the result of individuals gaining access
- the slow speed at which, often expensive, staff can use the Internet because they are neither familiar with it, nor trained in it.

Those who genuinely require access to the Internet have therefore to be trained and managed. Those who do not require regular access should be familiarised with it over longer periods of time so that eventually full effectiveness of use, as well as general availability, is achieved.

Any form of electronic mail or data access has, therefore, to be managed in exactly the same way as the rest of the communication process. E-mail is often simply an effective form of reinforcing what has been said during face-to-face meetings and discussions. It is also a quick and much more effective means of distributing organisational memoranda, newsletters, and more general information.

## Conclusions

Understanding and being able to apply the rules and principles outlined in this chapter are universal managerial and supervisory skills. They result in the ability to produce effective communications capable of being received, accepted and acted upon or responded to. All levels of communication should be monitored and remedial action where communication is poor or ineffective. Concentration on the barriers and blockages to effective communication is designed to reinforce

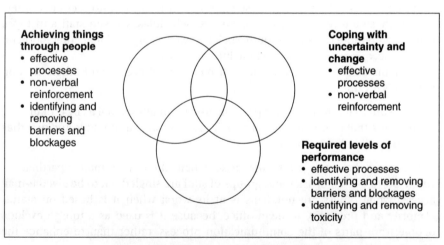

*Figure 3.2* Chapter and model summary.

the need for clarity of purpose and language – essentials for effective communications. As many channels as possible should be used, each giving the same message, so that the message received is complete and not subject to editing, interpretation or distortion. Moreover, where communications are not clear, they are necessarily unclear and so people will search for hidden agenda and meanings.

Organisations are responsible for creating the conditions in which effective communications can take place. Managers and supervisors must be familiar with both the content and processes indicated in this chapter. More generally, communication is the foundation of all effective interpersonal, professional and occupational relationships; relations between departments, divisions and functions; and between organisations and their suppliers, customers and clients.

Using the Model referred to at the start of Chapter 1 (Figure 1.1), the material in this chapter is summarised in Figure 3.2.

QUESTIONS

1. Of all the barriers to effective communication indicated in this chapter, which, in your view, are the hardest to overcome and why?
2. Identify the main strengths and weaknesses of television, radio and newspaper news and current affairs coverage. How are the stories weighted, distorted or presented from a partial point of view? How might this be remedied?
3. If you were required to use, or be a part of, a 'cascade' communication process, what steps would you take to minimise the difficulties inherent?
4. How might you prepare yourself for a meeting with someone who you know is going to use all of the trappings, furnishings and barriers at their disposal to make your life as difficult as possible?
5. Where do the main blockages and barriers to effective communication lie within your own department, and within the organisation as a whole? What steps could you, as an individual, take to a) identify these; and b) overcome them?

# ▼ **4** Presentation and advocacy

## Introduction

The presentation and advocacy aspects of management and supervision come a lot easier to some people than to others. It is, superficially, both easy and attractive to take refuge in the comfort zone of:

- unfamiliarity with public speaking and presentation
- the potential for embarrassment or mistakes
- lack of training or aptitude for public speaking, presentation and advocacy
- public speaking, presentation and advocacy is 'not the British way'.

This is reinforced by the fact that, in many cases, there is no overt encouragement to be competent from higher up the organisation. Indeed, it may be actively discouraged, because expertise in public presentation on the part of juniors may show up the shortcomings of seniors.

All of this is both understandable in general, and familiar in practice. Nevertheless, presentation and advocacy have to be learned because:

- These skills are expected by the staff. They require their managers and supervisors to be effective and successful on their behalf when acting as their advocate.
- These skills are required by peers and superiors. They expect their managers to be effective performers in committees and meetings, and when acting in the organisation's name with customers, backers, clients, suppliers and the community.
- These skills are expected by suppliers, customers, clients and backers, especially when dealing with problems and complaints.
- These skills are expected in the community. This applies not only to the professional and occupational community – meetings of professional bodies, cluster groups, seminars and away-days – but also to the community at large. If an organisation's representative is invited to speak to a professional or community group, the listeners expect at least a coherent and orderly presentation.

## Initial steps

The first steps towards effective presentations are taken by addressing the following questions:

- To whom is the presentation being made?
- What is being presented?
- Why is it being presented to this particular group of people?
- What is the nature of the information to be put across?
- What are people going to want to discuss as the result?
- Are there any difficult, unanswerable or awkward questions arising?
- How much time is available? How is this time best used?
- What do people need to get from the presentation? What are the aims and objectives?

Answers to these questions give clear indications of the following key aspects of the presentation:

- priorities
- main points
- structure
- specific issues and problems
- other likely matters arising
- how the material is to be most clearly presented (see Box 4.1).

## Box 4.1   Rules for the conduct of effective presentations

1. Say what needs to be said; write what needs to be written; demonstrate what needs to be demonstrated.
2. a) Decide on the best person to say what needs to be said; b) write or sign what needs to be written. If for any reason the best person is not available, be aware that this is likely to cause problems. This also applies to the signature on written material.
3. Use the time available. Do not cram too much material into too short a space of time.
4. Be aware that there are optimum timings; most people's attention starts to flag after approximately 35 minutes. If the period of time to be used is longer than this, vary the means of presentation, or give times for question and answer sessions along the way.
5. Deal with the most important issue first. If only a short period of time is available, then limit the presentation to this; if longer is available, more material can be covered.
6. Complicated figures and statements are always best presented in writing. If necessary, people's attention can be drawn to them during an oral presentation. Complicated figures and statements should always be handed out – never read from an overhead projector or slide presentation.
7. Give advance notification of date, time, duration and speakers; include synopses if appropriate.
8. Follow up all presentations in writing. At this point, it is often useful to ask for further questions; if these are forthcoming, then they must be answered.

9. Review the effectiveness of the presentation. There will often be something that has been forgotten.
10. Beware of factors outside your control (see page 59). Especially, be aware of the possibility or likelihood of having the time available cut.

**Notes**

- *Visual aids:* visual aids are there to support the presentation – they are never to become the presentation themselves. Overhead projectors, slide projections and video examples are only ever used with any validity in support of the material that the speaker is to present.
- The Brazilian, Ricardo Semler goes further: his golden rule for presentations is *'Never turn the lights off'*. His company requires that all presentations, whatever the subject matter, are kept to no more than ten minutes' duration.
- *Refreshments:* if people expect refreshments they have to be provided; if they are not provided, people will be antagonised, however valid or current the material of the presentation. It is best that refreshments are provided at the start, and at the end of the presentation, rather than in the middle.

In general, all managers and supervisors are likely to be required to make presentations to subordinates, superiors, peers, individuals, small groups, large groups, suppliers, customers and clients. So it is as well to be able and willing to do a good job.

# The great barrier

The great barrier to effective public speaking, presentation and advocacy is the widely held belief that top public speakers are born not made. This is simply not true.

It is true that some people have a greater aptitude, skill or talent for this than others. However, anyone with any talent for anything at all has to work hard at it in order to maximise it. And the absence of a particular talent does not mean that the capability to do a good job cannot be learned.

Managers and supervisors need to recognise this, and accept the need to make presentations as a key part of their professional and occupational position. It is necessary also that they become both interested in, and committed to, developing skills of presentation.

To do this effectively, other barriers must be recognised and addressed.

## Other barriers

These are:

- perception
- fear
- failure
- visibility.

## Perception

The two perceptions that have to be addressed are:

- the great barrier, that speakers are born not made
- that the standard of presentation required of managers and supervisors is the same as that required of orators, actors and newsreaders.

### Born not made

Great orators become so because they work at their purpose, scripts, appearance, voice and presentation. No great orator was born with any of this. Those that have the influence to do so, use and manipulate the media – newspapers, radio and television – to enhance and control their presentation (see Box 4.2).

## Box 4.2   Great public presentations

- It is illustrated below (see Chapter 13) that Hitler was manufactured as a leader; he was not born to lead. It is also true that his public presentations were manufactured.
- This is also true of Winston Churchill and his wartime speeches. Each was subject to expensive scripting, and rehearsal. The voice was tried and tested for effectiveness as a radio presentation. Only when Churchill and his advisors were completely satisfied that the desired effect would be created, did he go on to the radio and make the speeches.
- Richard Branson, Chairman and Chief Executive of the Virgin Group, ensures that he only has the media present when he is going to be shown off to best advantage. It appears spontaneous; in practice it is not.

It should be clear that all of this is the necessary background, and skill development for ensuring presentation of the highest order.

Those that do not have these advantages have to fall back on the argument illustrated in Box 4.2. Each of the examples used – Hitler, Churchill, Richard Branson – depended or depend on full knowledge, combined with rehearsal, cohesion and purpose, in order to generate the desired effect. This only leaves the voice – and this is the least important aspect. With confidence in the material, together with cohesion and purpose, comes strength of voice, and consequent conviction in the message. This, in turn, develops and enhances with the material. Those to whom the presentation is being made always prefer substance of content, adequately or even haltingly delivered, rather than slick but unsubstantial content produced smoothly. And those on whose behalf the presentation is being made, always much prefer that the substance, rather than the veneer of their case, is put across.

### Standards required

Actors and newsreaders use their voice and appearance from exactly the same point of view that a mechanic uses a spanner or a jack. These are the tools of those particular trades, developed and refined to levels of expertise through shear hard work and practice.

Managers and supervisors do not have this priority. They need rather to develop presentational capability to the point of competence and familiarity. As stated above, the source of this lies in knowing and understanding the material, its purpose, and its cohesion.

## Fear

The initial fear of making presentations arises from this being an unknown and unfamiliar territory. This is a completely legitimate and understandable feeling. Again, the best approach to reducing fear is to have confidence in the material and substance of the presentation.

Fear – or at least nervousness – are never subsequently completely lost. Teachers, lecturers, newsreaders, all of whom carry out presentations for a salary, invariably suffer butterflies or nerves before each class or each broadcast. Sales people invariably go into meetings with customers and clients nervous of unpredictable reactions. Sir Stanley Matthews, the great footballer, always said that he was physically sick before every game – and he played nearly 1,000 – such was the state of his fear and nervousness. Each of these groups of people state that the fear and nervousness is a reflection of interest, and the determination to do a good job; if they were not nervous, they would not be concerned about the outcome.

The important thing, therefore, is to recognise and understand that it exists, that it is inherent in all these situations. Most important of all, it is a reflection of the determination to succeed.

## Failure

Failure in presentations is perceived to arise from a lack of oratorial expertise. Failure in presentations actually arises from:

- not knowing, understanding or having faith in the material
- not preparing adequately
- not doing the material justice (which normally arises from a lack of preparation)
- not giving the audience what they expected or wanted (see Box 4.3)

- factors outside the presenter's control, of which the most likely and prevalent are: bad or hostile presentation environment, curtailment of time, meeting or event being dominated or side-tracked by a crisis, meeting or event being dominated or side-tracked by an over-mighty or over-influential attendee.

Whenever any of these happen, the need for written summaries or synopses of the matters in hand become even more important.

## Box 4.3   Giving audiences what they want

Giving audiences what they want comes in two forms:

- content
- presentation.

The content indicated or promised in any pre-presentation brief must always be delivered. If there is any indication at all that particular matters are going to be covered, then this must indeed happen. Failure to do so leads both to audience disappointment, and also to the integrity of the presenter being called into question.

It is quite true that audiences do prefer interesting and substantial presentations, smoothly and professionally delivered. However, they are certain to be extremely disappointed if the substance is not forthcoming; if the presentation is not quite up to the perceived or expected mark, this will be forgiven so long as the content is adequate and acceptable.

## Visibility

The other matter that has to be addressed at this point is visibility. Whether making presentations personally or in writing, or whether sending someone to act on your behalf, you are *visible* at this point. This cannot be avoided, diluted or dissipated – nor can responsibility for the content, style or objectives of the presentation.

If this is recognised and accepted at the outset, the inherent strength of a presentation is immediately assured. The standpoint adopted and specific aims and objectives can then be addressed so that they are put across in ways that do the particular case – whatever it is – the most justice (see Box 4.4).

## Box 4.4   Putting on a show

At the outset of any presentation those present are normally either supportive, or else at least, acquiescent in what has to be said. During the presentation, this support will continue for as long as the presenter is personally and professionally sympathetic to the needs of the audience. This remains true even where bad or adverse news is being put across.

Support for the presenter is however dissipated through: being over long, avoiding the main issues, resorting to blandness or flippancy, and relying on (rather than using) visual aids (see Box 4.1). Above all, support is lost through not leaving enough time for discussions or debate.

This last is especially used as a device by senior managers presenting bad news to the rest of the staff. They deliberately leave themselves insufficient time for full debate and discussion to take effect. This is known to be dishonest by those on the receiving end. As such, it always receives the same welcome if it is used by anyone, regardless of rank, expertise or length of service. Insufficient time for discussion – especially of adverse or contentious issues – is always viewed as a mark of dishonesty.

These barriers are present in all situations to some extent. It is therefore necessary to recognise and overcome them, rather than either denying their existence or avoiding presentations.

Having assessed the purpose, structure, timing, barriers and fear factors, attention must now be paid to more specific issues.

## Knowing your audience

The emphasis and delivery of a presentation clearly changes according to the nature of the audience. For example:

- presentations for Chief Executives or senior managers must include questions of cost and other resource implications;
- presentations for staff, peers or subordinates are certain to raise questions along the lines of 'How will this affect me?'
- presentations for suppliers, customers and clients raise questions of price, quality, value, delivery and payment interludes and schedules.

Wherever language is unclear or ambiguous, the following are certain:

- Chief Executives and senior management take the view that the matter is not well thought out.
- Staff, peers and subordinates suspect an alternative or hidden agenda.
- Suppliers, customers and clients suspect that terms of trading are to be made less favourable.

Each of these points reinforces the need to structure presentations with the audience, not the speaker, in mind. Each also emphasises the need to be completely familiar and confident with the material.

It is further necessary to understand that people bring their own opinions, prejudices and preconceptions to a particular situation. These may be well informed or not; they still have to be recognised and addressed (see Box 4.5).

## Box 4.5    Dealing with preconceived ideas and partial points of view

Where feelings on any subject are entrenched or running high (or both), there exists a potential for conflict and other serious problems. The point of view put forward must be respected and considered from the standpoint of the person expressing it if progress is to be made. This means understanding:

- why such views are held and why they will be defended
- any past history that has tended to reinforce such views.

It is also necessary to understand 'partial legitimacy'. For example:

- trade unions exist to represent their members' best interests and any dealings with them have to be seen in this context
- consumer and environmental lobbies come to any situation from a clearly expressed point of view and, similarly, this has to be recognised.

Any appeal to such groups to take account of 'the broader context' or other constraints will be unsuccessful unless there is something of substance in the wider scheme of things for the viewpoints that they represent. If, as the result, the presenter is likely to receive a rough ride, the best way to handle this is to be prepared, to present clear and unambiguous information, and to deal with the problems either as they arise, or through a commitment to sort them out within a few days.

# Cheerleading

Cheerleading comes in two forms, legitimate and illegitimate.

## Legitimate cheerleading

Legitimate cheerleading is:

- a celebration and promulgation of genuine organisational, departmental, group and individual achievement. Managers and supervisors must always be proud of special results, achievements and performance excellence achieved by their people as a whole, or as individuals or groups.
- celebrating and promulgating organisational achievements which help to secure its long-term future. While this may not have a direct relevance to all staff, the fact that they are now secure should be a cause of celebration. The two most common forms of this are securing long-term orders and contracts, and the award of funds (invariably from public bodies, government or the EU) to engage in pioneering work.

## Illegitimate cheerleading

Illegitimate cheerleading is:

- distributive celebration, in which one group within an organisation has gained at the expense or to the detriment of others
- celebrating the achievements of one group, but not equivalent results and achievements of others
- celebrating organisational results as personal triumphs (a common problem with senior management and boards of directors)
- celebrating tiny achievements as if they were major triumphs
- celebrating failure as if it were success (common in the award of senior management bonuses)
- celebrating organisational, group or team efforts as individual triumphs
- boasting and bragging, especially about small achievements, and when trying to turn small achievements into major triumphs.

## Cheerleading and presentation

The purpose of legitimate cheerleading is to gain recognition for those who have delivered outstanding performance or results. It consists of producing written and oral statements targeted at everyone who should know and recognise these results. If it is done properly, it acts as a form of encouragement to everybody. If it is consistently done, it means everyone gains the same recognition for their genuine achievements.

It can be corrupted – and therefore made illegitimate – if it becomes competitive, or a yardstick for judging managerial or supervisory performance. When managers and supervisors spend time putting forward the results achieved by their staff as a form of one-upmanship, this leads to an inevitable dilution in what is regarded as achievement.

It always becomes corrupted – and therefore illegitimate – if the pay and rewards of managers and supervisors becomes in any way dependent on the number of achievements put forward; or if something that happened by chance leads to an advantage to the organisation or someone within it.

---

EXAMPLE

A large County Council sent a junior member of staff on a weekend sailing training course. This course required participants to sail a schooner along the French coast to the Channel Islands, and then across the English Channel to Southampton, over the course of the weekend.

The member of the County Council staff was a young woman in her late twenties. She was a junior member of staff, on a fast-track graduate progression programme. She arrived at the training ship in Northern France and, together with others participants in the course, was put to work. During the course she was observed by a colleague.

The course instructors requested that course participants carry out a particular series of tasks and make ready to set sail. The participants disagreed and eventually the person from the County Council led a mutiny. Faced with this mutiny, the instructors changed their plans and allowed the participants to take full control of the weekend and sail the ship in their own way. The ship arrived in Southampton on the Sunday evening as planned.

---

When she returned to her office the following day, the woman was staggered to find that her mentor had suggested that she be disciplined, or even dismissed. A full inquiry was held by a Committee of the Council's Chief Officers. They were inclined to uphold the recommendation that she be disciplined.

However, they subsequently relented. Indeed, her promotion was further accelerated when it became clear that the whole escapade was to be published as a training film, and that this would show off her individuality (rather than rebelliousness).

## Lobbying and informal systems

Lobbying is the presenting of a partial point of view to the greatest possible advantage. Knowing the audience and cheerleading enable it to be done effectively.

It becomes a key management skill in medium-sized and large organisations, and in sophisticated managerial and administrative systems. It becomes necessary when it is known, believed or perceived that alternative, more straightforward, approaches have not worked, and so the manager looks for alternative routes to the required destination.

All lobbying requires give and take – lobbyists need to have something to give that others want. The purpose is to engage interest, support, resources and energy, in pursuit of the stated aim. Gaining credence for a point of view in this way normally requires:

- the ability to make appointments with key individuals or groups
- the ability to present in both informal and formal settings in order to gain credence for the particular matter
- the ability to gain the interest of the audience in a very short space of time
- the ability to influence the audience to act in the lobbyist's interests.

To be effective, a manager or supervisor must know and understand their own environment as fully as possible and be able to identify accurately what others want from this environment, what they are able to give, and what they are not able to give. It is also necessary to identify among target audiences:

- sources of access
- sources of power and influence
- the approach required by each in order to succeed (see Figure 4.1).

In advance of any attempt to lobby, the best trade union officials or representatives of customer and environmental lobbies always know the sources of access, sources of power and influence, and the approach required by each.

Lobbying is seldom completely wholesome or ethical. The best that can be said for it is that it normally involves using questionable means, personal knowledge and contacts, for wholesome departmental and group outcomes. It is a very short step from this to seeking out contacts who can provide personal and professional advancement. Nevertheless, it goes on to an extent in most organisations. In

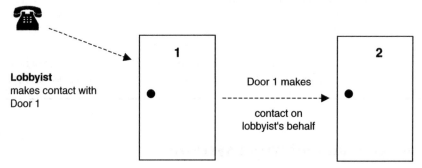

*Figure 4.1* The two doors. **Note:** Door 1 is used to gain access to Door 2, the real point of influence.

many cases also, it supersedes the formal channels and systems of organisations. Also, wherever lobbying and the use of informal systems becomes known, believed or perceived to be the most effective form of presentation, everyone does it – they have to.

## Leaking

Leaking is even more insidious than lobbying. The manager with integrity will do it only as a matter of last resort. Nevertheless, the formal systems of many organisations operate to dampen down quite legitimate dissent and discussion, and to restrict information. In these circumstances, leaking may be the only means open to managers and supervisors to get such matters into the open and to get them raised and discussed formally.

Integrity is further compromised because the leak has to be presented in such a way as to gain the desired effect and audience interest. This may – and does – mean showing or even tainting the message to ensure that it becomes a matter of legitimate concern all round.

Organisations, quite rightly, take a dim view of junior and middle members of staff using this form of presentation as a means of gaining influence or credence for their own advantage. Indeed, it is very often a disciplinary matter. However, alongside this, such organisations invariably need to review why these members of staff found it necessary to raise matters in such ways, and to question the overall effectiveness of their own formal systems. In general, leaks only take place either when the organisation knows something but refuses to do anything about it, because the formal systems simply do not work, or because the systems themselves are corrupt or toxic.

## Self-presentation

Self-presentation may be legitimate or illegitimate.

## Legitimate

Legitimate self-presentation is rooted in pride, enthusiasm, ambition, energy and commitment to the work of the department, to the teams and groups, and to the individual members. To be effective, it requires a knowledge and understanding of:

- each and every aspect of the work of the department, and of each group and member within it
- the hopes, fears and aspirations of each member of the department
- specific problems and issues that affect members of the department.

Effective legitimate self-presentation is founded on these bases. It is then enhanced through understanding the forms of approach required by, and important to, the organisation and its senior managers. This is then reinforced through the adoption of the required conventions and norms, including dress codes, forms of address and approach, written and oral delivery styles.

This, in turn, enhances the reputation of the manager or supervisor. As stated above (page 54), presentations are major occasions on which to bring to the attention of others a general reputation and reflection of the department, and of individual professional capability. Even when dealing with contentious issues or problems, the clarity with which the problem is understood and presented enhances the standing and reputation of the individual manager. The converse is also true – badly understood and poorly presented issues reflect not just on the individual manager or supervisor, but on their department and group as a whole.

Moreover, this level of knowledge and understanding brings both confidence and empathy, and tends to reinforce the self-awareness and self-assertiveness necessary to make effective presentations to any audience at all.

## Illegitimate

Illegitimate self-presentation is:

- when it is used to claim the credit for other people's work
- when it is used to blame individuals for mistakes in such ways as to divert attention away from the manager or supervisor in question
- when it cannot be supported with substance of activities or results
- when a particular problem or issue has been manipulated by someone to gain a wider audience for themselves

---

EXAMPLES

A large telecommunications company awards performance and profit-related bonuses on the basis of 'commitment to the organisation'. This commitment is measured solely on the basis of the hours in which the individual employees, managers and supervisors are present in the building. Consequently, whatever else they do, those individuals interested in achieving these bonuses make sure that they present themselves between 7.00 pm–8.00 pm on Monday, Tuesday, Wednesday and Thursday nights.

---

A junior social worker was dismissed from his position at a children's home in the county of Kent. He was found by an internal inquiry to have abused children in his care, and also to have stolen from the petty cash box of the institution where he worked. He was persuaded by his trade union official, a young man who had only been in the post for three months, to take the matter to industrial tribunal. This effectively required the inquiry to be reopened; it was also necessary to take statements for a second time from disturbed and vulnerable young people. The case was thrown out at tribunal, and the dismissal was upheld. However, the young trade union official gained a quick reputation for being prepared to represent anyone whatever the state of their circumstances. He consequently received two promotions within the space of the following year.

The line between legitimate and illegitimate is very fine. Again, if manipulating senior managers in these ways is known, believed or perceived to be successful, this will go on. It becomes a serious problem in many circumstances for those who wish to progress their careers but would rather do so on a fully wholesome basis.

## Presenting difficult and contentious issues

It is first necessary to identify areas of difficulty and contention. These normally come under one of the following situations:

- responses to legitimate customer and client complaints, responses to legitimate supplier complaints
- staff redundancies, redeployments and reorganisation, changes in technology and working patterns
- changes in management style
- the inability to meet expected or required pay rises
- dealing with unpopular work patterns and arrangements (e.g., mandatory overtime, night and weekend working).
- responding adversely to lobbies and requests from trade unions, staff representatives and other legitimate interest groups.

From a presentational point of view, these are always best handled by:

- confronting them early
- acknowledging the legitimacy of the concerns expressed
- identifying a priority order for such concerns, and a schedule for tackling them
- being prepared and willing to listen and adapt (see Box 4.6).

Each of the situations indicated above requires a visible presence from the organisation in question, together with a willingness and ability to discuss and resolve issues when they arise. This depends on the willingness of managers and supervisors to present themselves in these ways. It also depends on organisational recognition that those who do represent them need their full confidence, backing, and support; and that they also need full briefing and training. If anything does go wrong, if the issue is not resolved to the satisfaction of everyone, then this should become a point of review rather than blame.

## Box 4.6 Non-presentation: priorities, legitimacy and confrontation

It remains true that, in many cases, contentious issues are never confronted. This is because:

- It is less demanding for the managers involved. This is especially true for senior and top managers. When this happens, those further down the line are left to make the best of their own particular part of a situation. This requires them to work in isolation. This, in turn, leads to increases in staff grievances and disputes. It may also cause that an entirely unwarranted perception line managers and supervisors cannot control their staff.
- It is easier to hand tackling such issues to someone else. This is very often accompanied by parallel communications of which the two most insidious are: 'It gives junior managers and supervisors a chance to shine' – without ever stating the criteria by which they will be judged to be *shining* or not. Ordering junior managers and supervisors to 'bring solutions not problems' is actually impossible because the genuine problems and issues are not ordered or addressed at corporate level in the first place.
- Neglect, in which the attitude is 'If we do nothing about this, it will go away' or 'If we do nothing, the storm will blow itself out'. It is possible to pick many examples from overtly successful organisations where these attitudes have been known or believed to have worked. However, if the attitude becomes widespread, or becomes known as the corporate policy for addressing serious issues, there is always long-term damage to morale and output.

The language used should always be positive. This does not belittle the seriousness of the issues being raised, but it does reinforce the willingness of everyone involved to address and resolve the issues to everyone's satisfaction (see Box 4.7).

## Box 4.7 Using positive language

The greatest contribution to using positive language is to avoid the use of the words 'but', 'only' and 'never'.

**Negative**
This is excellent *but* it is very expensive
But he is *only* a cleaner
You will *never* get to the top unless . . .

**Positive**
It is excellent *and* it is very expensive
He is a cleaner
You will get to the top if . . .

Ambiguity often occurs because of a simple human failing to order the thoughts before speaking or writing, for example:

* she said 'she didn't mind what I did'
* she said she didn't mind what I did
* 'she,' said she, 'didn't mind what I did'.

Insidious ambiguity consists of the use of phrases such as 'There are no redundancies planned at present' and 'There are no plans for reorganisation at present'. A dual meaning is given – what is not said is whether there are future plans, nor is it clear how long the 'present' actually lasts.

The worst form of the use of non-positive language on a daily basis is the justification offered by managers and supervisors for over-emphasis on negativity, to the exclusion of all forms of positive language. One of the most common – and destructive – managerial and supervisory phrases in use is 'If my staff do not hear from me, then they know they are doing a good job'.

# Assertiveness and directness

A direct and assertive approach to presentations and advocacy arises from the point of view that any approach can only be effective if it is well thought out, its effect is understood in advance, and it the recipient knows quickly the aims, objectives and content of the presentation.

The following forms of behaviour and demeanour are essential to effectiveness:

* *Language:* clear, simple and direct; easy to understand and respond to on the part of the receivers. Words used are unambiguous and straightforward. Requests and demands are made in a clear and precise manner, and with sound reasons.
* *Aims and objectives:* precisely and clearly stated, recognising the effect that the presentation is likely to have on the recipient.
* *Delivery:* in a clear and steady tone of voice; where written, in a well-structured and easy-to-read format.
* *Voice:* always even, neither too loud nor too soft, and not involving shouting, threatening or abuse.
* *Persistence and determination:* where problems or issues are raised by the audience, the presenter sticks to the message, aims and objectives. The best presenters do not become side-tracked, but rather answer any problems that are raised without diverting from the main purpose.

- *Face and eyes:* the head is held up. There is plenty of eye contact with the audience. The gaze is steady. Delivery is reinforced with positive movements that relate to what is being said (e.g., smiles, laughter, encouragement, or a straight face when something has gone wrong).
- *Attention to the other non-verbal aspects:* uprightness of body, openness of hands and arms, no fidgeting or shuffling, no threatening gestures or table thumping or other displays of aggression (see Box 4.8).

## Box 4.8   Negative behaviours that affect presentations

The following approaches and attitudes normally destroy the credibility and effectiveness of presentations, whatever the audience:

- Aggression, shouting, swearing, table thumping and arguments. The matter in hand is lost as the aggressor (normally the presenter) strives to impose his/her point of view. Winning the argument becomes everything, rather than the substance of the presentation.
- Hostility – especially where the main emphasis is on the personalisation of the matters in hand. Often also characterised by shouting and swearing, the outcome is normally a personal attack – sometimes in public – on an individual or group.
- Defensiveness – characterised by nervousness, or oversensitivity, in responding to legitimate questions or concerns. Defensiveness often arises when either the presenter has no confidence in the material, or is unsure of the audience response.
- Inconsistency – according people and situations different levels of quality and value, and using different standards for different individuals and groups. This also extends to treating the same individual or group in different ways on different occasions.

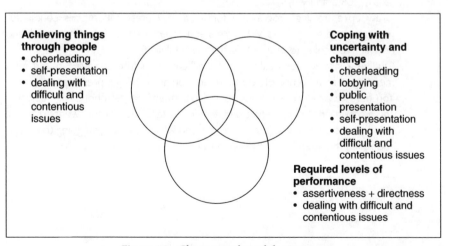

*Figure 4.2*   Chapter and model summary.

- Submissiveness – characterised by saying or doing anything that the audience wants so that the presentation can be finished with the overt minimum of fuss. In these situations, the presenters then remove themselves as quickly as possible.

# Conclusions

As stated at the beginning of this chapter, being a capable presenter is not always easy to achieve. However, by taking note of the points indicated here, great strides can be made in the development of an effective presentation style. This reflects personal and occupational standards, and levels of respect and value, accorded by managers and supervisors to the particular groups with whom they interact. It also reinforces personal and professional credibility, and mutuality of confidence and interest between manager and staff.

Effectiveness in presentation is required by staff, customers, clients and suppliers in a variety of situations. Above all, when problems need resolving, these groups expect someone with responsibility in the organisation to be able to speak quickly, clearly and with authority so that the matter is resolved.

Finally, effectiveness of presentation reinforces the personal standards and qualities present in the particular manager or supervisor, especially the qualities of integrity, enthusiasm, drive and commitment. These are reinforced by the attitude and approach to both self-presentation, and also the style of presentation adopted to deal with matters in public.

Using the Model referred to at the start of Chapter 1 (Figure 1.1), the material in this chapter is summarised in Figure 4.2.

QUESTIONS

1. Of all the barriers to effective presentation, which, in your view, are the hardest to overcome and why?
2. Draw up a training programme for a half-day presentation skills course for managers and supervisors. What aims and objectives have you set yourself and how are you going to ensure that these are fulfilled?
3. Outline a strategy for dealing with a difficult or unforeseen issue raised by a member of an audience of 100 to whom you are making a presentation.
4. You have to produce a talk for your department/college/cohort. The subject is *The organisation's annual report and review.* The talk is to last for twenty minutes. What points are you going to put across and why? How are you going to engage and retain the attention of the audience?

# ■ ⊻ 5 Motivation

## Introduction

Motivating people towards the attainment of goals and objectives is a key skill required of all managers and supervisors. Despite much research and study, no set of rules that apply to every situation can be offered, because the attitudes and behaviour of human beings can never be predicted with absolute certainty. Nevertheless, it is in everyone's interests to endeavour to attain the highest possible levels of motivation – not only is more productive and positive work output achieved for longer under conditions of high levels of commitment, but also the human aspects of belonging to an organisation are satisfied to a much greater extent.

Since the middle of the 20th century many studies of motivation have been carried out. Each of these brings a different focus to bear on the subject, and above all, indicates a particular set of managerial and supervisory skills that can be taught, learned and applied.

The headings under which motivation is studied are:

- motivation and attitudes to work
- motivation and needs
- motivation, satisfaction and dissatisfaction
- motivation, incentives and money
- motivation and expectations.

## Motivation and attitudes to work

### Theory X and Theory Y

McGregor (1961) looked at different approaches to motivating people, and classified managers, supervisors, and management and supervisory styles according to attitudes exhibited under two extremes. He called the two extremes Theory X and Theory Y (see Box 5.1).

The following points need to be noted:

- Under Theory X, there is very little that is positive; each point represents an assumption of negative, adversarial and conflicting working attitudes and practices, but without proposing anything other than more of the same thing.

## Box 5.1    Theory X and Theory Y

| Theory X | Theory Y |
|---|---|
| • People dislike work and will avoid it if they can. | • Work is necessary to people's psychological growth. |
| • People must be forced, bribed, bullied, cajoled or threatened to put out the right effort. | • People want to be interested in their work, and under the right circumstances, they can enjoy it. |
| • People would rather be directed than accept responsibility. | • People will direct themselves towards accepted and acceptable targets. |
| • People avoid responsibility. | • People will seek and accept responsibility given any encouragement to do so. |
| • People are motivated mainly by money. | • The discipline that people impose on themselves is much more effective and can be more severe than any imposed on them by managers and supervisors. |
| • People are motivated by anxiety about their security. | • Under the right conditions, people are motivated by the desire to realise their own potential. |
| • People have little creativity, except when it comes to avoiding rules and prescribed directions. | • Creativity and ingenuity are present in everybody and grossly under-used in organisations and work patterns. |

Source:  D. McGregor (1961) *The Human Side of Enterprise*, McGraw–Hill.

Adoption of Theory X attitudes is certain therefore, to lead to long-term decline in performance.
• Theory Y assumes an intrinsic interest in work, but without making it clear where that intrinsic interest is to come from in particular circumstances, e.g., repetitive or boring work (however well paid), work in extreme conditions (e.g., heat, cold), or working under bad or inappropriate management and supervisory styles.
• Theory Y assumes that self-discipline, together with intrinsic interest in work, obviates the need for more formal sanctions and disciplinary penalties when standards are not met. It is important to note that, just because work is intrinsically interesting, this does not mean that people will put all of their effort into it the whole time. It also does not mean that people holding down high quality, excellent and intrinsically interesting jobs are always human beings of the highest order (see Box 5.2).

## Box 5.2 Motivation and attitudes: anonymous examples

The following should all be considered in the light of the assertion that interesting work does not always lead to high levels of personal commitment. For example:

- one top international footballer was paid £70,000 a week over the course of a three-and-a-half-year contract with one of the world's top football clubs. This player happily accepted the money, but did not reciprocate with interest, effort or commitment on his own part.
- another top international footballer accepted a three-year contract from another of the world's top football clubs. Worth about £50,000 a week in 1997, the player himself knew that even for this money, he would be an understudy or a reserve – the club already had one of the world's leading exponents of the particular position
- in March 2000, a senior surgeon was dismissed by a large hospital Trust in the Home Counties of England for bullying, including striking a colleague. The fact of his supreme professional skill and quality, did not prevent him from conducting himself personally in ways unacceptable and abhorrent
- the Chief Executive of one of the UK's most well known national monuments, stated that he could only afford to take the job – which he had always wanted – because he had been able to earn a sufficiently high level of income in his previous job as Chief Executive of a large public authority.

It is therefore important to recognise that positive attitudes do not always follow intrinsic interests; and that intrinsic interest still has to be managed positively by those responsible.

It is also true that, during times of crisis, there is a behavioural shift towards the attitudes indicated in Theory X. In practice this is nearly always a managerial or supervisory shift – staff that respond to positive attitudes in good times, will respond to the same approaches when difficulties do arise, provided that things are explained to them clearly, directly and honestly. It remains true, however, that many organisations do compound initial difficulties by changing from a positive to a negative attitude when problems first become apparent.

# Motivation and needs

Maslow (1960) described a hierarchy of needs that explained different types and levels of motivation that were important to people at different times. This is normally depicted as a pyramid (see Figure 5.1).

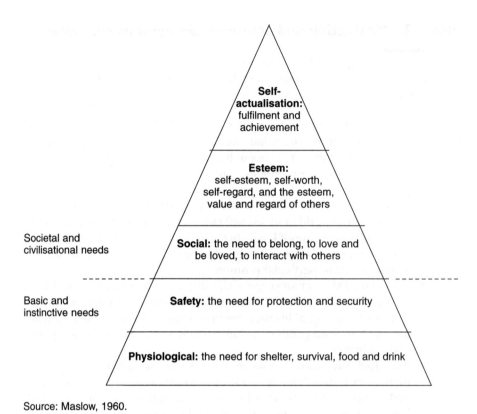

Source: Maslow, 1960.

*Figure 5.1*   A hierarchy of needs.

The hierarchy works from the bottom of the pyramid upwards, showing the most basic needs and motivations at the lowest levels, and those fostered by civilisation and society towards the top. The needs are as follows.

- *Physiological:* the need for food, drink, air, warmth, sleep and shelter.
- *Safety and security:* protection from danger, threats or deprivation.
- *Social:* a sense of belonging to a group or society, for example, the family, the organisation, the work group.
- *Esteem:* the need for self-respect and self-esteem; and also the respect, esteem, appreciation, recognition and status accorded by others.
- *Self-actualisation:* the need for self-fulfilment, self-realisation, personal development, accomplishment, material and social growth, and the development and fulfilment of the creative faculties.

Maslow reinforced this hierarchy by stating that people tended to satisfy their needs systematically. They started with the basic instinctive needs and then moved up the hierarchy. Until one particular group of needs was satisfied, a person's behaviour would be dominated by them. Thus, the hungry or homeless person will look to their needs for self-esteem and society only after their hunger has been satisfied or they have found a place to live. Maslow also pointed out that people's motives were constantly being modified as their situation changed; this was especially true of the self-actualisation needs in which having achieved measures of fulfilment and recognition, people nevertheless tended to remain unsatisfied and to wish to progress this further.

Accordingly, Cartwright (2000) adds a sixth level to the hierarchy. This, he calls the 'unattainable' – that which people strive for, but never reach, or never reach fully (see Figure 5.2).

This may then be broken down as:

- the constant striving for new directions, achievements, goals and direction
- the constant revision upwards of personal, professional and occupational expectations.

The following also need to be recognised in this context; and they are all negative.

- Childlike wishing or daydreaming that, in practice, is never fulfilled, usually because the person is unwilling to put in the effort necessary to achieve a stated goal.

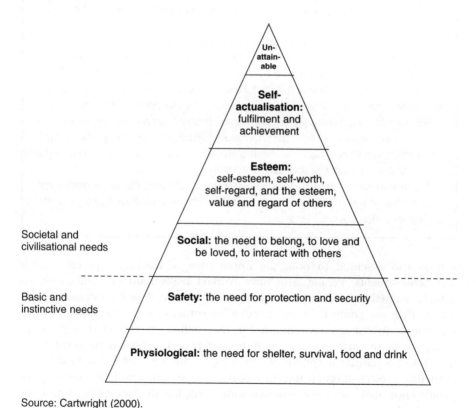

Source: Cartwright (2000).

*Figure 5.2*  A hierarchy of needs.

- Childlike foot-stamping, for example, the attitude of: 'I want to be leader/manager/pilot/hailed as a genius; and if I can't, then I'm not going to do anything'.
- Clinging to a position of real or perceived influence or authority for a period of years because it is at least is an outward sign of respect, esteem and fulfilment, for example the long-term serving shop steward, local councillor, professional association representative.
- Insisting on the unattainable or impossible, for example, when something suddenly becomes unavailable, the individual insists that he has to have it or else will not work.

---

┌─ EXAMPLE ─────────────────────────────────────────────

A highly promising architect gained a reputation early in his professional career for attention to detail. Consequently, he was initially extremely successful, because he thought of things that others would take for granted. His clients were always happy because he went into great detail as to what they were going to get; while those who were to build the finished design always knew more or less precisely what they were going to have to do from an early stage.

However, he became obsessive about details. In the end, clients started to turn away from him because he would insist on agreement on the minutest of items on his own terms.

The turning point in his career came when he lost two contracts. He lost a major hotel project because he insisted that only particular species of plants should be included in the reception area and that real flowers, and not plastic flowers, should be put on restaurant, bar and café tables; and also in the hotel rooms. When discussing furnishings for one of the bar areas, the manager on the client's side mentioned, in passing, that a particular strain of furniture was now out of commission and no longer produced. The architect insisted that, nevertheless, this particular type of furniture would be used – or else the project would not go ahead. Accordingly, the particular architect lost the job.

Because he was extremely well known in the profession, the word quickly got around that he was not to be used again; that his attention to detail had turned into a blind and unproductive obsession.

└───────────────────────────────────────────────────────

It is also essential to note the importance of marking and celebrating real achievements. People who have worked really hard and effectively to achieve something feel a sense of emptiness once it is completed. In the future, they are going to have to strive for something else of course; in the meantime, they need recognition for that achievement. Accordingly, it is becoming increasingly usual for both managers and organisations to celebrate the end of a particular sphere of activities, or the successful conclusion of a particular project, through having a party or celebration so that, not only do people know that they have achieved something, but the fact is also outwardly recognised.

## Other studies of needs

Other needs-based studies have sought to pin down more precisely the actual needs of people. Studies undertaken at Kent State University in 1997 highlighted six in particular:

- the need for recognition and identity
- the need for influence over people and circumstances
- the need to influence the course of life
- the need for influence over the environment
- the need to be in control of events (rather than at their mercy).
- the need for achievements and for those achievements tobe recognised

The Kent State University Studies also indicate that where one of these needs for influence cannot be satisfied, individuals will seek to remedy the matter elsewhere. Thus, for example, if people have no influence over others at home, they will seek it at the place of work; conversely, people who have influence in one sphere of life may (or may not) be satisfied with this. In particular, also:

- predictability, or a perceived inability to influence the course of working life, always leads to problems and disputes in the workplace
- perceived inability to control events, i.e., to be at their mercy, always leads to a general loss of motivation.

## Hidden needs

Packard (1958) studied motivation from a marketing point of view. He identified the following needs under the heading 'Marketing Eight Hidden Needs'. The needs identified were:

- reassurance of worth
- ego gratification
- creativity
- love and love objects
- sense of power
- roots and traditions
- immortality
- emotional security.

He then stated that, once the particular need for the product had been generated, the prospective customer or client then needed to provide satisfactory and comfortable answers to the two following questions:

- Am I good enough for the product?
- Is it good enough for me?

This study was of exceptional importance because it was the first to relate motivation to buying and consumer behaviour; it has great implications for marketing.

It also has much broader workplace application:

- *Reassurance of worth and ego gratification:* reflected in salary, status, trappings; size and location of office; personal, professional and occupational reputation; the name and reputation of the organisation; location of work (e.g., at head office or in the field); the ways in which the job is regarded in society at large.
- *Creativity:* the extent to which the individual can bring their own skills, knowledge and qualities into the work. Very often those working in rigid, highly defined roles experience great frustration as the result of having little scope to demonstrate their own talents. Historically, factory work removed creativity altogether, and many other occupations have sought to do this to a greater or lesser extent.
- *Love:* in work terms, this is reflected in feelings of respect and value, self-respect and self-value. There is always a form of identity between the organisation and its staff, and therefore, a relationship. Very high and enduring levels of motivation are present in those who can state with real pride that they work for a particular organisation – in addition to, not rather than, carrying out a particular job (see Box 5.3).
- *Sense of power:* job satisfaction is created through the ability to operate autonomously; produce individual, as well as team and group, results; and sometimes, to influence individual earnings. Each of these aspects reflects knowledge, belief or perception of a sense of power, and also the ability to influence the working situation.
- *Roots and traditions:* the strength of these become apparent when changes in current practices are proposed. Suddenly the old ways become wonderful points to cling on to because they are comfortable and familiar, in contrast to the new that is unknown and uncertain. This is a real barrier that has

## Box 5.3   Pride in the place of work

When they first came to work in the West, Japanese manufacturing companies went to a lot of trouble to ensure the motivation and commitment of their staff to the company itself. The main reason for this was purely pragmatic – the companies required full flexibility of working, and it was therefore extremely difficult to give people meaningful job titles. What they therefore set out to do was to engender and sustain a sense of pride in the organisation, the output of which was to be – and remains to this day – 'I work for Sony/Mitsubishi/ Toshiba/Toyota'.

This contrasts utterly with those carrying out high quality, technically expert, and supreme intrinsic value work in public services in the UK at the beginning of the 21st century. It is extremely difficult to get teachers, doctors, nurses, lecturers and social workers to take any pride at all in the institutions for which they work. This is because the management style has assumed a professional or vocational motivation; and consequently, no steps have been taken to achieve any organisational or personal commitment to the broader institution.

to be surmounted when developments are being implemented (see also Chapter 13).

- *Emotional security and immortality:* in terms of work motivation, people seek the illusion of security and immortality either in their work occupation, in their organisation, or in a combination of the two. From this point of view, there are advantages to companies that feel themselves able to offer job security or lifetime employment in 'guarantees'. It is worth noting that these, together with high wage levels, are present for example, at the Nissan Sunderland car plant, which is the highest output car factory in the world outside Japan and South Korea.

Packard's two final questions can be rephrased as:

- *Am I good enough for this company or organisation?* This requires attention to attitudes and behaviour at least as much as skills, knowledge and expertise. The relationship between organisation and individual has to be within the boundaries of comfort on both sides. No effective relationship can be achieved if the employee, however good they are technically, is overawed by their surroundings on the one hand, or not willing to work in them on the other.
- *Is the organisation good enough for me?* Only individuals can answer this question for themselves. Again, the relationship has to be seen as more or less in balance. If the answer is no, serious problems are certain to occur at some point because the relationship is based on expediency, convenience, comfort, or even contempt (see Box 5.4).

## Box 5.4   Packard's questions adapted

These questions can then be adapted as follows, so that a greater insight into individual and group motivation can be gained.

*Personal questions*

- Am I good enough for my manager? Am I good enough for my co-workers? Am I good enough for my subordinates? Am I good enough for my other colleagues?
- Is each of these groups good enough for me? Am I pleased and happy to be working with them? Am I ashamed to be working with them? Am I proud to be working with them?
- Am I good enough for the company's products/services/customers/suppliers? Are they good enough for me?

The following questions can then be addressed by managers and supervisors about members of their department or team:

- Is this person good enough for us? Is this person too good for us? Is this person not good enough for us?

And in answer to the second and third questions:

- What are we going to do about it?

And developing the point in ways similar to the personal questions:

- Are we pleased to have this person work for us? Are we proud of him/her? Are we ashamed of him/her?

This form of debate can go a long way towards establishing the extent to which a positive, productive, behavioural and attitudinal base can be created as the cornerstone of a long-term and positive working relationship.

# Motivation, satisfaction and dissatisfaction

Research carried out by Herzberg (1960) shed a different light on the subject of motivation. Relating studies of motivation directly to places of work, he sought to establish answers to the following questions:

- What factors lead you to experience extreme dissatisfaction with your job?
- What factors lead you to experience extreme satisfaction with your job?

These were then displayed as shown in Figure 5.3.

Herzberg suggested that the factors identified on the left-hand side of Figure 5.3 made people very dissatisfied, but did not, on the other hand, motivate them positively to work harder or more productively. Herzberg asserted that this was akin to 'removing unhappiness' rather than 'making people happy'. Or, calling them 'hygiene factors', he related them to the equivalent of washing your hands – keeping your hands clean would not give you good health, but allowing them to get dirty would quickly lead to health deterioration.

Factors on the opposite side of the diagram have little to do with money or style of supervision; they concentrate rather on achievement, recognition, responsibility, advancement and the content of the work itself.

If this view is adopted in order to understand and maximise motivation and morale, managers and supervisors have to be able to relate achievement, recognition, the nature of the work, the prospects for advancement and growth to:

- what is available, and therefore possible, in the circumstances
- whether these particular achievements are of value to the staff involved (see Box 5.5).

## Box 5.5   Motivation, satisfaction and dissatisfaction

Reference was made in Box 5.3 to the problems that public service managers have in motivating their professional staff. In particular, National Health Service management have great problems in this area with their medical staff.

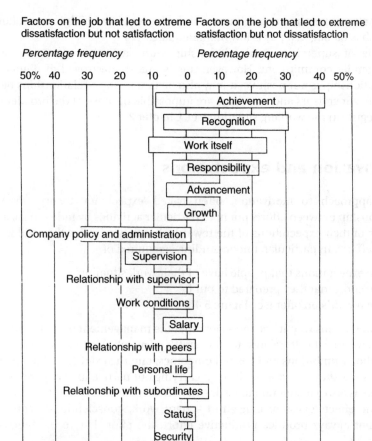

Factors on the job that led to extreme dissatisfaction but not satisfaction

Factors on the job that led to extreme satisfaction but not dissatisfaction

Source: Herzberg (1960)

*Figure 5.3* Two-factor theory.

Medical staff in the NHS seek recognition for their professional skills and expertise. They expect to be recognised for effective and successful treatment, and curing of patients according to medical needs and priorities.

However, the only recognition that they are accorded by their managers comes from whether they work within budget, manage waiting lists, are able to respond to short-term and expedient political priorities, and whether they can put through a demonstrable volume rather than quality of work.

This also requires an equally deep understanding of where things go wrong:

- If achievement and recognition are not present or not valued, then demoralisation sets in.

- Loyalty, respect and commitment cannot be bought with high wages; however, each is damaged if pay is low or inadequate.
- Style of supervision and relationship with supervisor does not of itself engender commitment. However, this is quickly destroyed or diluted if the relationship is not positive; it may also be that positive relationships between staff, supervisors and managers are impossible because of the broader lack of integrity in the working situation (see Chapter 2).

## Motivation and expectations

This approach to motivation, often called 'expectancy theory', draws the relationship between efforts put in to particular activities by individuals, and the nature of their expectations of the rewards that they perceive they will get from these efforts. In particular, understanding is required of:

- The expectations that people have of their work situation
- The effort that they prepared to put in
- The rewards on offer (see Figure 5.4).

Viewed in this way, it becomes clear that the management of staff expectations is a key priority. It relates to the staff's view of their work, expectations, aspirations, ambitions and desired outcomes, and the extent to which these can be satisfied at the workplace through carrying out particular occupations.

There is also a distinction to be drawn between the effort put into performance and the effectiveness of that effort – hard work, conscientiously carried out, does not always produce productive effort; the effort has to be directed and targeted.

There also has to be a match between the rewards expected and those that are actually available – a reward is simply a value judgement placed on something,

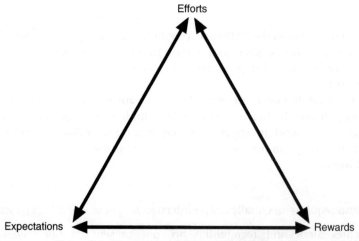

*Figure 5.4* Expectancy theory: a simplified model.

offered in return for effort, and if this is not valued by the receiver, it has no effect on motivation.

When the desired rewards are not forthcoming, therefore, demotivation occurs. When rewards are available for little effort, a lack of mutual respect occurs – if something comes too easily, people do not value it. If people have been given unreasonable expectations, they will see all their efforts have been put in for no good reason and again, will become demoralised.

# Motivation, money and incentives

It used to be thought that enhanced financial reward was sufficient to motivate anyone to maximum effort. Especially, those concerned with the management of production lines in their early days, felt that by overcompensating 'the workers' for lengthy spells on repetitive and boring tasks, they would make up for the lack of intrinsic worth in the work. However, what has happened here is a confusion of the terms 'motivation' and 'incentive'.

- Motivation springs from within – it is an attitude of mind that may be encouraged by external factors, but it is fundamentally firmly related to self-discipline. Motivation can also remain where the external influences that engendered it have ceased to exist.
- Incentives, on the other hand, belong to those forces that are applied from the outside and are designed as positive external influences to encourage improved performance. It follows, therefore, that people at work, even managers, may be encouraged to greater effort by an increase in financial reward, whether earned by effort, or through bonus payments, or profit-related payments (see Box 5.6).

## Box 5.6   Incentive payments

Research carried out by the Institute of Management (1994) and the Economist Intelligence Unit (1996) demonstrated that incentive payments had no discernible effect on performance. Both these, and also a study carried out at University College London (1997–98) drew particular attention to the fact that attendance allowances had no discernible effect on attendance. In particular, attention was drawn to the following two cases.

- Coal miners who received bonuses for attending the whole of the working week were likely to structure their personal finances around minimum rather than maximum attendance; they would attend the full week when they needed additional money, e.g., for holidays or outings.
- A large European bank offered its staff an extra week's holiday provided it took no time off sick during the course of the year. Members of staff who found themselves having to take a day off sick, would make sure that they took at least a further four days anyway.

In addition, it was found that some Chief Executives and senior managers of large corporations have deliberately publicised their own huge pay rises, very often supported by share options. The psychological purpose of this has been to generate for themselves an identity – notoriety – that compensates for their otherwise lack of intrinsic value in the job, or the identity that goes with it.

None of the studies found any evidence of where huge pay rises, or huge pay differentials, had any discernible long-term effect on performance.

Source: University College London (2000) *Management Studies Centre Working Papers*

## Principles of motivation

Each of the researched and theoretical approaches indicated above brings a particular slant to the central question of how to get long-term, sustainable, optimum levels of performance from staff.

There are no hard and fast rules. However, there are factors that are practised with success in many organisations and these are based on operational experience as well as the formal research indicated. They centre around the following aspects of work, and also, to some extent, indicate why people work in the jobs that they do.

Above all, managers and supervisors need to be aware of the fact that very few people work for money only – once a satisfactory income has been achieved, pay becomes a secondary consideration even though it may be given emphasis at different times.

Reasons for working differ between individuals, as do the factors that motivate them. However, the more of the following there are in place, the greater the opportunity for securing long-term positive motivation and commitment:

- *Security:* holding a job spells security. This is a common positive reason for working. Working in central and local government services, and company head offices, used to be considered extremely secure and therefore, people chose to remain within these areas. Japanese industrial companies working in the West also try to ensure a form of job security through great attention to training and development programmes, and full flexibility of working.
- *Status:* to be employed gives status within the worker's own social environment. Both socially and at work, some jobs are looked upon as having greater status than others and many people are motivated to achieve such a status.

  It is also essential that the individual's perception of status is recognised. For example, somebody may be happy to work as a 'sales representative' provided that they are actually called 'account manager'; or they may be happy to carry out any job provided that it is in a particular organisation (this is so that they can say to everybody, 'I work in a university' or 'I work for Shell/Toyota/The National Theatre/Chrysalis', and so on).

- *Use of skills and intelligence:* people are proud of their skills and work to employ them to best advantage. Dull, repetitive work is not calculated to motivate anyone to give the best possible performance. This form of work is extremely detrimental both to physical and mental health; and one of the findings of the Kent State Studies (see page 77) was that the effects of this form of work exhibited a lack of all of the influences required. As well as decline in physical and mental health and well-being, the inability to exert these influences invariably led to increases in both workplace and broader social problems.

  Work that does demand imagination or the use of creativity and initiative is much more certain of sustaining long-term positive performance. Dull, repetitive work should therefore always be positively managed to remove the dull and repetitive elements. The best ways of doing this are:
  - sharing out the dull and boring tasks equally between all members of the group
  - making sure that everybody can carry out every job required in the department, and then rotating them
  - developing and enhancing work methods within the department
  - ensuring that there are minimum and maximum lengths of time spent on dull, boring and repetitive work before a substantial change is made
  - training and developing everybody for future interesting work – and ensuring that this can be delivered.
- *Goals and aspirations:* everyone has goals and aspirations. Some people fulfil these through work, others elsewhere. In general, however, everyone at work responds to the opportunity to progress, develop and enhance their range of skills, qualities and experience. The extent to which each of these is progressing is best measured against goals and aspirations and very often supported through planned programmes of organisational, group and individual development, having regard to organisational professional, technical, occupational and individual needs (see Figure 5.5).
- *External aspirations:* to some people, job titles are important as a mark of social standing. To some people, the wider knowledge in their particular part of society that they are a Chief Executive, Head Teacher, manager, and so on, is a key feature of motivation. Others concentrate on earning sufficient money to be able to have a new car, take longer holidays, send their children to private schools, and so on.
- *A congenial work environment:* everyone is much more motivated when they know that they are going into a positive environment to work. This is a mark of the integrity of the working relationship between the organisation and its staff (see Chapter 2).
- *Managerial and supervisory styles:* bad and adversarial managerial and supervisory styles are always demotivating. Whatever style is adopted must be capable of recognition and understanding by those working in the situation; as stated in Chapter 13, as long as the style is founded on integrity, it does not matter whether it is autocratic, participative or democratic.
- *Type of industry or occupation:* many people are motivated by the fact that they work in a particular sector or carry out a particular occupation. Because

a)

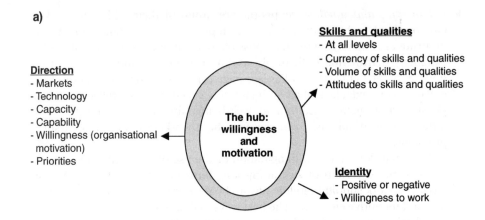

**Direction**
- Markets
- Technology
- Capacity
- Capability
- Willingness (organisational motivation)
- Priorities

**The hub: willingness and motivation**

**Skills and qualities**
- At all levels
- Currency of skills and qualities
- Volume of skills and qualities
- Attitudes to skills and qualities

**Identity**
- Positive or negative
- Willingness to work

b)

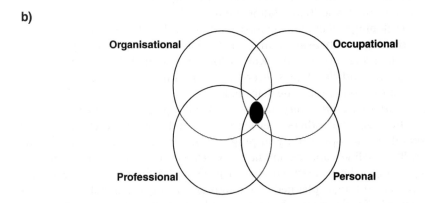

Organisational

Occupational

Professional

Personal

**Note:** To be fully effective, and gain maximum long-term benefits, personal and professional needs must be catered for, as well as organisational and occupational. This is explained in more detail in Chapter 10.

*Figure 5.5*   Criteria for effective development of (a) organisations and (b) individuals.

of the feelings of rejection and failure left on the part of the staff it is a serious problem for personal and social morale when an organisation closes down. For example, when many of the coal mines in the UK were closed down in the 1970s and 1980s, towns and villages lost their identity and their sense of community as a consequence. When the Longbridge car factory was sold on by BMW in March 2000, it caused a great sense of social demoralisation, because people did not know what was to happen as result.

- *Engendering commitment:* it is being increasingly recognised that motivation is a function of commitment. If organisations require commitment from their staff, then they should be committed to their staff. They need to take whatever actions are necessary in order to ensure that this commitment is present; and that the maintenance of this commitment is a part of long-term policy and objectives.

- *Engendering fairness:* where money and financial rewards do contribute to motivation, this is in terms of value, worth and, above all, fairness. People will work in any set of circumstances provided that they believe that the rewards for doing so are fair. If they know that the rewards for doing so are not fair, they will remain in the situation only so long as it serves their own interests to do so. Moreover, no long-term and enduring positive relationship or loyalty is engendered.

- *Achievement:* everyone should be rewarded for their achievements, both financially and otherwise. People deserve recognition for what they have done. It is extremely demoralising when managers and supervisors take praise for the successes of their staff, but blame them when things go wrong.

- *Respect and value:* everyone requires to be treated with respect and value whatever their occupation. It is a mark of human dignity as well as sound workplace practice. Where people are treated with neither respect nor value, they will seek to leave the situation as quickly as possible. Moreover, when dealing with disciplinary or grievance matters, managers should concentrate on the professional, technical and occupational aspects. People's personal character and integrity should never be called into question. This constitutes a loss of self-respect, self-value, and self-worth and is certain to lead to increases in resentment, disputes and grievances.

## Motivation in practice

If financial incentives are not effective as true motivators, then what steps can managers and supervisors take to create positive motivation in their staff?

There are a number of factors that are generally accepted as being of value in achieving some measure of success in encouraging positive attitudes and commitment:

- *Atmosphere:* an atmosphere of cooperation, trust and openness must be generated between managers, supervisors and their staff. This leads to the creation of an atmosphere of mutual respect. Autocratic, adversarial and confrontational management styles simply lead to conflict.

- *Recognition:* human beings have a need to be esteemed and recognised. Managers who realise this, and recognise the achievement of their subordinates, are much more likely to be successful in motivating them positively. Recognition of individual and group efforts is also necessary. All employees like to feel that their efforts are appreciated, particularly if some improvement in performance or some contribution outside the narrow requirements of the job has been achieved. Words of praise or encouragement raise the morale of everybody so long as they are justified.

- *Involvement and participation:* apart from anything else, involvement and participation, and rights to information, are legal requirements in all matters concerning workplace practice. In the future, this is certain to be extended to include financial information, business direction and performance, so long as the UK remains a member of the European Union. More generally, however, people always respond better when they feel fully involved in a situation. They understand it, and can therefore become committed to it. The basis of this involvement and commitment is trust, integrity, communication and information. People understand much better when they know why they need to work in particular ways; and what the consequences of working or not working are. Ideally, therefore, it is necessary to draw everyone into contributing to planning and decision-making (see Figure 5.6).

This should all be supported by informal discussions between managers, supervisors and subordinates on matters concerning work practices. This is a major contributor to building morale and trust; and is also an early warning system for problems.

● *Work satisfaction:* clearly people expect financial rewards from their place of work. They also expect development, variety, enhancement and the opportunity to progress, whatever their chosen field of work. It must be made clear, therefore what is and is not available to people as the result of working in a particular occupation or organisation. Increasingly, it is being recognised that organisations should demonstrate the limitations of working at a particular place so that when staff are ready, they can move on with the blessing of their employers to something else that they would like to do. And, if they do wish to stay in the organisation, then, in order that

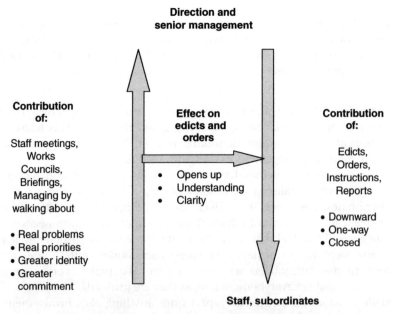

*Figure 5.6* Participation and involvement.

their commitment remains secure, they must be offered opportunities when they arise.

## Conclusions

People clearly work better when they are highly motivated, and there is a direct relationship between quality of performance and levels of motivation and commitment. Conversely, the volume and quality of work declines when motivation reduces, or when demotivation is present. The need to motivate, and be motivated, is therefore continuous and constant. It is essential to recognise the following:

- Motivation comes partly from within the individual, and partly from the particular situation. It is therefore subject to continuous adaptation.
- It is clear that no genuine motivation exists where value, esteem and respect are not present. Value, esteem and respect are basic human requirements extended to all places of work and all occupations (and indeed, to every walk of life).
- The key features of an environment in which it is possible to generate high and continuing levels of motivation and morale are: integrity of relationships, high levels of knowledge and understanding, general prevailing attitudes, and an understanding of people's expectations and needs.
- People respond positively to equality and fairness of treatment, and negatively when these are not present. They also recognise when equality and fairness of treatment are present, and when they are not.
- The main obligation lies with the organisation to provide the conditions in which high levels of motivation and morale can be generated. If they do this, organisations are entitled to expect a positive response and continuing high

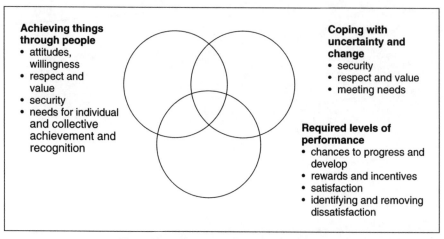

*Figure 5.7*  Chapter and model summary.

levels of commitment from those who come to work for them, provided that the environment does not deteriorate.

Using the Model referred to at the start of Chapter 1 (Figure 1.1), the material in this Chapter is summarised in Figure 5.7.

QUESTIONS

1. To what extent is the motivation to work a) similar, and b) different in respect of:
   - factory staff
   - doctors
   - charity volunteer workers
   - professional sports players (those not at the very top of their chosen sport)
   - the manager of a village grocery store.
2. Under what circumstances, if any, does the Theory X view of the world apply? In such circumstances, what actions can be taken by managers and individuals to improve the quality of the working life?
3. Outline the advantages and disadvantages of engaging in job enrichment and job enlargement programmes for unskilled operative and clerical staff. How might these be measured for success or failure? What are the pitfalls that have to be overcome?
4. What are the main effects – positive and negative – on motivation and morale at your place of work, university or college? What action should be taken by those responsible within the institution to address the problems? Produce a summary of the 'general state of motivation and morale' at the institution.
5. Identify your own motivators and demotivators. Which are your overriding concerns and why? What steps might be taken in order to a) overcome the demotivators, and b) enhance the motivators?

# ▼ 6 Appraising and measuring performance

## Introduction

Appraisal and measurement of performance are the processes of checking, monitoring, reviewing and evaluating the short-, medium- and long-term progress and direction of organisations, departments, divisions, functions, groups and individuals. This is conducted with the object of establishing:

- what is going well, and why
- what is going wrong or could be improved, and why.

It also involves taking steps to understand and develop what is going well and to understand and develop what is going wrong.

Appraising and measuring all aspects of performance are essential managerial and supervisory activities; yet they continues to be carried out poorly or inadequately (if at all) across all sectors. This is because:

- Everything is driven by the interests of one dominant stakeholder; this is overwhelmingly the shareholder, demanding that actions are taken with the sole purpose of driving up the short-term share value.
- There is no time (i.e., time is not made) to do the job fully, and so it gets done at best sketchily, at worst, not at all.
- Appraisal and measurement systems (especially staff performance appraisal systems) are not believed in, valued or respected.
- Appraisal and measurement systems (especially staff performance appraisal systems) are overwhelmingly bureaucratic, amounting to little more than form filling exercises.
- Appraisal and measurement activities may also throw up uncomfortable truths (see Box 6.1).

### Box 6.1  Performance appraisal: initial examples

- 'I work in a technical support group. Our manager decided that the best measure of our performance is the number of calls we take in a day. Since we have three phone lines, our staff have found that using one line to call yourself on another line will give you credit for a call.'
- 'Bob was assigned an urgent project with a very high priority which involved designing a new product in a very short period. Bob worked 18-hour days for weeks. He treated weekends just like week days. He only

went home to sleep. The project was completed on time and Bob's boss was congratulated heartily by the organisation's top management. The next week was time for Bob's performance review. The meeting took five minutes. The manager sat Bob down and said: 'Bob I think you may be a little disappointed with the rating I have given you. Generally speaking, you have been working well; however, there are two problems you have which need to be addressed. First, I have never seen you go a whole day without unbuttoning your shirt and loosening your tie. Second – and this is more important – you have a habit of stretching out at your desk and kicking your shoes off. Frankly that is offensive. If it were not for these problems you would rate a solid "competent". As it is, you are scruffy and I am afraid that means you are "developing".' (Source: S. Adams (1996) *The Joy of Work* – Box Tree.)

- **Lastminute.com:** an institutional investor placed millions of pounds in the share flotation of Lastminute.com. After an immediate initial rise, the share price sank and by the end of three months' trading, the shares were trading at little more than half of their initial sale price. The particular institutional investor appraised his performance thus: 'The PR was a disaster. What were they doing putting up a grinning schoolgirl? [i.e., Martha Lane-Fox, aged 27]'. He went on to assert that what was required to resurrect Lastminute.com was someone with gravitas to be seen running the business. 'You don't need to be young to run a new economy operation. We want to see a heavyweight there. It's not sexist to say the City would like to see a bloke who knows what he's doing.' (Source: C. Blackhurst *Blackhurst's Diary – Management Today*, May 2000.)

## Appraisal and measurement process

Appraisal and measurement can only be effective if they are carried out against specific aims and objectives. Herein lies a major perceived problem. Because everything – production, output, service levels, human resource performance and return on investment – takes place under circumstances that are never fully predictable or controllable there is a tendency to:

- try and make everything linear or simple, e.g., measuring simple percentage return on investment, devising performance league tables (hospitals, schools, police), giving sales people volume or income targets
- reduce everything to a series of sub-objectives and detail so that by measuring component parts, the whole can implicitly be measured
- engage in extensive paperwork and form-filling that *prove* that work has been carried out to the satisfaction of everyone.

None of these addresses the key questions of:

- what is being measured
- why it is being measured, where, when, or by whom.

# Aims and objectives

Aims and objectives arise from the planning process (see Chapter 7). The outcome needs to be a series of short-, medium- and long-term targets, set in context, and directed at effective performance. Herein lies the next problem – identifying what for particular groups and individuals actually constitutes effective performance in particular sectors, organisations, departments, divisions and functions.

To be subject to effective appraisal and measurement, performance has to be related to the major components of the planning process – its economic and environmental context, pressures, elements of risk, and contingencies. Aims and objectives are best set in the context of past and current performance, and future projections, and an initial or present appraisal determines whether past and current performance is acceptable or not, and what changes need to occur in their own context.

Once this is established, then a further look is required. This is to address the reasons why aims and objectives are to be measured in the ways decided. The usual answer is one of the following:

- It is the only way that we can think of or understand, or nobody can think of a better way.
- It is the only way acceptable to, or recognised by, staff, customers, clients, shareholders, unions.
- It has been decided upon by a particular figure or department who cannot afford to be seen to be wrong, or to back down, or to change their mind.
- Everybody else in the world/sector/country/locality does things this way, so we must to.
- Everything can be kept very general so as to avoid tackling real issues that the process might bring to light (see Box 6.2).

## Box 6.2   Key issues: examples

- The first submarine was built in 1821. It was deemed to be 98% successful on the grounds that it could be submerged when required. Unfortunately, it could not resurface.
- The missile weaponry used by NATO during the war against Yugoslavia in 1998 could avoid detection from defence systems, and was electronically guided. Unfortunately, it would not work when there were clouds in the sky.
- In 1992, the Deputy Chief Executive of a County Council produced a briefing for colleagues on the Council's services without once mentioning the clients and communities that they were supposed to be serving. The same Deputy Chief Executive had also endorsed a proposal at the same time to go ahead with an exclusive housing developing on what was known to have been a toxic waste site.

- In 1999, the Chief Executive Officer of a health care trust denied that prescription budgets were allocated on a postcode basis. When the next audit demonstrated that, in fact, prescription drugs were indeed allocated on a postcode basis, he was promoted with double salary to a Department of Health central corporate function.

## Why?

On the face of it, this seems a very silly question! Of course performance *must* be measured for success, failure and the lessons to be learned. However:

- Success and failure are subjective value judgements driven by the whims and self-interest of individuals and groups; and in any case, they are often left at that, without ever being reviewed or assessed as to why particular activities or staff members were known, believed, perceived or deemed successful, or otherwise to have failed.
- Nobody wants to be associated with failure, nor are they particularly keen to learn from their own professional and occupational mistakes. Goodworth (1990), writing about recruitment and selection, states that 'People will tend to do in the future what they have done in the past' rather than change their approach or attitude to work, or more specifically and importantly, their values, priorities and ways of working.

All organisations, departments, divisions, groups and individuals need to know how they are getting on, and the overall and interim aims and objectives against which they are being assessed. They also need to know, understand and accept the consequences of this. Therefore, whether it is departmental, divisional, functional, organisational or human resource performance that is being assessed, full clear briefing is required.

## When and where?

The best measurement and appraisal of all performance is carried out:

- on a daily basis by walking the job, identifying problems and issues before they become serious, reinforcing the positive and dealing with the negative on the spot
- on a weekly or monthly basis at short staff meetings at which issues can be raised and debated more widely, and which are then confirmed in short notes or memoranda
- on a formal basis, at least quarterly, at which progress is checked and confirmed in writing.

This is in contrast to most measurement and appraisal activities that are carried out:

- on an annual or bi-annual basis in general terms only
- by concentrating on forms and paperwork rather than specific aspects

## Box 6.3   Bland and innocuous terms: examples

- *Human resource appraisal:* the blandest of questions asked in human resource appraisal processes is: 'What do you do badly? What could you improve upon?' Since anybody answering these questions honestly is likely to be disciplined or downgraded for incompetence, the rehearsed answer to these questions normally include: 'I find it impossible to go home at night', 'My loyalty to the company outweighs everything else', and 'I work too hard and find it impossible to relax'.
- *Investment appraisal:* the worst forms of blandness in investment appraisal measurement concern reports to shareholders. These are very often written up in company annual reports as: 'another record year', 'we are doing no better/worse than anyone else in the sector', 'our share price continues to perform at least to expectations', 'markets are buoyant/difficult/growing'. Only on the rarest of occasions do shareholders' representatives try and get at the heart of what is being said, much less understand what the general terms state or imply.

- by aspiring to fill in the forms in bland and innocuous terms that bind nobody to anything (see Box 6.3).
- by stating everything in generally positive terms, to give the overwhelming impression that everything is alright, or that there is nothing to worry about; certainly that there are no serious problems to worry about; certainly also that there are no serious problems that need addressing.

## Who?

Whatever the appraisal being carried out, it needs to be a joint process, addressed by all concerned, and directed and facilitated by the particular manager or supervisor. It is not to be used to apportion blame or find scapegoats. Whatever performance appraisal scheme is in place needs to be made to work to best advantage for all concerned, and for the good of the organisation, department, division, function or individual in question.

Particular roles that exist in the process are:

- *The immediate superior:* who has the most detailed and up-to-date knowledge of what the department, group or individual has been doing.
- *The grandparent (the immediate superior's superior):* to take a wider view, and ideally an overview of the performance.
- *Peers:* the great advantage of peer appraisal is that a person's colleagues have an excellent appreciation of what is being carried out, and the circumstances under which this is done.
- *Subordinates:* this is especially effective on questions of management, staff, volume and quality of communication and management style (see Box 6.4).

# Box 6.4   Appraisal by subordinates

Ricardo Semler (1992) states that 'If you ask subordinates to appraise managers, they may actually tell you what they think. So we do it anyway'.

Most organisations do not. They prefer effectively not to know what their staff really think of the environment, the work and, above all, the management style.

For any organisation to stand any chance at all of achieving near to its full potential, appraisal by subordinates has to be carried out. Some organisations nod in its direction with exit interviews when staff leave, to see if they can find out what has really driven them away.

It is also true that this form of appraisal may bring to light issues that can be treated in purely positive ways. For example, if an organisation with the best will in the world can only keep technological expertise for a maximum of five years before people move on, then it can:

- concentrate on maximising output from those staff during that period
- develop opportunities for them
- attract them in the first place with a promise of an excellent five-years' experience that will act as a springboard to a very prosperous and fulfilling future elsewhere.

- *Specific experts:* who can give a truly informed view on the activities being carried out, the likely and possible outcomes, any remedial and developmental actions necessary.
- *Other stakeholders:* because they have their own specific demands. The most influential are:
  - customers, clients, and suppliers, who appraise organisational performance in terms of their willingness, or otherwise, to conduct repeat business
  - shareholders and backers, who measure performance by their willingness, or otherwise, to put funds into the business, or to retain their interest in it
  - and the media.

---

**EXAMPLE**

The year 1999–2000 was widely deemed to have been a bad year for Marks & Spencer. During that year, turnover went up; but profits were sharply down. This led to a change in the Chief Executive Officer and top management team. One media report castigated the company for complacency, claiming that it had distanced itself from its core customers, and its values. This was compounded early in 2000 when the company announced that it would cease using UK and European suppliers; but would rather look overseas for comparable quality at cheaper costs, in order to reduce its overheads.

---

The media coverage was driven by a perceived loss of confidence on the part of customers, suppliers and backers and the adverse nature of that coverage reinforced the anxieties of each of these groups. The company's organisational, managerial and sales performance was deemed to be poor. At least a part of this was due to the perceptions gained as the progress of the company was written up in the media. The company's profits for the period were £420 million – down 20% on the previous year, but still a substantial volume in a flat sector.

Whoever measures performance requires the following skills and expertise:

- Knowledge and understanding of what is being measured, when, where, how and by whom
- Knowledge and understanding of the full constraints of the situation
- Knowledge and understanding of the specific aims and objectives in question
- Knowledge and understanding of the performance indicators present and why, how and by whom these are being used.

## Performance indicators

Performance indicators arise as the result of a combination of function, planning and required output. They are:

- precisely identified, legitimate points of inquiry into all aspects of performance
- precisely stated aspects of performance existing in organisations, departments, divisions and functions.

The following sections illustrate some useful performance indicators.

### Human resource performance

- The number of tasks carried out well or badly, and the reasons for this.
- The number of strikes, disputes and grievances; movements in the numbers of disciplinaries and dismissals; the extent of movements in the operation of disciplinary, grievance and disputes procedures.
- Movements in numbers of accidents and injuries; movements in the numbers of self-certificated absenteeism.
- Levels of disputes and grievances among those who have enjoyed perceived high levels of job satisfaction and security.
- Movements in staff turnover; movements (especially decreases) in organisational, departmental, divisional and functional staff stability.
- Increases in administration and support functions at the expense of frontline operations; increases in the administration and reporting workload placed on frontline operations.
- Pay differentials between top and bottom of the organisation; movements in pay differentials; the presence or otherwise of benefits based on status rather than operational necessity; the allocation of performance-related and profit-related pay.

## Production

- Production targets, especially where production output bears no relationship to targets set; this is as much a cause for concern when targets are far exceeded as when they are not met.
- Production, volume and quality, especially where these fall short of projections, or wildly exceed them.
- Increases in customer complaints about one aspect of product performance; increases in customer complaints about total product performance; increases in customer complaints about packaging, delivery, appearance, durability and after-sales.
- Supply-side issues, especially increases in supply problems, access to components and raw materials.
- Maintenance issues and problems with production and information technology; management of the balance of preventative and emergency/crises maintenance.
- Extent and nature of training offered, demanded and available; extent of obligation to understand this/make it available.
- Identifying where blockages occur, why, what causes them, their frequency, their effects on total effectiveness.
- New products, development and innovations: proportion of new products that get to market; actual and required research; development capability and expertise; research, development and innovation as a percentage of total organisational activities/fixed costs (see Box 6.5).

## Box 6.5   Performance indicators in public services

The supposed ease with which industrial and commercial production can be measured causes those in public services to seek to look at their own situation in similar ways rather than to establish a valid standpoint from which to measure the specific performance of these services.

The knowledge, expertise, judgement, attributes and qualities of a public service manager are critical. These form the context in which the following broad and narrow perspectives can be taken:

- *Broad:* the state of the work environment (school, classroom, library, hospital ward, laboratory, prison); the availability, use, value, quality and appropriateness of equipment to service users and consumers; cleanliness, warmth and comfort; general ambience; professionalism of staff; currency of professional expertise; interaction of staff with clients; prioritisation of activities; resource effectiveness, efficiency, adequacy and usage.
- *Narrow:* application of absolute standards of service delivery; speed of response to clients; nature and content of response to service users; nature and volume of complaints, failures and shortcomings; attitudes of service users to providers and vice versa; acceptance of professional

responsibility and standards; acceptance of professional development; personal commitment.

This is the context for measuring performance in public services. It requires concentration on the output of specific services and has no legitimate reference to inter-functional comparison or league tables. This is the best basis for judgement of and intervention in the performance of such services. It has to be carried out by service experts and analysts, and those who understand the full context and limitations of the situation.

## Marketing and sales

- Currency and effectiveness of marketing information and research.
- Sources of customer satisfaction and dissatisfaction; the benefits that customers expect to accrue from purchase and ownership of the products and services; the benefits that actually accrue, and where the differences between the two lie.
- Changes in customer perceptions, especially from positive to negative (though a change from negative to positive may cause increases in demand with which the organisation is unable to cope).

The following also reflect marketing reference, especially when this falls blank of projected targets:

- Organisation perceptions of *good value* are seen by customers as *cheap*.
- Marketing and promotion campaigns do not have the desired/projected effects on sales; problems arise due to a lack of full investigation, assessment and analysis.
- Lack of full market knowledge and understanding, often based on market research that generates 'generally favourable impressions' (e.g., 'Would you buy?' rather than: 'Will you buy – if so, how often and under what circumstances; if not, why not?').
- Poor public relations which is usually symptomatic of organisational lack of surety, capability or faith in what it is doing.
- Marketing rebounds – unlooked for (usually negative) consequences of marketing, advertising and promotion activities; this may also be a problem when very high ratings are scored and the organisation is unable to satisfy increased demand.

---

┌─ EXAMPLE ────────────────────────────────────────────────

In the spring of 1999, commuters coming off the trains at Euston station to begin their day's work were amazed to be met by young men and women offering small glasses and paper cups of beer. This was part of a major promotion for a nationally recognised, high-brand, premium-priced lager. Partly as the result of this marketing push, an extensive promotional campaign was undertaken on the television and through sponsorship activities in the media and at public events.

The promotion was never fully successful, and sales did not reach projected targets. However, only when the company called in marketing experts, were they made to understand that the initially 'generally favourable response' generated by the free offers was certain to lead to misunderstanding. There was a world of difference between accepting a free offer and translating this into changes in regular buying behaviour.

## Communications and information

- Quality and volume of written, oral, formal and informal communications; usefulness of this quality and volume.
- Extent and content of grapevine.
- Extent and nature of communication blockages and misunderstandings.
- Frequency and value of team, group, department, division and functional meetings; their agenda, outputs and outcomes.
- Extent and use of formal communication channels; length of time taken; general effectiveness; effects on operations, administration, decision-making processes.
- Information management systems, especially use, value and effectiveness of internet usage, website access and usage, e-mail, and intranet systems.
- Website design, usefulness and value; website objectives; number and frequency of 'hits' on website.
- Information systems: ease of access to information; capacity for the acquisition, storage, retrieval, analysis and processing of information.
- Language used: the simpler and more direct this is, the more likely it is that what is said will be understood; and the more likely it is that what is said will be valued.
- Integrity of communications: the extent to which people say what they mean and mean what they say.
- Hidden/secondary agenda: the messages that are actually received by those receiving them; the messages that the organisation is actually putting across, reflected in the nature and language of what is said and written.

The best organisations also identify and use performance indicators in order to assess and appraise the more general aspects of organisation well-being. The main areas covered are:

- staff motivation
- value of activities
- confidence and expectations.

## Staff motivation

Highly motivated and committed staff produce high-quality work over sustained periods of time. The highest levels of motivation occur in organisations which:

- respect and value their staff; treat them equally; offer opportunities on an even and equal basis; concentrate on performance not personality; and pay and reward their people well

- generate positive and harmonious cultures and working environments; take early action to remove negative attitudes where they start to emerge; reward contributions to organisational performance
- recognise that everyone has personal, professional and occupational drives, aims and objectives that require satisfaction; and take steps to harmonise and integrate these with organisational purposes
- recognise the key behavioural features of expectation, effort and reward; recognising and rewarding achievement, development and progress
- balancing the attention given to the work in hand, the function of work groups, and individual and overall performance
- paying specific attention to levels of: absenteeism; turnover; accidents, sickness and injury; disputes, personality clashes and inter-departmental wrangles; approaches and attitudes to problems; the ability to offer fulfilment, recognition and accomplishment to all levels and grades of staff
- the level and nature of identity that staff have with the organisation; the extent to which status, esteem and rewards are issued for productive output as distinct from adherence to procedures.

---

**EXAMPLE**

A large hospital in southern England employs nurses on a four-weekly working cycle. Each week they are required to work 3 × 12.5 hour shifts – a total of 37.5 hours. These shifts are either from 7.00 am to 7.30 pm, or from 7.00 pm to 7.30 am; that way there is always an overlap between shifts coming on and going off, allowing for effective handovers to take place.

In 1999, the hospital authorities introduced a change to this arrangement. Every four weeks, the nurses were required to work a thirteenth shift in order to make up for the time consumed by mealtimes and tea breaks.

The hospital currently has 150 nursing vacancies. Any attempt to appraise, measure or improve performance has to be seen in this context.

---

## Value of activities

The purpose of measuring and appraising value is to establish where the elements and activities that add value to the organisation's activities lie; and conversely, where value is lost or deducted. Measuring value may be related to products, services and support activities. All departments, divisions and functions should be assessed in this way.

The components to be addressed are:

- length, frequency and intensity of usage
- depreciation/appreciation of resources
- maintenance, repair and replacement; development and improvement
- returns on investment, activity, energy and effort.

Each aspect of performance, as well as the use of products and services by customers, should be measured using each of these elements. This enables attention to be switched to those areas where value is being lost and

## Box 6.6  Adding value: appraisal and assessment

'Veronica had an observant boss who noticed that many of the ideas coming out of her work group were hers, but it was often someone else in the group who trumpeted the ideas around the office and got credit for them. The boss told Veronica she should take more credit for her ideas. But Veronica was not comfortable doing that. She tried it, and found that she simply did not enjoy work if she had to approach it as a grabbing game. She liked the atmosphere of shared goals and was comfortable in the knowledge that she was part of a group effort. Striving to get credit for herself felt like a lonely and not very admirable endeavour. Trying to follow her bosses advice made coming to work a lot less fun'.

This constitutes the correct appraisal of someone who is adding value to the work of her group, and also to herself. Many managers and supervisors do not notice this, however. It is usually those who 'trumpet' ideas and initiatives that get the credit for them, rather than their true originator.

Source:  D. Tannen (1992) *Talking from 9 to 5*, Virago.

not maximised. It also enables the strengths and weaknesses of each activity to be measured in terms of the positive and negative aspects brought to the organisation as a whole (see Box 6.6).

## Confidence and expectations

Everyone who comes into contact with an organisation, or who has a legitimate stake in it, expects to have confidence in it – confidence in the strength and quality of the overall relationship; confidence in products and services; confidence in continuity, reliability and stability; confidence in continuing long-term success and effectiveness.

People join and work for organisations, make purchases, and avail themselves of services, with certain expectations in mind. They anticipate that their expectations will be fulfilled. Problems occur when these expectations are not fulfilled. Levels of expectation are set as follows:

- *Staff:* the need to be well rewarded; to gain job satisfaction, fulfilment, development and achievement; to be associated with a positive and prestigious organisation or occupation; to be valued, respected and esteemed.
- *Shareholders and backers:* there is a need to receive regular positive returns on investment.
- *Customers, consumers, clients and users:* expect satisfaction and utility from the products and services; in many cases, they also expect esteem, respect and value to be enhanced.
- *Communities:* expect to feel pleased and proud to have certain organisations established and working in among them.
- *Suppliers:* expect to engage in a long-term secure, productive and profitable relationship.

Problems arise when a lack of confidence sets in and when expectations are not met. Part of the wider appraisal and assessment of managerial performance is therefore to understand what the nature of confidence is, and what the expectations of the particular stakeholders and interested parties are. Steps can then be taken to ensure that, as far as possible, these can be satisfied.

## Appraisal, rewards and punishments

There are specific problems with performance measurement and appraisal when they are known, believed or perceived to be directly tied in with rewards, advantages, punishments and sanctions. This is a serious and enduring problem above all with staff performance appraisal schemes, but it also relates to year-end and period-end performance reviews by shareholders' representatives and media analysts.

### Rewards

Rewards that accrue as the result of measurement and appraisal normally take the following forms.

- Bonuses, either cash or else company shares if the organisation has demonstrated the level of profitability required by shareholders. The main problem is that organisation activities tend to be skewed towards maximising short-term shareholder value and demanded short-term profit requirements, rather than long-term viability.
- Profit-related or performance-related pay as the result of having 'met or exceeded' stated objectives.
- Promotions as the result of having demonstrated good or excellent performance in the present job or role.
- Training and development as the result of having identified particular needs, wants and opportunities. It is most important that this is structured to address:
  — organisational priorities
  — professional priorities
  — occupational and departmental priorities
  — personal priorities (see Figure 6.1).

### Balancing individual and group rewards

In order to sustain long-term high levels of morale and output, this balance has to be addressed. It requires specific application to every individual set of circumstances and it is very difficult to make hard and fast rules. However, there are principles that must be adhered to as follows:

- Individual performance must be genuinely recognisable as such, and capable of being sustained as such, in open argument.

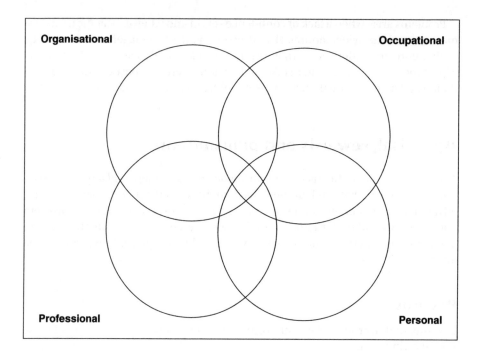

If one is addressed at the expense of others, the consequences are: *Organisational:* the individual becomes institutionalised and ultimately narrow and unmarketable; *Occupational:* the individual comes to learn one way of doing the job only, rather than gaining a broader perspective; *Professional:* the individual is effectively using the organisation for their own professional advancement that may, or may not be, in the best interests of the organisation; *Personal:* the organisation is sponsoring the individual's own preferred priorities and direction.

*Figure 6.1*   Organisational and individual development mix.

- Provision must be made for where individuals (and groups) *genuinely* meet or exceed stated objectives; and again, this position must be capable of sustenance in open argument.
- Describing individual and group performance as 'excellent' must be capable of rebutting any charges of elitism or favouritism.

These aspects also need consideration when powerful and/or expert individuals use their personality or command of expertise to enhance their own rewards either above and beyond others with whom they work or, worse still, at the expense of other people. This is to be resisted at all times.

## Punishments and sanctions

Appraisal should never be used as a vehicle for attributing penalties or punishments – the place for doing this is the organisation's disciplinary system (see Chapter 9). Disciplinary systems must always operate fully independently of performance measurement.

It may come to light that the performance measurement process shows serious shortcomings in the performance of both individuals and groups. This must then become the focus for individual, group and organisation development, not punishment and sanction.

When it becomes apparent that organisation performance is falling or declining, this also ought to be tackled in the same way. This does not always happen, normally because:

- chief executive officers and other senior managers have golden handshakes and termination bonuses built into their reward package, which may encourage their efforts to depart rather than seek effective solutions to real problems
- shareholders' representatives demand particular courses of action with the purpose of ensuring a short-term rise in share price rather than long-term problem solution
- consultants are brought in to advise and recommend courses of action and these are then blindly accepted and followed by the particular organisation
- the ability to blame individuals and/or departments for wider shortcomings draws attention away from any senior management or institutional malaise.

When remedial action is required, it should be agreed by all concerned and specific aims and objectives drawn up. These should then be the subject of further progress review on pre-agreed dates. Overall progress can then be evaluated as above, and any further remedial action identified.

## Organisation development

Organisation development (OD) is the generic term given to strategies and initiatives for improving organisational effectiveness through developing the capabilities, capacities, qualities and expertise of the staff.

OD implies a direct relationship between the development and enhancement of staff and long-term commercial success and service quality advancement. It follows from this that a very high priority is given to training and development activities in order to take the organisation and its departments, divisions and functions in the required directions.

The OD process is aimed at changing, forming and developing culture, values, attitudes and beliefs in positive and constructive ways. In order to do this successfully, the following are required.

- A measure of conformity and the willingness of staff to go down the paths required
- Obsession with product and service quality
- A strong customer and client orientation
- Universal identity with the organisation at large on the part of all staff
- Setting a moral or value-led example and taking an active pride in the organisation and its works.

The OD process requires expertise and understanding in all its component parts. Above all, this refers to:

- performance, assessment and appraisal
- problem raising and acknowledgement
- openness, honesty and trust
- access to information
- inter-group activities and cross-fertilisation of ideas
- organisation assessment and evaluation of the development process.

There will be a framework around the OD aspects and activities at corporate, department, divisional, team, group and individual levels. In order for it to succeed it is essential that it is fully resourced. This framework then involves:

- setting aims and objectives
- devising processes, approaches and priorities
- addressing problems and issues
- setting and maintaining time scales and deadlines
- addressing each of the four key components of organisational, professional, occupational and individual development
- establishing monitoring, review and evaluation processes (see above)
- keeping staff fully informed on progress.

The benefits to be realised are as follows.

- Organisations gain a high level of commitment and a strong sense of identity.
- Organisations set their own positive attitudes, styles and values rather than allowing these to emerge.
- The approach provides niche openings and opportunities along the way that can be exploited.
- The approach provides opportunities for behavioural, attitudinal, structural role and functional development on the part of all concerned.
- A creative and positive environment is created, and this makes the identification of, and solution of, problems and blockages more effective.

OD depends for its success on long-term commitment. Investment in performance assessment, and the development activities that arise, is often only realised over a period of years. Its benefits are also virtually impossible to measure in narrow or linear terms and many managers and organisations are not even prepared to look at the consequences of not following this approach. It nevertheless remains the fundamental approach used by companies such as Nissan, Sony, Toyota, Honda, Virgin and Body Shop (see Box 6.7).

## Box 6.7 Organisation development, profitability and effectiveness

- *Nissan UK:* in line with its activities elsewhere in the world, Nissan UK spent an average of £10,000 per member of staff on induction, orientation, initial and job training. The staff are required to train until they are fully competent in all aspects of work. The company also pays for any evening classes that the staff may wish to undertake.

- *Lucas CAV:* this company also operates a policy of paying for staff evening classes. These may or may not be work-related – however, the company insists that all staff undertake some form of training and development every year that is not directly work related.
- *Body Shop:* the Body Shop insist that all members of its staff work for one day per month on community projects. These may involve: environmental restoration; working with the disabled or disadvantaged; or running fundraising activities on behalf of a named national or local charity or not-for-profit organisation.

The purpose of each of these examples is for demonstrate the distinctive nature of the relationship required between staff and organisation. This is not to the liking of everybody. However, it does indicate the lengths to which some organisations will go to secure effective long-term output and commitment from their staff.

## Conclusions

There is a clear right way to do things for all types and aspects of performance measurement and appraisal. This is often distinct from what organisations are prepared to do or to sanction, and the resources that they are prepared to commit.

Nevertheless, appraisal and measurement remain key managerial and supervisory tasks. They complex and requires a high level of contextual

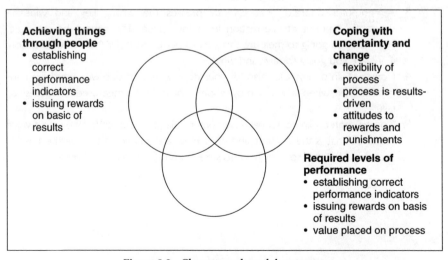

**Achieving things through people**
- establishing correct performance indicators
- issuing rewards on basic of results

**Coping with uncertainty and change**
- flexibility of process
- process is results-driven
- attitudes to rewards and punishments

**Required levels of performance**
- establishing correct performance indicators
- issuing rewards on basis of results
- value placed on process

*Figure 6.2*  Chapter and model summary

knowledge and understanding, as well as the capability to choose the right means of measurement and the required points of inquiry.

It done effectively, the following can be pinpointed:

- those activities that contribute to effective, successful and profitable organisational performance
- those activities that do not make any direct contribution to performance
- those activities that detract from successful and effective performance
- specific diversions, blockages and barriers to progress
- specific organisational, occupational, personal and professional issues.

Only by measuring and assessing all aspects of organisation performance and relating these to the broader context in which activities take place can actual success or failure be judged. Measurement and appraisal enable known, believed or perceived successes and failures to be further quantified and examined, and the reasons found. They indicate areas where improvements can, should and must be made and are key to effective short-, medium- and long-term resource utilisation. They are essential if lessons are to be learned from the past and current range of activities so that the future may be better prepared for. Above all, it is essential that every manager and supervisor learns to understand the importance of measurement and appraisal, and to commit themselves to carrying them out.

Using the Model referred to at the start of Chapter 1 (Figure 1.1), the material in this Chapter is summarised in Figure 6.2.

QUESTIONS

1. a) In an ideal world, how would you like to measure the performance of your staff/ department? Why would you take this approach? b) What is preventing you from doing this at present?
2. Discuss the view that shareholder and staff performance requirements and measures can never totally be reconciled.
3. A computer operator inadvertently presses the wrong key and wipes a substantial amount of information from the system. This cannot be retrieved. How are you going to measure this part of performance? What remedial action, if any, are you going to take, and why?
4. Construct an outline OD plan for your department, or one with which you are familiar. How, when, where and by whom should this be measured for success or failure?
5. Construct an outline personal development plan for yourself for the next twelve months. What is the content, and why? How are you going to measure this for success or failure? How might others measure it for success or failure?

# ▪ ⌄ **7** Planning

## Introduction

Planning is the process of assessing and implementing the priorities and activities of organisations, departments, divisions and functions. It exists in all organisations at the following levels:

- *Corporate:* responsible for the short-, medium- and, above all, long-term future prospects, success and effectiveness of activities; and to develop new products, services, markets and outlets.
- *Strategic:* patterns and series of decisions taken to ensure the success of the short-, medium- and long-term direction established at corporate level.
- *Operational:* patterns and series of decisions taken at departmental, divisional, functional – operational – levels, to ensure that the short-, medium- and long-term direction of the organisation is translated into action.

From this, initial points become clear.

- Planning is not an end in itself. All effective managerial planning is based on the ability to adjust, improvise, identify and maximise opportunities; identify and avoid threats; and respond to changing circumstances.
- It is not linear. It is a process that is constantly subject to responding to forces inside and outside the control of organisations, their managers a nd supervisors.
- It is dependent upon the quality and accuracy of decision-making at all levels (see Chapter 8 below). It is a key responsibility, and therefore key skill, of all managers and supervisors (see Box 7.1).

## Box 7.1   Planning has a bad name

Both planning and forecasting (see below) have a bad name among managers and supervisors. The main reason for this is that corporate head office functions are known, believed or perceived to carry out planning activities in isolation from those on the ground – those responsible for producing outputs, products and services.

Most people have a bad experience, or apocryphal tale to tell, about planning. For example, an oil company flew its senior management team to an exotic location, and put them up in five-star accommodation, so that they could plan redundancies at the frontline. A government department produced a three-year strategic plan *after* it had been informed that it was to close. A social services department was required to plan for home visiting services for its elderly clients after it had been told that these services were to be cut altogether.

More generally, planning is known to result in *plans*. Produced by corporate head office and cast in stone these have been known to take no account of possible or likely changes in circumstances.

'Planning is everything, the plan is nothing' – when anything that purports to predict future outcomes is cast in the belief or perception of certainty, it is certain to fail, and therefore becomes discredited. This also applies to forecasts; as these are drawn up, it becomes very easy for them to assume a life of their own. Then, when the precise set of circumstances in which the forecasts were made change, the forecast also is discredited.

Above all, however, the reason why effective planning activities are not undertaken more widely is because they are not understood by those who have to prepare and implement them.

Source: R.A. Dixon (1992) *Investment Appraisal*, Kogan Page

## 'Planning is everything, the plan is nothing'

These words were spoken by General Dwight D. Eisenhower on the eve of the D-Day landings in Normandy in June 1944, towards the end of the Second World War. 'The plan' was to invade Europe by landing an army on the beaches of northern France.

Eisenhower went on to say that the operation had in mind the clear objective of getting the army ashore to begin the invasion of Nazi-occupied Europe. As the result, what were considered sufficient resources to do the job properly had been gathered together. However, they had to be prepared to respond to the situation as it unfolded, and to be prepared to adjust the operation in the light of the resistance and response offered by the opposing army. They also had to be prepared for heavy casualties, and to expect delays and hold-ups. Above all, before the invasion could even take place, half a million men and their equipment had to be taken on a ten-hour sea journey between the south of England and northern France – and the weather might have been bad (the weather in the English Channel is always unpredictable – see Box 7.1).

Both Eisenhower and Firth (see Box 7.2) – and everyone else – need the following to be successful:

- To gain a full understanding of the whole context in which they are to be operating, including factors inside and outside their control.
- The ability to provide sufficient resources to do the job completely and effectively.

## Box 7.2 Farming planning

John Firth, a farmer with extensive sheep and arable interests in southern England, puts all of this much more succinctly. He says: 'I plan every activity on the basis that it will take twice as long as I expect, and cost twice as much. That way I always come in within time and budget. If I expect nothing to go wrong, I am always disappointed. The harvest might break down, the weather might be too wet, too dry, too hot or too cold. If, on the other hand, I plan on the basis that anything that can go wrong will go wrong, I have time and resources to spare'. This approach has kept the farming business for which he works in profitable business for over half a century.

Source: Hastings Chamber of Commerce (1999).

- Contingency arrangements to ensure that resources are available in the event of things going wrong.
- To identify the priorities that the situation demands, and be prepared to re-order these if the situation changes, and therefore produce the means by which all efforts are to be coordinated and controlled.
- The ability to provide sufficient time for the resources involved to do their job.

# The planning context

Understanding the planning context involves:

- understanding the environment, both internal and external
- having and using information forecasts and projections
- making an initial match between resources, aims, objectives and priorities
- contingency planning.

## Understanding the environment

The best and simplest way of doing this is to use the PEST, SWOT, and Five Forces techniques.

### PEST analysis

PEST stands for Political, Economic, Social and Technological. It involves itemising all the factors affecting the environment in which planning is to take place under these headings as follows:

- *Social:* social systems at the workplace, departmental and functional structures, work organisation and methods.
- *Technological:* the effects of the organisation's technology, the uses to which it is put and the technology that may become available.

- *Economic:* financial structure, objectives and constraints at the place of work.
- *Political:* internal political systems, sources of power and influence, key groups of workers, key departments, key managers and executives.

PEST analysis is carried out to evaluate the strengths and influence of forces largely outside the control of the organisation, or of the particular manager or supervisor, but which nevertheless constitute the boundaries and pressures within which activities have to be carried out. PEST analysis works as shown in Figure 7.1.

In each of the cases illustrated in Figure 7.1, the overriding pressures and forces can be pinpointed. However much outside the control of the particular manager

(a) **Model**

| Political | Economic |
|-----------|----------|
| Social    | Technological |

Each of the points raised can then become the subject of further investigation if required. It can be used to identify and evaluate the forces present in any situation, macro or micro, as follows:

(b)  **PEST for centralised personnel services in a large organisation (simplified)**

| Political | Economic |
|-----------|----------|
| *External* | • Fixed costs incurred |
| | • Secondary costs |
| • Employment law compliance | • Accommodating meetings |
| • Identification and management of external issues | |
| *Internal* | |
| • Need for professional advice | |
| • People expect a personnel or HR function in large organisations | • Information systems and databases |
| • Social and welfare workplace roles | • Data protection regulation compliance |
| | • Security |
| Social | Technological |

*Figure 7.1*  PEST analysis: examples.

(c)  **PEST for a corner shop (simplified)**

| **Political** | **Economic** |
|---|---|
| • Opening hours<br>• Sales restrictions, e.g. alcohol, tobacco | • Opening hours<br>• Prices charged<br>• Range of goods<br>• Fixed costs |
| • Convenience<br>• Opening hours<br>• Range of goods<br>• Social roles, e.g. message forwarding<br>• Meeting point | • Reordering<br>• Security<br>• Accounting and charging |
| **Social** | **Technological** |

(d)  **PEST for a unionised production line crew (simplified)**

| **Political** | **Economic** |
|---|---|
| • Role of union<br>• Legal factors<br>• Need for industrial relations specialists | • Costs and benefits of unionisation<br>• Costs of time spent on unionisation and union matters |
| • Expectations of belonging to union<br>• Divided loyalties (?) | • Production process<br>• Automation and alienation<br>• Work and job rotation (?) |
| **Social** | **Technological** |

*Figure 7.1*  Continued.

or supervisor some of these things may be, at least a good understanding of where problems and issues may come from is generated.

## SWOT analysis

This is carried out by identifying the component features of an organisation department, division, function, product or service under the headings of:

• *Strengths:* the things that the organisation and its staff are good at, and for which they have a high reputation.

- *Weaknesses:* the things that they are bad at or for which they have a poor reputation.
- *Opportunities:* directions that could be profitably explored for the future.
- *Threats:* external threats from competitors; the potential for internal threats from strikes and disputes, resource or revenue constraints.

SWOT analysis works as shown in Figure 7.2.

## Five Forces

The Five Forces approach is used:

- to assess the position of organisations within the markets in which they operate, by placing the organisation at the centre of the four main forces with which they have to interact – suppliers, buyers, substitutes, and potential new entrants or new competitors

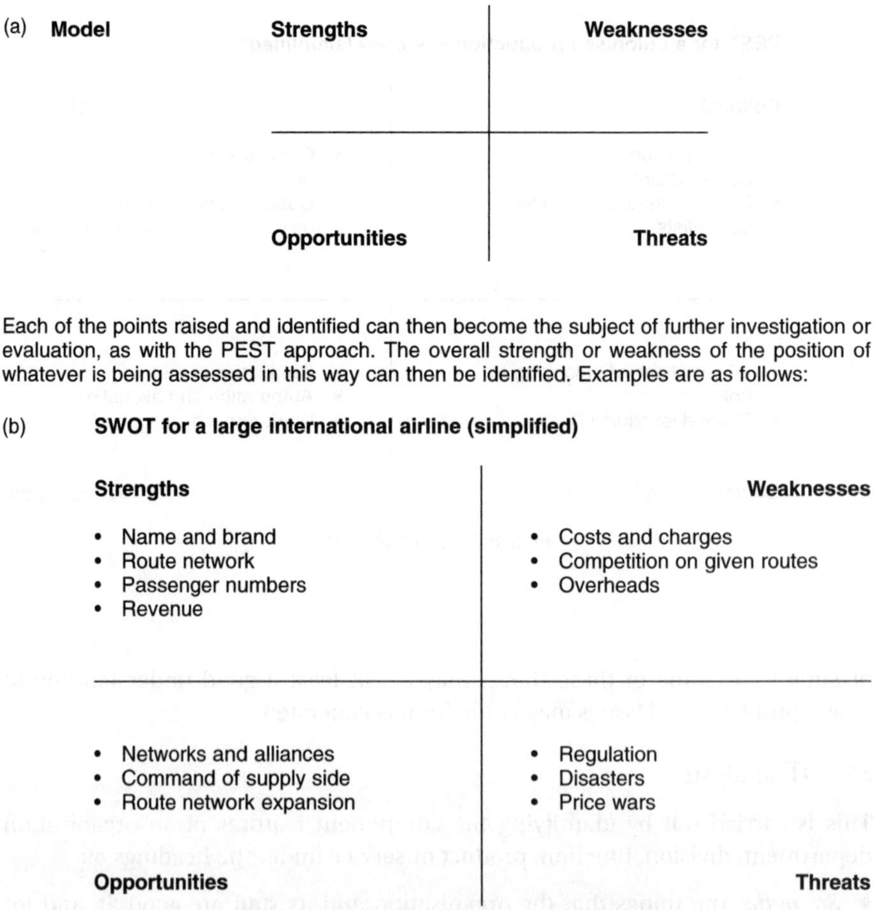

(a)  **Model**

|  **Strengths**  |  **Weaknesses**  |
|---|---|
|  **Opportunities**  |  **Threats**  |

Each of the points raised and identified can then become the subject of further investigation or evaluation, as with the PEST approach. The overall strength or weakness of the position of whatever is being assessed in this way can then be identified. Examples are as follows:

(b)  **SWOT for a large international airline (simplified)**

| **Strengths** | **Weaknesses** |
|---|---|
| • Name and brand<br>• Route network<br>• Passenger numbers<br>• Revenue | • Costs and charges<br>• Competition on given routes<br>• Overheads |
| • Networks and alliances<br>• Command of supply side<br>• Route network expansion | • Regulation<br>• Disasters<br>• Price wars |
| **Opportunities** | **Threats** |

*Figure 7.2*  SWOT analysis: examples.

(c) **SWOT for a small hospital in a country town (simplified)**

| Strengths | Weaknesses |
|---|---|
| • Knowledge of services<br>• Public confidence<br>• Range of services | • Public sector costs<br>• Range of services<br>• Opening hours, e.g. for accident and emergency<br>• Retaining expert staff |
| • Development of services<br>• Development of community facility | • Political pressures<br>• Health economics<br>• Health service costings |
| **Opportunities** | **Threats** |

(d) **SWOT for a new information systems installation (simplified)**

| Strengths | Weaknesses |
|---|---|
| • Excitement, opportunity<br>• State of the art<br>• Training for staff<br>• 'Everyone else' has one | • Cost<br>• Teething troubles<br>• Access to advice and problem solving |
| • Develop expertise<br>• Develop quality access and use of information<br>• Develop staff<br>• Change culture (if required) | • Costs, on-costs and hidden costs<br>• May be at the mercy of suppliers<br>• Staff may not like it, and will not use it |
| **Opportunities** | **Threats** |

*Figure 7.2*  Continued.

● to assess the position of departments, divisions and functions within the organisations in which they operate by placing each at the centre of the four related pressures on them – the link in the chain before them, the link in the chain after them, alternative ways of doing things within the department, and alternative means by which the job might get done elsewhere.

## Organisations and their markets

The Five Forces analysis is carried out as shown in Figure 7.3.

## Departments within organisations

This is carried out as shown in Figure 7.4.

Five Forces analysis is particularly useful when trying to assess where cost savings can be made, and where alternative methods of doing things might be found. Of particular importance are:

- the supply side, where managers and supervisors assess the supply chain for alternative sources offering comparable or acceptable quality at reduced prices, greater convenience, frequency of delivery (physical supply) and access (physical supplies, and also information and the Internet);
- substitutes, where managers and supervisors assess what different means and methods might be used to deliver particular parts of their activities or processes. This may also serve as a prelude to reorganising or reconstructing the location of work, work patterns and work skills, qualities and expertise.

None of these approaches need take long, though it is most useful if such a structured approach is adopted. It gives clear pointers for further investigations. It can also highlight more serious gaps in knowledge and understanding, and these can then be filled before taking steps into the unknown. See Box 7.3 for another approach.

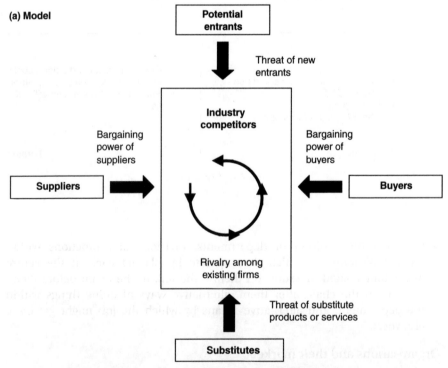

*Figure 7.3* Five Forces analysis: examples (1).

**(b) Five Forces for British Telecom (simplified)**

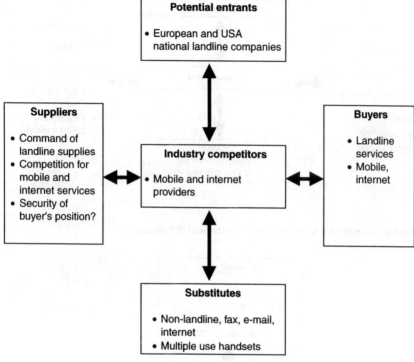

*Figure 7.3* Continued.

# Box 7.3  SPECTACLES analysis

Cartwright (2000) takes a very much more detailed approach to organisational, environmental and operational factors, features and elements. He identified a ten-point approach under the acronym SPECTACLES, as follows:

- *Social:* changes in society and societal trends; demographic trends and influences.
- *Political:* political processes and structures; lobbying; the political institutions of the UK and EU; the political pressures brought about as the result of, for example, the Social Charter, market regulation.
- *Economic:* referring especially to sources of finance; stock markets; inflation; interest rates; local, regional, national and global economies.
- *Cultural:* international and national cultures; regional cultures; organisational cultures; cultural clashes; culture changes; cultural pressures on business and organisational activities.
- *Technological:* understanding the technological needs of a business; technological pressures; the relationship between technology and

**(a) Model**

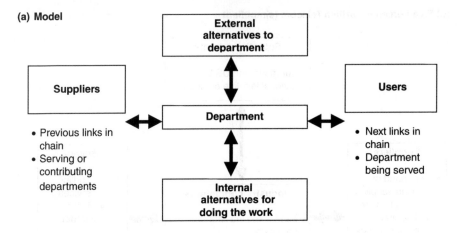

**(b) Five Forces analysis for centralised personnel/HR function**

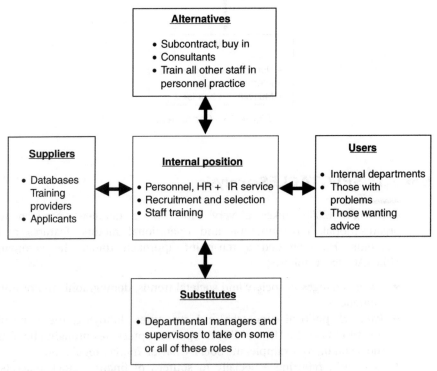

*Figure 7.4*   Five Forces analysis: examples (2).

work patterns; communications; e-commerce; technology and manufacturing; technology and bio-engineering.

- *Aesthetic:* communications; marketing and promotion; image; fashion; organisational body language; public relations.
- *Customer:* consumerism; the importance of analysing customer bases; customer needs and wants; customer care; anticipating future customer requirements; customer behaviour.
- *Legal:* sources of law; codes of practice; legal pressures; product liability; health and safety; employment law; competition legislation; European law; and whistle-blowing.
- *Environmental:* responsibilities to the planet; pollution; waste management; farming activities; genetic engineering; cost benefit analyses; legal pressures.
- *Sectoral:* competition; cartels and monopolies; competitive forces; cooperation within sectors; differentiation; and segmentation.

Cartwright states that his intention is '*to widen the scope of analysis that needs to be carried out in order to include a more detailed consideration of the culture within which an organisation must operate, the customer base, competition within the sector, and the aesthetic implications, both physical and behavioural, of the organisation on its external operating environment*'.

This is a far more precise and detailed approach. It clearly indicates specific points of inquiry, many of which are implicit in the PEST, SWOT and Five Forces models indicated above. It requires managers to take a detailed look at every aspect of their operations within their particular environment and niche. It is also much more likely to raise specific, precise, detailed – and often uncomfortable – questions that many managers (especially senior managers) would rather not have to address.

Above all, the approach can be used by managers at every organisational level in order to make themselves think more deeply about all the issues present in their own particular domain.

Source: R. Cartwright (2000) *Mastering the Business Environment*, Palgrave Masters.

## Forecasts

Forecasts are never completely accurate. Nor are they absolute predictors of future activities or performance. It is rather a statement of possible, likely or probable future performance or outcomes, calculated from data gathered for the purpose.

Herein lies the main problem. So much of business and management activity changes very quickly; forecasts and projections have therefore to be generated on the back of less than complete information. This is in direct contrast to weather forecasting, where a steady stream of data from a complete range of sources is used to provide regular updates – and even this is not always accurate. By contrast, the sources of information available to managers and supervisors for their purposes can change at any time – sudden shifts in markets, government policy, currency values, can be assessed from a very broad basis only. Managers and supervisors therefore have to rely extensively on the following:

- *Secondary information:* that gathered by others for their own uses, and for which a connection has to be made and very often inferred. Such sources include libraries, archives, databases held by government, professional bodies, trade unions and professional associations; as well as information held by the organisation and its sector. This is in contrast to primary information.
- *Primary information:* gathered by the users for their own purposes directly from their own sources. When projections and forecasts are required in quick time it is very often not possible to gather more than the sketchiest of primary information (see Box 7.4).

## Box 7.4   Information gathering

In order to ensure that whatever information is gathered has at least some consistency, it is useful to structure some form of questionnaire. A questionnaire is an instrument for gaining information from an informant for a particular purpose. It has, therefore, to be designed with specific understood purposes, aims and objectives. If at all possible, it should be piloted or tested to check that it does fulfil these purposes, or that it is likely to do so.

If it is possible to get this right, it is a most valuable format for the gaining of equivalent information from a variety of sources. It may be used as a means for structuring an interview, or as a more precise way of asking specific questions; and of ensuring that the same questions are asked to different people or sources.

- Questions used may be open: where the subject is invited to expand their own response in their own words or style on given matters. Such questions are led by words like 'who', 'what', 'where', 'why', 'when' and 'how'.
- Questions used may be closed: in which a precise answer – usually a yes or no response, or a numerical figure – is requested.

Whichever method is used, it is usual to address questionnaires to a sample population – either a number of people or sources selected at random; or a percentage of those who have the knowledge or information required. Except for very small problems, it is most unusual to be able to address the entire population under question in this way.

The information thus gathered is then used to inform planning and also decision-making processes. If further information is then required, or if the amount of time required to carry out the assessment accurately is beyond the scope of the manager or supervisor, then information and statistical specialists can be engaged, or else the services of outside research agencies can be used.

Even if it is possible to gather good quality information, this still has to be used, judged and evaluated. Projections of likely and possible outcomes have to be made in order to assess:

- best, medium and worst outcomes (see Chapter 8)
- feasibility and viability of proposed courses of action, schedules and activities
- risk of things going wrong.

## Risk

All managers and supervisors need to understand risk. In all situations there is a risk of an accident or emergency occurring. At the very least, this has to be assessed. It is also essential that all managers and supervisors understand the elements of lack of certainty, potential for accidents, and factors inside and outside their control as part of a broader assessment of the general situation.

The background to risk assessment is covered in Chapter 8. At the planning stage, it is nevertheless useful to engage in discussions and investigations around the vagaries and uncertainties of the broader situation, and as a vehicle for bringing these out into the open (see Box 7.5).

## Matching resources with planned activities

A simple way of looking at this is to itemise resources on the one hand, and activities, proposals, and priorities on the other (see Figure 7.5).

An initial assessment can then be made as follows.

- Too few resources for the proposed activities require a fresh prioritisation.
- Too many resources for the proposed activities mean that the organisation or department is being inefficient and wasteful. This often leads to a fresh set of problems; it then becomes necessary to address such matters as:

## Box 7.5 'What if?'

A simple and straightforward way of starting to think of risk at the planning stage is to ask questions with the prefix 'What if?'. This approach can be:

- *Precise:* e.g., 'What if the machine breaks down?'
- *General:* e.g., 'What if my deputy/superior were to leave?'
- *Possible:* e.g., 'What if our supplier/distributor goes bankrupt?'
- *Possible but unlikely:* e.g., 'What if we have an epidemic of flu in the department?'
- *Fanciful:* e.g., 'What if national interest rates double/halve tomorrow?'

As with many other planning techniques, this need not take long. It also need not be particularly substantial. However, conducted properly, it does make people think; and this then leads to a broader overall view. It gets people thinking outside their normal realm of activities. It may also bring to light things that people know exist but would rather not consider.

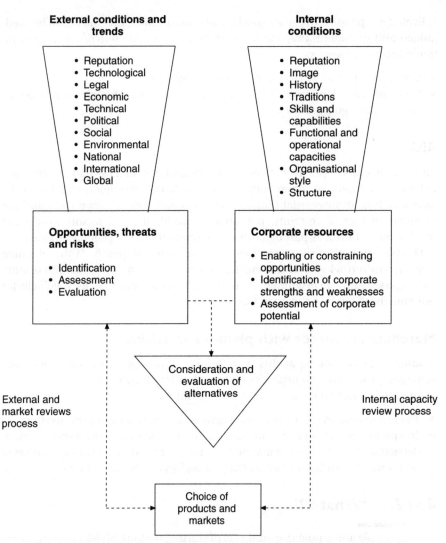

*Figure 7.5* Matching opportunities and planned activities with resources.

— can resources be kept back?
— will we lose resources if we don't use them up?
— is there anything else we would like to do?
— is there anything else we need to do (see Box 7.6)?

Any match of resources with planned or proposed activities is therefore clearly subject to pressures and events outside the control of individual managers and supervisors. Planning activities undertaken with a great deal of thought, care and expert local knowledge and understanding may be diluted or reprioritised by those in higher authority. This is entirely outside the control of individual managers and supervisors. However, the fact that it goes on has to be recognised so that contingency plans can be made.

## Box 7.6 Acquiring resources

The answers to some of the questions indicated in the text clearly depend on the actual ways of working of the organisation as a whole. In most public services, for example, nobody ever admits they have too many resources, because these then would simply be lost.

The problem is compounded because of traditional resource bidding systems that require managers and supervisors to draw up estimates of what they require to operate effectively over the coming period. These are then invariably cut by budget and fund holders on the grounds that:

- everyone overbids, so cuts are made anyway;
- it is a ritual negotiation, akin to collective bargaining (see Chapter 10);
- these cuts are made to judge the ability of managers and supervisors to work under pressure and constraint (a spurious line of reasoning, but it happens very frequently).

UK managers and supervisors also know that if they put in bids for staff training, re-grading, bonuses for their people, these are certain to be cut if the organisation for any reason requires reductions in expenditure. So they tend to bid for them anyway.

## Contingency planning

It is usual to recognise the following types of activity:

- steady-state or mainstream activities comprising the overwhelming majority of organisational or departmental activities;
- research development and pioneering activities, making investigations and proposals for the future; and forays into the unknown;
- maintenance activities, that have the purpose of ensuring that both staff and equipment continue to function effectively;
- steering activities: akin to the *hand-on-the-tiller*, so that when circumstances change, the manager or supervisor is able to respond;
- crises and emergencies that are planned for on the basis that they will be kept to an absolute minimum.

Each has its own contingencies, as follows:

- *Steady-state:* may be required to change at short notice due to sudden losses of orders; sudden gains of orders; or shifts in market and priority.
- *Research development and pioneering:* may require additional resources to finish off a particular project; may also require resources to be written-off if the particular pioneering activity comes to nothing.
- *Maintenance activities:* while the ideal is to plan maintenance, it is

nevertheless essential that machinery breakdowns and/or computer crashes, can be accommodated and fixed when they do occur.

- *Steering:* in the normal course of events managers and supervisors will be aware of proposals for at least the short-term future of their departments; they may nevertheless have to respond at short notice to a sudden shift in priorities ordained from on high.
- *Crises and emergencies:* resources available at instant or very short notice to cope with genuinely unlikely or unforeseen circumstances.

In all of these cases, the likelihood and specific contingency components of each can be recognised and therefore planned. For example, if the organisation regularly accepts rush orders for which overtime is required, then arrangements can be made in advance to forewarn the staff, and to gather in the required supplies. When the matter then arises, people are prepared for the request to work overtime. It only becomes a serious problem if either people are not warned, or else if the approach used is known, believed or perceived to be coercive or the effect of a lack of general understanding and forward planning.

## Crises and emergencies

All organisations and departments have crises and emergencies from time to time. Clearly any contingency planning approach is designed to ensure that these are kept to a minimum. The two biggest issues to address are:

- to assess and evaluate both human and operational aspects for a full range of what can possibly go wrong and have procedures and practices in place (or at least something in mind) to deal with matters when they do arise;
- to assess and understand the likelihood and prevalence of having priorities and objectives changed from on high, the regularity and frequency with which this occurs, and the consequences to mainstream operations and staff morale as the result.

Problems can also arise when the ability to resolve crises and emergencies is a key organisational or managerial performance indicator (see Box 7.7).

### Box 7.7  Attitudes to crises and emergencies: the problem-solving dilemma

Consider the following:

- In early 2000, the manager of a team of social workers working with vulnerable adolescents in Central London took early retirement, aged 43. This was on health grounds – he was suffering from severe stress, high blood pressure and heart problems. He had worked for the particular council all his working life, having joined them upon qualification as a social worker. He had risen rapidly through the ranks because of his ability to solve problems. His energy and commitment far exceeded the call of duty. He regularly received excellent reports from his superiors, and additional increments, for his ability to tackle crises. Only when he left, did it become clear that most of the crises were of his own making, and that he received recognition for his ability to resolve them purely because it was the only thing that his own bosses within the Borough council were bright enough to understand.

Now consider the following:

- 'One sales manager sits in the reception area reading the newspaper hour after hour, not even making a pretence of looking busy. Most modern managers would not tolerate it. But when a Semco pump on a oil tanker on the other side of the world fails, and millions of gallons of oil are about to spill into the sea, he springs into action. He knows everything there is to know about our pumps and how to fix them. That's when he earns his salary. No-one cares if he does not look busy the rest of the time'.

Source: *Metro* (3 March 2000); Ricardo Semler (1992) *Maverick*, Free Press.

The ability to deal with crises and emergencies, and to solve these problems, is overwhelmingly recognised in corporate HQs in both private and public sectors. The matter is compounded when those who run well-planned and well-ordered departments know, believe or perceive themselves to be disadvantaged in relation to those who have first allowed chaos to occur, and then very publicly resolve it (see Box 7.8).

## Box 7.8 The 'White Knight Method'

The 'White Knight Method' is described by journalist Sharon Barnes who works in New York for an American business publication syndicate.

Sharon Barnes contrasted the way two managers, a man and a woman, handled the switch in an office from manual to computer operations. The woman foresaw the need for computerisation and gradually hired secretaries with computer experience so that the transfer to computerisation took place without a ripple.

The man did not prepare, so when the time came to switch to computers, his staff were in revolt. He mollified them by arranging a lunch at which a consultant taught them what they needed to know.

The man's troubleshooting was rewarded with a letter of commendation and a bonus.

Sharon Barnes calls this the 'White Knight Method', in which problems are allowed to happen, and then are ostentatiously solved. This attracts attention, whereas making sure the problems do not arise in the first place is likely to go unnoticed and unrewarded.

Source: Sharon E. Barnes 'The White Knight Method'
(*'Executive Female'*, January/February 1991).

## Priorities

Priorities are established to ensure concentration of organisational resources to best commercial or service advantage in the pursuit of long-term customer, client and user satisfaction, and to the satisfaction of those concerned with the overall direction of the organisation.

In practice, it is rarely possible to achieve everything desired or required. This is either because:

- resources are not adequate to carry out the full range of matters required
- priorities are imposed by organisations and their senior managers for their own particular purposes (the need for a triumph, the need to be seen to be doing something themselves).

It is possible to distinguish two basic approaches to the organisation of priorities (see Figure 7.6).

There is nothing intrinsically right or wrong with either approach. The main issue at the outset is to know and understand which approach is being taken, and the opportunities and consequences of that choice. For example, approach A is extremely commonplace in public services because politicians and senior figures in government bodies have overwhelming pressures placed on them to be seen to be doing things.

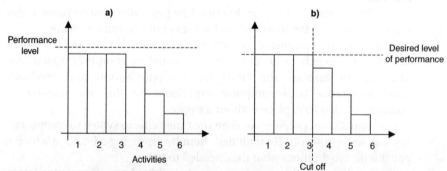

(a) **Everything is attempted, but unsatisfactorily; (b) Those things which cannot be completed satisfactorily are not attempted.**

*Figure 7.6*  Priorities.

# Time

It is usual to define work time as follows:

- *Productive time:* engaged in prescribed directed activities.
- *Maintenance time:* engaged in repairing and refurbishing machinery and equipment; and in training and developing staff.
- *Down or waiting time:* in which there is an amount of slack as the result of machine or system breakdown, or staff absence.
- *Overtime:* which is worked and paid above, and beyond, normal working hours.
- *Meeting time:* spent in staff meetings, consultations, briefings, and/or with customers, suppliers and clients.
- *Social time:* non-working staff interactions at the place of work.

It is also necessary to acknowledge:

- time to think
- time to plan
- time to do
- time to review.

Except for 'time to do', this list is largely ignored.

The mix and balance of this clearly varies between organisations, departments, divisions and functions. In all consideration of time usage at work, there are two certainties only:

- there is never enough time in the day/week/month/year to do everything required
- time is invariably seriously mismanaged and wasted, above all by senior managers (more junior managers, supervisors and operatives are simply left with the consequences of this).

## Time is money

This phrase has been used so often that it must be true! It is however the ways in which time is used that decide whether it is cost effective or extremely expensive.

---

**EXAMPLES**

A senior British Telecom executive was interviewed by the BBC. The BBC reporter was anxious to ascertain whether BT was paying its middle and senior managers for genuine productive and commercial output, or for working long hours. This was because a report had recently been published drawing attention to executive burnout and stress brought about as the result of working long hours. Junior and middle managers at BT at the time were adamant – they had to put in the long hours, to be seen at the office early in the morning and late in the evening, or else they would not receive performance bonuses. The BT senior executive was equally adamant – that only by working these long hours were more junior staff showing the commitment required to a company. (Source: *Panorama*, BBC1, 10 September 1992).

---

'Managers spend up to 20% of their time or the equivalent of one whole day per five day working week in meetings. Furthermore, they spend up to a third of their working time on paperwork, routine and administration. The main time wasters identified were interruptions from colleagues, handling telephone calls that a junior or subordinate should have fielded, and dealing with untargeted bureaucracy and memoranda. The main operational cause of hold-ups was found to be computer problems and systems failures'. (Source: UK Industrial Society, *Management, Pressure and Time*, March 1993).

'The best kept secret in business is that great leaders are nearly always extremely lazy as well as being capable of bouts of intense work. This is not just a weird coincidence. It is because laziness means time to think; and thinking time leads to good ideas, and good ideas rather than unthinking toil gives the edge in today's business world. The answer to the problem of laziness is therefore not to try to banish it, but to embrace it as a vital life tool. Every business needs idlers'. (Source: Tom Hodgkinson, *Management Today*, May 2000).

Value and expectations of time, as well as pure demands, have therefore to be assessed before work is ordered and scheduled.

Clearly, the great majority of time is allocated to organisational, departmental and divisional priorities and demands. The best, most widely used, and easy to understand way of ensuring that this is effective is the critical path plan (see Figure 7.7).

## Efficient and effective use of time

The distinction has to be drawn between the two. Efficient use of time is very narrow; effective use of time requires a much broader view (see Box 7.9).

## Box 7.9  NHS hospital beds

NHS hospital beds are, in simple terms, now managed very much more efficiently than ever before. Patient throughput times are calculated with great precision. As a bed is vacated, so it is cleaned and made up afresh. In many cases, beds are left unoccupied for less than an hour. Bed managers are employed in most NHS hospitals to ensure that this is done efficiently. This process has enabled the NHS to reduce its bed numbers from 500,000 to 130,000 over the past forty years.

Time efficient it may be. Time – and cost – effective it most certainly is not. The bed management system has to be costed, paid for and supported. Staff have to be employed to work this system, rather than to deal with patients. Patient throughput has fallen at exactly the time that bed usage efficiency has increased. This means that fewer patients are being seen and treated less effectively, and more slowly, with a greater need for repeat visits and care.

**a) Model**

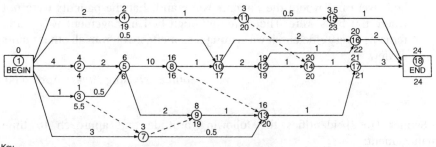

Key

(4) Activity number    Critical Path (1) - (2) - (5) - (8) - (10) - (12) - (14) - (17) - (24)

4 Time unit

→ Operational progression

- → Operational tie-ups

19
○ Time completed (cumulative)    The number on top is the earliest point at which the activity can be completed, the number
19                                below is the latest point by which it must be completed.

*Purpose:* a project/operational schedule; a planning tool; a model against which to measure actual progress. Identification of critical incidents (those on the critical path). Identification of potential problems, blockages and hold-ups. Doing this part of the job properly, also requires the other indications and provisions for contingencies to be taken into account and in-built as follows before a full assessment of effective time can be achieved.

**b)  Delivery schedules**

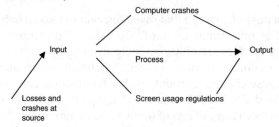

**c)  Production output**

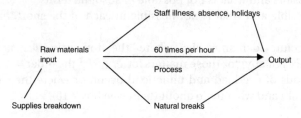

**d)  Information output**

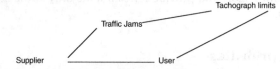

*Figure 7.7*  The critical path plan.

A broader – effective – consideration would have recognised that the beds were not where the patients were; and that the patients were not where the beds were. Therefore, although bed management was – and remains – very efficient, it was wrong (i.e., ineffective) from all other points of view.

Source: Nursing Times – April 2000.

Semler (1992) identifies the following attitude and approach to time management:

- Begin at the end; set a time when you will finish work each day and obey it blindly.
- Manage interruptions by blocking out periods in the day when you will a) wander the job; and b) be available for consultation and discussion.
- Acquire a second waste paper bin in which to put all of those interesting, but diversionary, papers that cause real work to pile up.
- Consider everything not directly related to organisational or departmental activity from the point of view of 'What is the worst thing that can happen if I do not read or keep this?'
- Keep meetings short and provide refreshments only at the start, if at all (see Chapter 3).

## Time and priorities

Time and priorities can then be related to:

- what is possible and what is not possible in absolute terms
- what is possible and what is not possible in each of the short, medium and long terms
- where absolute demands lie; where the top priorities lie; and the consequences (if any) for those matters lower down the order
- where periods of overload and underload occur, or where they are likely to occur (if at all) and what to do about them (see Box 7.10).

## Box 7.10   Overload and underload

There is a Russian proverb that says: 'You cannot make a baby in one month by working nine times as hard'. Operational pressures requiring over-capacity to be met are only genuinely sustainable in the very short-term. Where it becomes the norm – especially in health and public services – staff leave because of stress burnout, work-related illness and demoralisation.

Underload also has to be managed. Long periods of inactivity also bring about their own form of loss of morale and commitment. Staff come to feel undervalued and become alienated. Boredom sets in; and when productive effort is at last called for, it invariably cannot be achieved.

# Conclusions

It is clear that planning is a process, not an activity (see Figure 7.8).

When seen in this way, and when broken down as indicated above, it is clear that this is a key managerial and supervisory skill and activity. It also becomes clear that effective planning has little to do with all of the things that have gained it a bad name in the past:

- large irrelevant documents produced by remote corporate functions
- corporate daydreams produced either at head office, or by external management consultants
- fashions and fads such as total quality management and business process re-engineering.

It has everything to do with taking certain simple steps and actions to ensure that:

- priorities can be set and met
- provision for contingencies is in-built
- external and internal pressures are recognised and, as far as possible, addressed.

Above all, by understanding planning from this point of view, and by adopting the methods and techniques illustrated in this chapter, simple, direct and effective plans can be drawn up. These are also much more capable of being understood and accepted by those working for the particular manager or supervisor than something that is overtly more substantial, but which actually lacks in credibility. Many problems arise in organisations when things are unworkable or unvalued, and, in the past, corporate, strategic, managerial and supervisory planning activities have fallen into both of these categories.

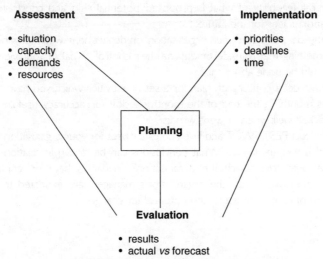

*Figure 7.8*  The planning process: summary.

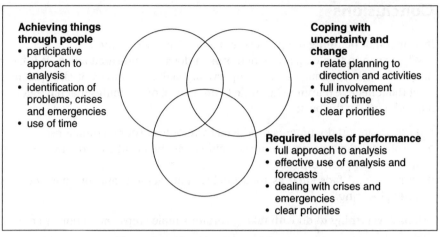

**Achieving things through people**
- participative approach to analysis
- identification of problems, crises and emergencies
- use of time

**Coping with uncertainty and change**
- relate planning to direction and activities
- full involvement
- use of time
- clear priorities

**Required levels of performance**
- full approach to analysis
- effective use of analysis and forecasts
- dealing with crises and emergencies
- clear priorities

*Figure 7.9*   Chapter and model summary.

Finally, this approach ensures that everything is capable of, and subject to, review and evaluation. If things go wrong, they can be traced back to points in the planning process where they were first allowed to go ahead, and a proper evaluation can then take place. This is in contrast to simple responses to corporate or remote direction, delivered out of context, and which nobody is ever going to evaluate or review.

Using the Model referred to at the start of Chapter 1 (Figure 1.1), the material in this chapter 15 summarised in Figure 7.9.

QUESTIONS

1. For a set of organisational or departmental plans with which you are familiar or to which you have access, produce a short critique and analysis addressing: the overall feasibility of what is proposed; potential risks and constraints; potential opportunities for the future.
2. Why do people in your organisation or department work long hours? Is this something that is inside or outside their control? What in your view could and should be done about this?
3. Construct a critical path plan for a set of activities which you have to complete this month. At the end of the month check it for: accuracy; usefulness; where it worked well; where it went wrong.
4. Conduct PEST, SWOT and Five Forces analyses for your organisation, or one with which you are familiar. What conclusions can be drawn in relation to: external pressures over which the organisation's managers have no control; internal direction over which the organisation's managers are expected to have some form of control; pressure and potential for change?

# ▼ 8 Decision making

## Introduction

Decision making is a constant and integral part of all managerial and supervisory activities. All managers and supervisors must therefore be able to make effective decisions and understand the processes involved in their implementation. Decisions are taken at:

- strategic and policy level
- operational and project level
- group and divisional level
- levels concerned with day-to-day administration and maintenance of individual, group and departmental activities.

At whatever the level the decision is required, there are certain fundamental considerations that have to be made if the process is to be effective and successful. There are different stages that must be understood.

Current decisions and patterns of decisions arise from that which has previously occurred, combined with the pressures of the present situation. Decisions taken at present have direct impact and implications for the future. Decisions taken, for example, in a marketing department have implications for, and effects on, production, sales, human resource management, purchasing and supplies. Decisions taken by a human resource department (for example, when new staff are taken on, inducted and trained) have implications for the subsequent profitable and effective performance of the organisation.

Elements present in all effective decision making are:

- *Problem or issue definition:* this is the starting point of the process. Once the problem or issue has been defined, the likely effects and consequences of particular courses of action can begin to be understood. Failure to do this may lead to considerable waste of time, effort and resources. Failure to do this accurately may lead to a range of misperceptions and misunderstandings being present from the outset for the entire duration of the process.
- *Process determination:* much of this depends on culture, structure and environmental and other pressures surrounding the organisation or department involved. It also depends on ways of working and the personalities and groups involved.

  There may also be key groups, staff, suppliers, customers, vested interests, pressure groups and lobbies who must be consulted on particular matters. If these groups are consulted, then they feel that their views have been respected and valued. Not to consult such groups, especially when they carry particular influence, is normally wrong; and the effects of antagonising such groups should always be considered.

- *Time scale:* time is involved heavily in process determination. There is also a trade off between the quality and volume of information that can be gathered and analysed, and the time available to do this. The longer the time scale, the better the chance of gaining adequate information and considering it and evaluating it effectively. However, this also increases the cost of the eventual course of action. On the other hand, quick decisions may involve hidden extras at the implementation stage if insufficient time has been spent on the background.

  It may also be possible to timetable either the whole process, or else particular parts of it; if this is possible, the risks involved become minimised if, due to changing circumstances, the proposed course of action is then either modified or cancelled.

- *Information gathering:* very few decisions are taken with perfect information. Conversely, decisions made without any information are pure guesswork. Both quality and volume of information are required; and means for the understanding, evaluation and review of that which is gathered are also essential. In some cases, this will mean hiring or acquiring the expertise necessary to draw conclusions from the particular information.

  The better the information on which it is based, the more effective the decision is likely to be. Both the quality and accuracy of the information are also important. In some cases, where highly specialist or technical information is required as the basis for arriving at an effective decision, the managers or supervisors concerned find themselves having to place themselves in the hands of experts, and having to accept the interpretation of this information by those experts as the basis for taking the particular decision. Some decisions are therefore taken by managers and supervisors based on someone else's evaluation of the situation.

- *The alternatives:* alternatives are always available – in any situation, there is always the option of doing nothing. At this stage, the consequences of not following proposed courses of action will also be evaluated. Having understood that, it is now also necessary to fully evaluate all of the possible positive steps that are now open as a result of following the previous stages.

  In addition, possible opportunities will now start to present themselves. Specific matters and details such as costings, profits, losses, costs and benefits that will, or may, accrue also now start to become apparent (see Figure 8.1).

- *Implementation:* this is the point of action. The point of implementation is arrived at as the result of working through the previous stages of the model, together with related implications and considerations. The choice made affects future courses of action; as well as the choice, it is essential that the reasons it was made are also understood. All decisions, in turn, affect others and likely future consequences should also be extrapolated.

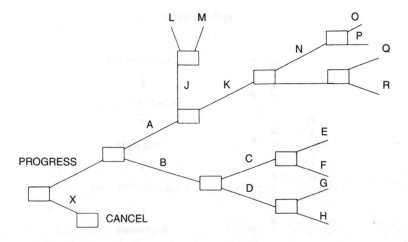

*Purpose:* to illustrate proposed courses of action, and likely and possible outcomes of them, from a given starting point. In this particular example, Option X – CANCEL – is evidently not on the agenda, as the consequences of this are not extrapolated. What is illustrated are the ramifications that accrue once the decision is taken to progress; and assuming two positive choices (i.e. other than cancellation) at each stage. The tree is a useful illumination of the complexity and implications of the process, and of the reality of taking one decision.

*Figure 8.1* The decision tree.

Decisions normally require both resources and people to implement them. It is essential that those directly involved are at the very least consulted on the proposed course of action. The action required may also indicate the need for further organisational planning.

This is a process that, if understood and followed as fully as possible, minimises the risks and uncertainties of the resultant courses of action. It is not a prescription for the provision of perfect activities, but rather a means by which the opportunities and consequences of following particular courses of action, and taking particular initiatives, may be evaluated.

All decisions should be subject to monitoring and review, to ensure that changing circumstances and factors outside the manager's control are not ignored, and also to ensure that they remain consistent with other organisational priorities and objectives (see Figure 8.2).

# Programmed and non-programmed decision making

It is usual to divide decision making into programmed and non-programmed. It is considered good management practice to have as many decisions as possible in the first category, provided that this does not diminish effectiveness of managerial activity, nor ignore changing circumstances and factors beyond the manager's control.

**a) Progression**

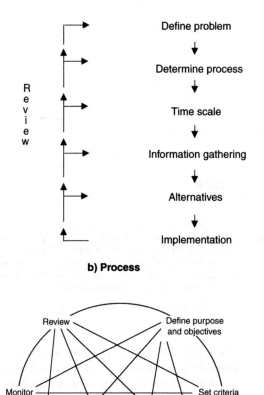

**b) Process**

*Purpose:* to draw the distinction between the two elements of progression and process. The former is a schematic approach; b) is that from which the former arises, and which refines it into its final format. Effective and successful decision making requires the confidence that is generated by continued operation of the process.

*Figure 8.2*   A decision making model.

Programmed decisions are simply those that are taken automatically in any given set of circumstances. They are normally taken to address simple and relatively certain operational issues. An example is that of stock replenishment. If it is a rule that the stock of a certain product should not fall below 1,000 units, then the decision by the supervisor to replenish the stock when this level is reached is programmed. The amount to be ordered will also be programmed by the setting of a maximum stock holding figure, the reorder amount being the difference between maximum and existing stock. Other such decisions, normally taken with the aid of computer programmes and record keeping, fall into this category.

Non-programmed decisions require the exercise of managerial and supervisory judgement. Decisions such as investment or development of new buildings, plant, machinery and equipment require informed and expert judgement of a very high order.

Judgement at all levels is nevertheless required where the decision is not automatic. Even programmed decisions or certain ways of working can be disrupted by sudden changes in the price of commodities that are ordered on an automatic basis. Should the firm be offered a quantity of the product at a very attractive price, a judgement would have to be made as to the wisdom of departing from the normal policy and whether sustaining an additional stockholding at such an attractive price would be outweighed by the fact that other premises and capital assets would be tied up in its storage.

## Organisational, managerial and supervisory adjustments

This is where the decision making process is limited or constrained. The normal result is that the organisation, or the particular manager or supervisor, alters, adjusts or limits activities in some way as the result of having to respond to circumstances outside their control.

Sufficient time and resources must be set aside to ensure that effective monitoring, review and evaluation takes place if organisations are not to be at the mercy of circumstances outside their control.

Organisational, managerial and supervisory adjustments may also have to occur as the result of ethical pressures or those brought to bear by internal and external pressure groups (see Figure 8.3).

Effective decisions are therefore arrived at through a combination of the preferred and chosen direction, together with recognising and accommodating the means by which this chosen direction can be made successful; and by acknowledging the limitations and pressures that are present.

## Participation, consultation and involvement

Participation, consultation and involvement are necessary where wide measures of support from among the workforce, community or public at large are required. The purpose here is to generate understanding and acceptance of courses of action.

It may also be necessary to consider:

- legal constraints affecting all aspects of business and organisation practice
- public interest, public pressure, lobby and special interest groups (see Figure 8.3)
- economic, social and political groups including consumer groups, environmental lobbies, local and public authorities, public agencies and

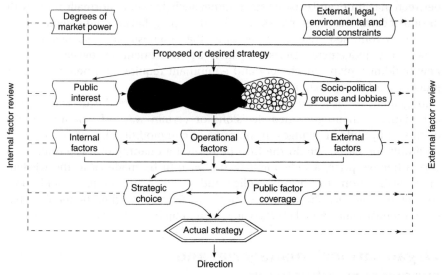

*Figure 8.3*　Model of decision making.

statutory bodies, industrial lobbies and staff representative bodies including trade unions

- committees and other formally constituted boards
- media interest and pressure.

Increasingly, there are statutory duties to consult where proposals are certain or likely to affect:

- internal ways of working, patterns of employment, technology and job occupations
- external disruptions to the environment, changes to the community, changes in the relationship between the organisation and its community
- commercial relations between the organisation and its suppliers on the one hand, and its customers, consumers and clients on the other.

# 'Wait a minute'

All managers and supervisors should have a mechanism in some shape or form that constitutes a 'wait a minute' facility.

This will be present in the formulation of policy or direction, the taking of operational decisions, and in the implementation of departmental aims and objectives. At junior management and supervisory levels, the purpose is to ensure that no inconvenient operational precedent is being set by taking a particular line to resolve what may seem a simple and one-off problem.

'Wait a minute' is neither an abdication of decision making ability, or of decision making itself. It need not take a 'minute'. It is simply a mechanism to ensure that what is to be done has been questioned from every conceivable angle. It is more generally part of the monitoring, review, early and late warning systems that should be integral to all aspects of the manager's task.

The presence of a 'wait a minute' facility does not, of itself, ensure that the right decision is taken. It does at least afford a moment's further consideration. If that is all that is necessary to confirm that what is being done is truly for the good of the organisation, and is fair and equitable treatment of the staff concerned, it is a moment well spent. It may also help to head off other problems that could easily have been foreseen, if only a moment's further consideration had taken place.

---

**EXAMPLE**

In 1999, a large holiday package company was required to pay £100,000 damages to one of its clients. On arrival at the destination, the particular client had walked straight through a glass window without realising it was there. The client was badly injured; however, if the holiday company had admitted liability and had paid reasonable compensation, together with providing instant high quality medical treatment, the £100,000 damages would not have been necessary.

In 1999, a university in south eastern England cut its travel expense payments to part-time staff from 40p per mile to 16p per mile. This, the university supposed, would save it in the order of £17,000 per annum from its travel and mileage bill. The same year, the university incurred newspaper advertising recruitment bills to the order of £89,000 to replace the staff who had left because they had felt slighted by the reduction in travel expenses.

---

# Risk and decision making

It is impossible to predict with certainty the outcome of decisions. It is possible to take certain steps to assess the possible range of outcomes. Much of this is dependent upon the volume and quality of information available and gathered (see above); and on the process used (see above). This can then be organised to gain answers to the following questions:

- Is what is required possible, likely or probable in the circumstances and in the desired time scale?
- What is likely to go wrong, and what can possibly go wrong?

---

**EXAMPLE**

Following the carnage of the First World War, the military elite of Europe and North America determined that the blueprint for future wars would consist of 'bloodless airborne warfare'. Military targets would be bombed with precision. Civilians would not be killed; neither would armies in the field – because they would not be in the

---

field. Fighting would be limited to targeting, the effective and precise destruction of key strategic installations. This, it was stated, would remove all the risk from military activities.

Within hours of putting this policy into practice for the first time in November 1939, it became apparent that it was unworkable. The risk to those who flew the planes had simply not been considered. The risks incurred as the result of a universally known, recognised and understood strategy had not been considered. Moreover, the technology necessary to deliver this form of precision bombing had not been invented (and in the early 21$^{st}$ Century this still remains true). This has not prevented governments, military establishments and defence equipment manufacturers from seeking to develop this form of military hardware. However, it should be noted that on the last occasion on which this form of military hardware was in substantial use (in Kosovo in 1999), it failed largely because it could not cope with the uncertain Balkan weather.

Source: Channel 4, *Great Military Blunders*, 2000.

- Extrapolation of decision-tree approaches to project the longer-term opportunities and consequences (see Figure 8.4).

It should be apparent that all decisions can be fraught with the problems of uncertainty, and errors can have the most far-reaching repercussions.

As a result, many organisations now go to great lengths to try and assess the risk inherent in particular decisions. They have extensive databases and employ expert analysts in order to try and gauge the effects of the range of possible outcomes in advance of decisions being taken. Approaches to the assessment of risk normally try to present the potential outcome in terms of best, medium and worst scenarios; and risk assessment information databases include factors outside, as well as inside, the organisation's control.

In the management of risk, all organisations try to have early warning systems available. Again, their effectiveness is based on having complete and high quality information concerning the state of markets, products and services; and also taking active and positive steps towards assessing the state of the workforce, the effectiveness of production processes, prevailing attitudes and so on.

To try and take some of the risk out of decisions, management now also try to make use of sophisticated mathematical, statistical and computer-based techniques. It is essential to remember, however, that these are only tools to aid managers. The decision still has to be taken based on the manager's judgement and evaluation of situations and the information presented.

Most decisions have to be taken by particular deadlines. There is, therefore, a balance to be struck between the volume and quality of information required and the deadline by which it is necessary. The longer the deadline, the greater the ability to gather information; however, in practice this is not always possible. If a decision is required in a short space of time, it has to be taken on the basis of the information that can be made available by the deadline.

**(a) Arriving for an appointment**

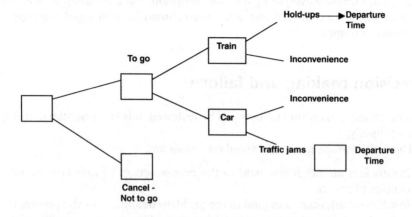

**(b) Installing a new production plant**

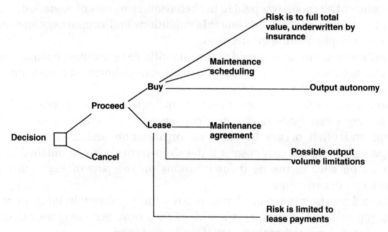

*Figure 8.4*   Decision tree examples.

Organisations also need the facility for taking crisis and emergency decisions. This means ensuring that all managers and supervisors have guidelines to work to when they are affected by crises and emergencies. Crises and emergencies should never become excuses for guesswork.

# Decision making and success

Decisions that have successful outcomes must always be evaluated and reviewed. This is to establish the basis on which success was achieved, to understand what made the particular process and activities so effective, and to draw lessons on which to build for the future.

Many organisations do not review their successes. They either take them for granted or else base everything on an assumption that they are infallible. Worst of all, many organisational successes are claimed by individual managers as their own triumphs.

## Decision making and failure

It is much more likely that failures will be reviewed. It is still essential that this is done properly.

The main reasons for unsuccessful outcomes are:

- Insufficient attention was paid to the consequences of following particular courses of action.
- Insufficient attention was paid to the problem definition; or the problem was defined wrongly for some reason (either a simple error or an unwillingness to face the real issue).
- Insufficient attention was paid to the behavioural aspects of operations, above all, to creating effective and suitable conditions and support systems as the basis for implementing the decision.
- Insufficient attention was paid to the quantifiable performance requirements of management and supervision, and to the establishment of proper aims and objectives along the way.
- Short-term results were prioritised at the expense of long-term activities. This very often leads to the over-consumption of resources in the short term and often occurs because the organisation and its managers and supervisors can see easy results if the short-term course is pursued. It also occurs because of the need for triumphs on the part of key figures and particular departments.
- Artificial constraints and deadlines, overwhelmingly driven by budget systems and reporting relationships, gain a life of their own, becoming the reason for decision making, rather than part of the background.
- Priorities are established for reasons other than performance effectiveness, especially for reasons of publicity, kudos, status and the demands of key figures.
- Unreasonable deadlines for the achievement of particular objectives are set. It is usual that the deadlines are unreasonably short. However, it should also be noted that over-long deadlines can also have a deadening effect, and lead to almost certain failure.
- Feelings of complacency are allowed to emerge, often based on long histories of success, continuity and past achievement. These tend to lead, in turn, to feelings of infallibility and immortality. As a result, decision taking ceases to be orderly and there is a loss of focus, as well as insufficient attention to monitoring and review.

# Other factors

Other factors that require consideration are:

- perfectionism
- hurdle removing
- procrastination.

## Decision making and the sin of perfectionism

Perfectionism is nearly always an excuse for inertia or procrastination. The standpoint taken is that unless we can achieve 100% success in an ideal way, we will not start at all. It can be demonstrated in any set of circumstances that this is not possible so the decision to progress is never taken.

People then revert to comfort using such phrases as:

- 'Aren't we unlucky?' (Robert Baden-Powell, 1929 – the usual excuse for missed opportunities).
- 'The timing was wrong.' (J. Edgar Hoover, 1961, excusing the American's inability to get a person into space before the Russians).
- 'Complete information was not available.' (Neil Kinnock, Labour Party Leader, 1992, on general election defeat by John Major – complete information is never available).
- 'I may not win the race so I won't enter.' (David Bedford, Olympic trialist, 1972 – he had a great reputation for being able to race against the clock, but was perceived not to be able to race against other human beings).

As a consequence, nothing is achieved.

Worse still is where a manager or supervisor pretends, or conspires with the view, that a perfect set of circumstances is available, in pursuit of a narrow personal objective. This is always a problem because the negative or limiting factors that are present in all situations are simply ignored. Possibly if they were not ignored, the decision would be taken effectively, because the full context would be understood. However, by failing to recognise the effects of certain elements, full success becomes impossible to achieve.

## Hurdle removing

Objections, barriers and hurdles to progress are raised by groups and individuals from organisational, occupational, professional and personal standpoints. These may be legitimate or non-legitimate. These hurdles may also be raised on the basis of ignorance or prejudice. Either during the consultation or in the run up to implementation, hurdles become apparent. The usual way in which these are raised is to say, 'Yes, but'.

- 'Yes, but', is the phrase used when those affected raise objections, problems or issues (whether legitimate or not) that represent barriers to progress. These need to be dealt with on the spot as far as possible and on their own individual merits.

'A Bridge Too Far' is the name of the film made by Richard Attenborough in 1978 depicting the Arnhem landings of 1944.

The Arnhem mission was a military disaster. The aim was to drop a paratroop army of 10,000 men at Arnhem, Holland, 60 miles behind enemy lines in order to secure bridges across the Rhine that would speed up the progress of the invading US and British armies into Germany.

The planning process is well documented. The idea was dreamed up by Field Marshall Bernard Montgomery, because he needed a military triumph, having failed to secure overall command of the invasion of Germany. As a result, the following 'Yes, buts' were not addressed:

- 'Yes, but there are three photographs of a German army in the field where our people are going to land'.
- 'Yes, but the weather is unpredictable and we might not be able to get enough planes up during breaks in the weather to get the army over to the zone where they are to be parachuted in'.
- 'Yes, but the Germans may have anti-aircraft fighter cover, and defensive positions which we may not be able to break through with an army of 10,000 paratroops'.

These three questions were raised in the precise form of 'Yes, but'. They were ignored, or not addressed fully. Above all, they represented three barriers to the execution of the particular plan, and implementation of the decision that, because they did not fit in with people's preconceptions, were simply ignored.

Source: 'A Bridge Too Far', Richard Attenborough (1978).

- Providing and producing additional information: those who do not know the full story, often ask for additional information to be provided or produced. This is a legitimate hurdle and needs addressing when the information demonstrates that something either will not work at all or will not work in the ways envisaged. It is illegitimate when it is used by professional and occupational groups, and vested interests, to advance a partial point of view – and this can happen either to try and hurry the decision along, or to try and block it.

The management skill lies in recognising the nature of the hurdles and barriers, and dealing with them quickly on their own merit. Illegitimate barriers and hurdles must lead to a review of proposed direction. If illegitimate barriers and hurdles are allowed to gain credence, this is always symptomatic of a deeper malaise:

- over-influence of vested interests, personalities, occupational and professional groups
- using this as a prelude to raising real issues
- legitimate concerns for job or work security (even if this is a non-legitimate way of raising these concerns)
- elitist, negative or defensive mentalities that for some reason have formed in the groups or individuals raising the objections.

So long as each barrier – legitimate or not – is dealt with openly and honestly, real issues can be addressed, and the veracity, or otherwise, of objections established. And if the objectors are proven or demonstrated to have a serious point, this should always be considered.

## Procrastination

Procrastination occurs when, for whatever reason, the manager is, or feels, unable to choose a particular direction. The reasons for this are:

- the known or likely unpleasantness that will occur as the result
- unwillingness or inability to deal with known or perceived consequences
- unwillingness or inability to deal with difficult or contentious questions or matters arising as the result
- unwillingness or inability to deal with known or likely emotions on the part of those affected, especially anger, despair, loss of motivation
- unwillingness or inability to deal with strong or strident personalities or vested interests, especially trade unions, professional groups and specialist lobbie.

---

**EXAMPLE**

In 1997, a scandal broke at the Bristol Royal Infirmary. It concerned surgical practice in the hospital's paediatric department. It was found that of 67 patients operated on by a particular surgical team, 33 had died.

The two surgeons who carried out this work had been allowed to carry on in practice, in spite of the fact that it was well known that their work was producing these results. It was also well known among the surgeons' managers. However, because of the strident personalities involved, the managers had found themselves unable and unwilling to approach the surgeons because they could not face the unpleasantness of the result.

---

These matters are only effectively dealt with face-to-face with the protagonists, and supported by concise, accurate written notes and summaries. The process is:

- to prepare a summary of the position in advance of a face-to-face meeting
- to make a verbal statement based on a summary at the face-to-face meeting
- to listen to the concerns – legitimate and otherwise – that are raised
- to deal with them face-to-face, if possible, or, if not, to make a commitment to getting answers by a particular deadline and sticking to this rigidly
- to deal with the emotions through listening to the concerns, recognising where they are coming from, and agreeing or conceding anything that is genuinely legitimate and within the remit of authority on the spot (see Box 8.1).

## Box 8.1 Techniques for managing procrastination in decision making

Minimising the effects of procrastination is essential if an effective management or supervisory style is to be engaged. Some of the techniques that are used are:

- *Repeating the question:* in which the angry person is allowed to storm out their particular point; when they have finished making their statement, the manager asks them to repeat the question.
- *Using the phrase 'What do you want from me?':* and then writing down the request as it is dictated out. This always draws the distinction between legitimate and non-legitimate concerns – the particular protagonist is always happy for genuinely legitimate concerns to go forward elsewhere.
- *Letting people have their say:* ensuring that everyone has the opportunity to let off steam, air their views, raise concerns, air prejudices even – and then leaving time at the end of the discussion to produce a working summary (subsequently to be published as a written document).
- *Pushing at an open door:* in which as many demands as possible are acceded to on the spot; this technique is used to build up quickly areas of common ground and agreement.

Moreover, if these techniques are adopted, procrastination becomes impossible. Everything is conducted out in the open. Procrastination can only take place behind closed doors – and it quickly becomes a feature of a management situation that is either toxic or dishonest.

# Decision making and other pressures

The following points have always to be considered. No decision is ever taken in isolation; everything is subject to limitation (see Figure 8.4). The main pressures that have to be considered are:

- *Limitations of laws and government direction:* representing national, local and social constraints and restraints. They require evaluation by managers and supervisors to ensure that what is done is not only commercially viable, but also culturally acceptable in the particular part of society in which it is to be implemented.
- *Public interest:* public interest is a reflection of the general social ethos; it consists of dominant public opinions, received wisdom, the activities of pressure groups, and the acquiescence of the majority. It includes such abstract values as freedom, respect for life, respect for the individual, telling the truth and helping the needy.
- *Eco-socio-political groups:* more or less organised constituencies that organisations have to consider, and which ultimately effect decision making

activities and policies. They include consumer groups, environmental lobbies, local and public authorities, public agencies (e.g., the Health and Safety Executive), industrial lobbies and trade unions. They also include pressure groups formed by those whose environment or locality is to be affected by the implementation of particular decisions. Some social values lack institutional voice or political muscle. Some social benefits are defeated by institutional deadlocks. Some powerful groups and lobbies do not represent the public interest. However, they all have voices, and these must be considered when they arise, and reconciled where necessary. The greater the level of understanding by managers and supervisors, the greater the ability to harmonise the effects of each of these groups into effective decision making techniques.

- *Public factors:* public factors often conflict. Both business and public decisions must, therefore, take account of this and, where necessary, try to reconcile these matters, a new bypass scheme, for example, is certain to cause environmental and construction blight, but may take a lot of traffic pollution away from built-up areas. This adds to the complexity of making choices into which there may be included ethical as well as social, political and commercial dimensions.
- *Internal factors:* where the organisation considers specific aspects of its own operations, and the ways in which these will affect the implementation of particular decisions.
- *External factors:* including the necessity to open up for discussion the public interests on which particular decisions are to impinge. This includes opening relationships with trade association or trade union bodies; particular public bodies; and where required, pressure groups and lobbies. It is important to note that the effect of pressure groups and lobbies are rarely diminished through ignoring them – at some stage, where they exist, they have to be dealt with.

## Gaining commitment

The final part of the decision making process is gaining commitment. In order for this to be achieved successfully, the proposed course of action has to be capable of being understood and be capable of standing up on its own merits. It is usual therefore to consult on particular decisions.

## Consultation

Consultation is a behavioural and organisational process, the essential purpose of which is:

- to gain the commitment of the staff. This is only achievable if the process is communicated via all means at the disposal of the organisation, and if adequate and full briefings, meetings and discussions are held and supported by clear and concise documentation

- to gain the commitment of any other interested parties in the same way
- to ensure that everyone understands and values the necessity of what is being done. This must include coverage of the reasons and the time scale and progression in ways understandable to those being consulted
- to address the needs of particular groups. For staff, this will include matters concerning relocation, redeployment, retraining, redundancy, changes in operational or behavioural patterns and organisation expectations. For those who do not work in the organisation, it requires addressing particular pressures and influences on the environment, transport schedules, motorways and link roads, noise, heat and dust levels generated, and so on. No useful purpose is served in the long-term by ignoring such matters when they are known to exist.

Consultation is therefore concerned with implementation and understanding. It does not exist to dilute or affect what is to be done unless the process of consultation itself throws up an operational barrier or caveat. It is likely to impact on all aspects of work, whatever is being proposed. Consultation must be fair and reasonable. Normally, such a period will be for at least four weeks; this relates to relatively minor changes or decisions. For a major exercise – relocation for example – a period of up to a year may be necessary. For major projects that impact on the environment, it will normally be necessary to consult with local community representatives as to what they want in the particular set of circumstances. In all cases, a true balance has to be struck between the pressures on the organisation, the needs of the staff, and the demands of the community.

Consultation is an active process, and one that must be led and directed by managers and supervisors. It is not enough simply to give a period of notice that a decision has been taken. Responsibility for gaining the understanding, commitment and support of staff in such matters is an obligation placed on all managers in every organisation. They are required to direct the consultation process and ensure that it happens in the ways indicated (see Box 8.2).

## Box 8.2  The negative decision

Negative decisions are often hard to take. They are often equally hard to convey.

The essence is to keep the transaction adult, businesslike, open and above board.

Operational requests should never be turned down for personal reasons. No request should ever be turned down without a full explanation.

- It must be made clear to the individual that the decision has been well thought out and is not arbitrary.
- It must be based on operational logic and soundness, and communicated in this way.
- The word 'no' should be used to underline a point.
- The transaction should end in suggestion or direction towards the positive and towards alternatives if these are feasible.

- The negative decision should always be followed up in writing – and the writing must match exactly the words used during the transaction.

No manager should ever hide behind procedural issues or niceties of phrase in such a situation. The employee, or member of the community, is entitled to the respect and openness implicit in the above approach.

## Implementation

Implementation of decisions can be summarised in terms of the following:

- *Distributive effect:* where a decision benefits one group at the expense of others, or one project at the expense of others, or where resources are allocated to one set of activities at the expense of others.
- *Integrative effect:* a decision benefits all groups, projects and activities.
- *Avoidance of cop-outs:* e.g., 'I left London to visit Edinburgh, I only got as far as Newcastle, therefore I was 75% successful'.
- *The best, medium, worst (BMW) effect:* this is effective as long as the full consequences of the *best* are effectively evaluated (e.g., a decision may be so initially successful that it skews the whole strategy and direction of the organisation or department in its favour), the full consequences of the *worst* are fully evaluated (including, as precisely as possible, a definition of the 'nightmare scenario'). (See Figure 8.5).
- *Getting to win:win* (i.e., the integrative effect); and understanding the consequences and fall-out from:
  — *win:lose* – a version of the distributive effect in which you succeed at the expense of other people
  — *lose:win* – in which other people receive benefits at your expense (this also needs extremely careful management)
  — *lose:lose* – in which a bad decision is taken from every point of view.

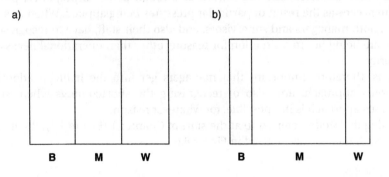

a)                                                    b)

    B        M        W              B        M        W

**Each is defined precisely**        **Best and worst are defined; too little attention is paid to the medium**

*Figure 8.5*   Best, medium and worst outcomes.

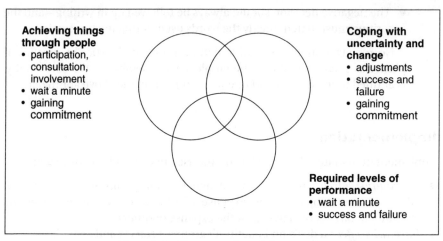

Achieving things through people
• participation, consultation, involvement
• wait a minute
• gaining commitment

Coping with uncertainty and change
• adjustments
• success and failure
• gaining commitment

Required levels of performance
• wait a minute
• success and failure

*Figure 8.6*  Chapter and model summary.

It is also necessary to acknowledge the factors outside the control of the particular manager or supervisor. These may be as diverse as imposed changes in organisation policy or direction, interest rate and exchange rate changes, sudden losses of staff, or machinery or equipment breakdowns.

## Conclusions

The purpose of considering decision making from this point of view is to ensure that all managers and supervisors get into the habit of giving all matters as full a coverage as possible.

It is also essential that the imperfections and subjectivity inherent in all such situations is recognised. Complete objectivity is only possible in a small proportion of programmed circumstances. There are nearly always elements of risk. Many decisions also are arrived at through personal prejudice, personal influence, or as the result of particular pressures being applied. When this is the case, both managers and supervisors, and also their staff, have to recognise that they are being put in a situation for reasons other than operational necessity or priority.

It is, therefore, important that managers get into the habit of adopting a rigorous approach, and also of recognising the shortcomings where such a rigorous approach is not possible, for whatever reason.

Using the Model referred to at the start of Chapter 1 (Figure 1.1), the material in this Chapter is summarised in Figure 8.6.

QUESTIONS

1. Can decision making be an entirely rational process? In what ways is decision making limited by inadequate information and by the style of management in an organisation?

2. What are the essential differences between the approach to decision making at strategic and operational levels?
3. To what extent are the consultation processes in use at your organisation/college adequate? How do these work? How would you recommend they be improved?
4. Give examples from your own experience of ways in which the 'wait a minute' approach would have enhanced the effectiveness of decisions.
5. How might those responsible for the running of flexible and non-standard patterns of work engage in effective participation and involvement at the point of implementation of decisions?

# ▐ ⱴ  **9** Problem solving

## Introduction

At the core of all managerial and supervisory activities lies the ability to solve problems. This is because operational and functional effectiveness has to be maintained so that effort, priority and resources can be directed at the aims, objectives and priorities of the particular organisation, department, division, function or group.

In fact, this is rarely straightforward because:

- there is often pressure from superiors, peers, subordinates, suppliers, customers and clients to provide a quick answer (whether or not this is the right answer)
- some visible problems (e.g., staff absences, customer complaints) may be symptomatic of deeper malaise
- many organisations measure their managers and supervisor's performance on their ability to solve problems (see Chapter 7) so managers and supervisors find problems to solve and then, ostentatiously, solve them (see Box 9.1).

## Box 9.1  Solving problems

It is stated at the end of Chapter 1 that a guiding principle is 'to know when to seek help and where to seek it from'. However, it is important to note that this is a principle only. It has to be seen in context, and can be a double-edged sword. For example:

You are the manager of a production line. You have a serious staff management or industrial relations problem that needs to be resolved quickly. You are not quite clear how to go about it, though you do know the desired outcome, so you go to the organisation's industrial relations department for help.

At this point there is a fundamental conflict of interest. You want the matter sorted out; on the other hand, the industrial relations department is the support function that now has the opportunity to justify its existence, to demonstrate its value and to work itself into a job. What do you do?

The lesson is that anyone seeking help from an outside department, expert (including consultants) or other agency needs to be aware of the fact that there is always a potential conflict of interest. The issue is compounded by the fact that their expertise may bring to light other issues that you were not aware of, and they also need to be tackled.

The broader context is further complicated by the following:

- The right answer may not be acceptable.
- The acceptable answer may not be right.
- There may not be enough time and resources to do the job in an ideal way, so that the best that can be achieved is a holding job, or staged approach.
- Capabilities in problem solving may be measured in terms entirely outside the control of particular managers and supervisors.
- The presence and operation of sophisticated bureaucratic and hierarchical systems tend to mean that praise and recognition for problems solved go to those at the top of the hierarchy, while blame for problems unresolved is apportioned to those responsible for dealing with them at the frontline.
- Today's priority is likely (some would say certain) to be submerged under tomorrow's pressures.

Very often, all that managers and supervisors can do is recognise which of these constraints they are required to operate within.

## Problem identification and sources

The following are the usual sources of problems and issues in organisations:

- *Proactivity:* keeping a constant ear and eye open; developing an early warning system; walking the job; listening to staff, subordinates, peers and superiors; listening to suppliers, customers and clients; listening to people in the previous and subsequent links in the business process or chain. This is the best way of identifying matters early before they become serious and urgent.
- *Responsiveness:* to sudden issues and crises – blockages and breakdowns on machinery; rows and arguments; computer and information systems crashes; customer, client and supplier complaints; spillages; accidents.
- *Management style:* management style provides an institutional definition of what a problem actually is (see Box 9.2).

### Box 9.2   Staff problems

Examples of different attitudes as to what constitutes staff problems are as follows:

- *Ford:* the management at Ford Dagenham was faced with problems of inter-racial and inter-cultural strife. This was exacerbated by the knowledge and belief that most of the frontline production staff are from the Asian community, while supervisors and managers were from the white community. Over the period 1985–2000, the company paid out a great deal of money in damages in order to settle cases where racial harassment was alleged, proven or strongly indicated.

- *North Yorkshire Police:* in 1998, the Force paid out compensation totalling over £300,000 to two women police officers. These officers had complained for years that they had been the subject of serious sexual harassment. The matter was only resolved when one of them began proceedings against a male colleague for a serious sexual assault.
- *Somerfield/Gateway supermarkets:* during the course of his managing by walking about, a store manager found two members of staff in a storeroom engaged in sexual relations. The man was very much older than the girl. The following day, the store manager received a complaint from the girl's mother, who wanted to know why her daughter, a fifteen year old on work experience, had been treated in this way. The store manager was subsequently sacked.

In each of these cases, the organisations concerned either refused or failed to recognise that there was a problem at all. The management style, culture and priorities meant that it was effectively easier to respond to specific situations, rather than create an environment where such problems could not possibly occur.

The response to the problem is also clearly driven by the style adopted or allowed to emerge:

- *Institutional forums, meetings and committees:* which bring to light problems and issues from their particular domains and remits.
- *Changes:* in ownership, direction, priorities, culture, management style, technology and working patterns; changes in staffing arrangements and union recognition; changes in key positions and appointments; changes in managerial and supervisory appointments (see Box 9.3).
- *One problem leads to another:* this is where:
  - someone raises an issue as a euphemism for another (e.g., 'I've hurt my chin' as a euphemism for 'Person X punched me');
  - someone raises one issue as a prelude to another (e.g., 'I don't feel very well' as a prelude to 'Because I've got heart problems and will have to have surgery, and will therefore be off work for six months');
  - someone raises one issue in the hope or expectation that the manager or supervisor will see the real issue (e.g., 'I don't feel very well. Can I go home?' in the hope that the manager will see that what is really being said is 'My life is a misery. I'm being bullied and victimised. Please help').

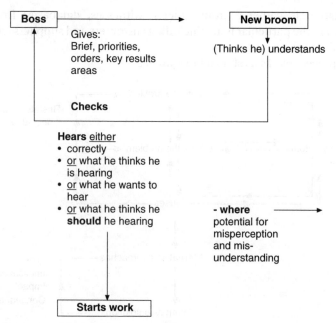

*Figure 9.1*   The new broom: initial perception and misperception.

## Box 9.3   The new broom

Unless recognised and carefully managed, 'new brooms' can do as much harm as good, often with the best will in the world. A key part of the problem is initial perception and misperception (Figure 9.1).

This process determines whether or not the new broom gets off to a good start, and sets the tone for their immediate and medium-term future at the very least. Difficulties are compounded when there is:

- sufficient briefing in what is required, but insufficient in how it is required
- or sufficient briefing in how to work, but insufficient attention to what
- or where the briefing is too general all round; or where there is no briefing at all.

In these cases, new brooms have to sort out the what and how for themselves.

## The basis for solving problems

There are three key features for an effective basis for problem solving:

- *Information gathering:* gathering as much as possible in the circumstances and time allowed (recognising that there are likely to be time constraints).

Information is gathered from experts, witnesses, databases; from those involved in the particular issue (including customers and suppliers where they have raised the matter).

The process works as shown in Figure 9.2.

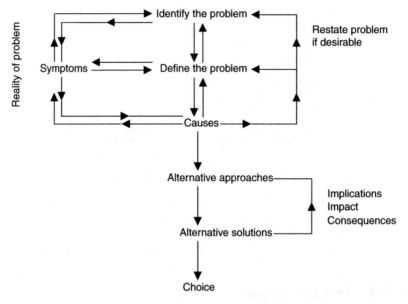

Purpose: to ensure that a rigorous and disciplined approach is recognised and understood as being necessary in all situations; or that it is adopted. Points for consideration throughout the process must also include: the context and nature of it; when it is occurring; where it is occurring; why; its impact on the rest of the organisation, department or division; the extent to which it can be avoided; the extent to which it can be controlled; the consequences and opportunities of not tackling it (which is always a choice).

Figure 9.2   A problem solving model.

- *Information assessment, analysis and evaluation:* putting what has been gathered and discovered into some sort of order; separating out the main points and priorities from the rest; identifying key features; establishing an order of priority, aims and objectives for tackling the particular matter; and from this, establishing the order in which the matter, or matters in hand, are to be tackled.
- *Face-to-face:* preaching perfection, everything should either be resolved or confirmed face-to-face, and supported in writing. The only genuine exception to this is the management of some customer complaints where the lack of face-to-face is effectively over-compensated by replacement and refund policies, the issuing of vouchers and discounts.

┌─ EXAMPLE ────────────────────────────────────────────────

Chiltern Railways was established in the early 1990s as part of the UK railway privatisation. The service offered by the company quickly deteriorated. The company responded by painting the trains in a distinctive livery, giving their staff smart new uniforms, and by offering a wide range of drinks and snacks on refreshment trolleys on the trains.

However, customers did not want any of this. Their priority was, and remains, punctual and reliable services.

Chiltern compounded the problem when, during a serious power failure at Reading, all senior managers removed themselves from the location, and left young junior staff to repeat a pre-rehearsed apology to frustrated and increasingly irate passengers.

This approach to customer complaints is wrong on every score. The only reason it is sustainable in these precise circumstances is because there is a relatively secure and captive market, with little alternative means of customer satisfaction.

Source: 'World in Action', Granada TV (March 1998).

With major customers and suppliers, even if the matter has to be resolved by telephone, fax or e-mail, it should always be followed up with a short personal call if at all possible.

With staff problems, any failure to meet with the person who has raised the issue is always seen as a mark of lack of respect or value. The person has, after all, found it important enough to raise the matter in the first place – it is clearly a concern to them, and deserves to be treated as such.

The management and resolution of staff problems is compounded where managers of individuals who do raise issues have to go to their own superiors for an answer; and their own superiors then refuse to explain their decision to the individual concerned. This is usually because:

- they do not see it as important
- it is beneath their perceived dignity or status
- they are frightened
- they cannot be bothered.

The best that individual managers or supervisors can do in these circumstances is to try and persuade their superiors to change their mind. Otherwise it becomes yet another constraint within which they have to operate.

## Problems

The major problems that managers and supervisors have to resolve are:

- *Staff problems:* disciplinary, grievance, disputes and dismissal; redundancies; sickness, absence and turnover; serious problems including vandalism, violence, assault; accidents and emergencies.
- *Peer and superior problems:* managing pressures from outside the department.
- *Supplier and customer complaints:* keeping suppliers and customers satisfied, and addressing the source and validity of specific issues.

This also includes dealing with powerful and difficult people from whatever source – inside or outside the organisation; powerful or influential personalities; shareholder and union representatives; dominant or major customers and suppliers.

## Staff problems

By law, all organisations are deemed to have procedures that cover discipline, grievance, disputes and dismissal. These must be in writing, available for inspection, be understood by all, and be followed in all cases. The first duty of managers and supervisors is therefore to ensure that this takes place.

Everyone concerned must understand their general rights and duties, and specific rights and obligations.

## Discipline

Staff discipline is a reflection of the standards of attitudes, behaviour and performance required in the particular situation. Disciplinary procedures are present to ensure that when there is any deviation from these standards, there is a proper, fair and even way of resolving the matter.

All disciplinary standards and procedures must state the circumstances in which they are to be conducted and applied. The following circumstances are normally covered.

### Poor and unsatisfactory performance

This is where for some reason the individual is incapable or unwilling to do the job for which they are employed. This requires a clear statement by the manager or supervisor of when, where and why the performance is falling short, followed by another clear statement of a programme for action to put it right. This is then subject to regular monitoring, evaluation and review, and is concluded with a clear statement to the employee that either performance is now satisfactory, or performance is still unsatisfactory and further action is to be taken.

### Misconduct

This includes negligence, unacceptable behaviour, failure to follow procedures, failure to act in the organisation's best interests, insubordination, gratuitous rudeness to colleagues and bad timekeeping. It may also include persistent self-certificated absenteeism in some circumstances (though very great care must be taken with this).

Misconduct may also include victimisation, bullying and harassment, though ideally, these should all come under the category of gross misconduct.

### Attitudes and demeanour

These are harder to pin down, but it is quite legitimate to make provision for dealing with negative, poor and sloppy attitudes, and where individuals place their own priorities above those of the organisation.

Other matters include attitudes to others – for example, where someone engages in a constant or persistent attitude of blame or denigration towards others; or where somebody adopts an inappropriate attitude towards a customer or supplier.

## Serious and gross misconduct

Organisations are required to have and make known to staff what constitutes serious and gross misconduct. The usual form of presentation of this is a list. This list need not be exhaustive. It should give clear and wide-ranging examples. The usual matters covered under this heading are:

- theft, fraud, sale of confidential information, other dishonesty
- vandalism, violence, attacks on staff, equipment and premises
- sexual misconduct
- serious or gross negligence or inattention to duties and the organisation's interests
- using foul and abusive language, swearing in front of customers and clients
- dishonesty in dealing with staff, customers and suppliers
- denigration of the organisation to other staff, customers, clients, suppliers and the public
- failure to follow safety procedures, endangering life and/or equipment
- bullying, victimisation and harassment.

Serious and gross misconduct may also arise as a result of persistent misconduct. This includes persistent bad timekeeping, persistent absenteeism, persistent insubordination and rudeness. The outcome of serious and gross misconduct cases is normally – at the very least – a final warning, and it invariably leads to dismissal.

## Operation of disciplinary procedures

All disciplinary procedures must have a series of warnings and these must be followed. Only in the case of serious or gross misconduct may an investigation be held that may lead to dismissal. Procedures must be operated as follows, whatever the level of misconduct alleged:

- Individuals facing discipline by their organisations must be allowed representation. Where a trade union is recognised, and where the individual is a member, representation is normally through that union.
- Individuals must always be told that they are facing discipline in advance of the hearing. This notification may give an indication of the range of outcomes. It must never prejudge the issue.
- Individuals facing discipline are entitled to hear the charges against them and to face their accuser/accusers in person. They are entitled to respond to the charges and call witnesses and evidence in support of their case.
- Individuals who have been disciplined must be afforded the opportunity to appeal. They must be notified of the person/official to whom the appeal should be made and the deadline by which it should be made.
- Individuals facing discipline must be notified in writing of the outcome of the case. A copy of this is placed in their personnel file. When a warning is issued, a copy of this should be given to the employee and a copy placed on their file. This applies to both oral and written warnings. It should state what the warning was for, any remedial action necessary, what is to happen if there is any repeat, and how long it is to remain current.

## Other factors

### Suspension

This is used quite legitimately in serious and/or contentious cases. Especially in cases of serious and gross misconduct, it is often essential that the individual concerned is removed from the scene while a full investigation is held. If it is decided that there is a case to answer, the individual must then be allowed time to prepare a response.

Suspension may be with or without pay – it is usual to suspend on full pay. The guiding principle must be that people are innocent until proven guilty. The guiding principle must be that people are innocent until proven guilty. If charges are found to have no substance, any pay due must always be made up at the point at which innocence is proven.

### Dismissal

This is the final sanction. It occurs either when an individual persistently refuses to improve their performance, attitude, behaviour or conduct or as the result of being found to have committed an act of gross or serious misconduct for which dismissal is the penalty.

### Arbitration

It is both useful and legitimate to make provision for arbitration. It is used most often when an impasse is reached. In these cases, both parties usually agree to the appointment of an arbitrator, and to be bound by the arbitrator's findings.

The arbitrator hears presentations from both parties, and then arrives at a preferred solution. This may be holy in favour of one party or the other; or a compromise, or a solution not previously considered.

Arbitration, in any form, should only be used as a last resort. It should never become a substitute for strong effective staff discipline and general management. If used too often, it becomes a crutch on which managers and supervisors eventually become dependent. It also places the capacity, independence and autonomy to resolve issues in the hands of an outside party.

## Grievances

All employees have the right to raise grievances against their employers, or against other employees. Grievance procedures are the formal means by which anyone working in, and for, an organisation may raise such an issue. This normally only occurs when the matter has first been raised in conversation between the employee and their superior with the request that it be resolved, and that this has not happened to the employee's satisfaction.

Grievance procedures must have at least two stages:

● The employee's right to raise an issue with the immediate superior, to have it heard; and to receive a response confirmed in writing giving the employer's view of the matter and the reasons for their decision.

- The employee's right to raise the issue with their superior's immediate superior for review and resolution if they are not satisfied with the outcome of the first stage.

The following must also be understood:

- Where serious allegations (e.g., discrimination, victimisation, bullying and harassment) are being made, the case must be heard without delay and the problem (if it turns out that there is one) nipped in the bud.
- Employees must never be discriminated against, victimised, bullied or harassed as the result of raising grievances or complaints. If the complaint turns out to have no foundation, the reasons why it first became apparent (usually misunderstanding or misinformation) should be made clear. If the complaints turns out to be malicious it should then be dealt with through the disciplinary procedure.
- The aims of all grievance procedures, and the management of grievances, must be to support the principle of dealing with problems as quickly as possible. The ideal outcome is always one that is satisfactory to both employer and employee. Where this is not possible, time must be taken to explain clearly to the employee why the matter was refused or turned down, and this must be capable of being sustained.

## Handling staff management issues

All cases start when a problem becomes apparent, and which has to be solved to the satisfaction of all concerned. In all discipline and grievance cases, the onus is placed on managers and supervisors to prove or demonstrate that:

- they acted fairly and reasonably, and with honesty and integrity
- they followed procedures, criteria and any recognised standards of best practice
- the outcome would have been the same for anyone in the same, similar or equivalent set of circumstances
- alternative courses of action were considered, evaluated and rejected
- where dismissal has resulted, the stated reasons for this were the real reasons for dismissal.

## Disciplinary cases

When it becomes apparent that there is to be a disciplinary case, the matter must be investigated as quickly as possible. This involves gathering evidence from existing records, and from witnesses. In particular cases, the following is required:

- *Poor performance:* copies of performance appraisals with dates; details of training and development undertaken with dates; copies of previous warnings; actions taken to remedy this in the past.
- *Bad timekeeping:* copies of clock cards, signing in registers, print-outs of keyed in or other electronic registers with dates; copies of previous warnings with dates; actions taken to remedy this in the past.

- *Absenteeism:* copies of absence records with dates; copies of previous warnings with dates; actions taken to remedy this in the past; acceptable and unacceptable levels of absence and the means by which these are promulgated throughout the organisation.
- *Misconduct:* dates and times on which the misconduct occurred; those who saw and/or were affected by it; previous warnings for this or similar misconduct; acceptable and unacceptable standards of conduct.
- *Attitudes:* identification of those aspects of behaviour which prove or indicate unacceptable attitudes, statements from others affected or in contact; the effects of a bad/negative attitude on others and on organisational and individual performance.

Once it is clear that they are required, investigations should become a high priority. They should be conducted as quickly and as thoroughly as possible. For minor cases, this need be no more than a quick trawl through the information indicated above. For more serious cases, a thorough investigation is essential. Under no circumstances is any manager or supervisor to spoil a strong case against a bad employee because they have not done this part of their job properly. Neither are conclusions to be arrived at before the full spread of evidence is gathered and available. Carrying out a full investigation enables a complete assessment of all the facts and merits of the case. This enables any disciplinary hearing to be carried out with full confidence. It enables all areas of doubt to be brought out into the open. Any question that the employee is being victimised is avoided. It also underlines a genuine concern that all managers and supervisors should have when their staff are either not happy or not performing.

## Relationships with peers and superiors

Effective relationships with peers and superiors are based on the following:

- Developing approaches based on a combination of role, function and personality, adding a personal strand to the professional and operational. This means developing measures of trust, warmth, liking and respect as a part of professional and operational dealings.
- Developing approaches based on individual influence. This involves recognising the nature of the influence of particular individuals, and the ability to present it in ways useful to others within the organisation.
- Developing networks of professional, personal and individual contacts and using these as means of gaining fresh insights and approaches to problems and issues.
- Developing funds of bargaining chips – equipment, information, resources and expertise – which can, if required, be used in trade-offs and for mutual advantage and satisfaction.
- Developing a clarity of thought around the entirety of organisational operations and activities. This is based on the one hand, on what is important, urgent and of value, and to whom; and on the other, what facilitates progress,

and what hinders or blocks it. This also involves recognition of where the true interests of the organisation, its managers and supervisors, and its frontline staff, actually lie, and how these can best be served in particular situations.

Different forms of approach are required for particular situations in which these points are used, managed and combined. A different approach may also be required to the same individual or group where there is interaction on more than one basis. For example, a production supervisor may be able to request financial information from the accounts supervisor in one way; however, the approach to the same supervisor will vary considerably if the accounts supervisor were also the local union lay official representing a grievance on the part of a member of the production team.

## Supplier and customer complaints

The issues here include the following:

- Deciding who is to handle the complaint and, if necessary, giving the authority to do it. For example, at Nissan UK, customer complaints are handled directly by the team that actually made the particular car.
- Assessing the validity of the complaint. This always includes:
  — ensuring that the complaint is fully understood. This can only be effective again through talking to everyone involved
  — ensuring that the complaint made is as stated and not symptomatic of something else, especially a deeper dissatisfaction with the overall business relationship.
- Ascertaining what the customer or supplier wants to happen as the result of having made the complaint, and ascertaining whether or not this is possible. If it is possible, it then has to be determined whether or not this is a suitable response. If it is not possible, then the reasons for this have to be made clear. If it is not possible, it is necessary to have alternative proposals to put forward.
- Knowing and understanding the expectations and components of satisfaction that the customer or supplier has in their dealings with the organisation in question.
- Knowing and understanding the certain, likely and possible effects of offering particular remedies to problems. There are some pretty well established rules and substantial legal protection in many circumstances.

### Wholesale and retail products and services

Faulty goods and products bought from shops or wholesalers are normally refunded or replaced without question. The reason for this is quite simple – it is a lot easier and much more cost effective to replace faulty products than dissatisfied customers, who invariably go off and tell friends, relations and colleagues of the poor service they have received. The only occasions on which these refunds are ever resisted is if there is overwhelming evidence of fraud, or if the customer has made a genuine mistake and returned the product to the wrong outlet in error. Even then it may be difficult to resist (see Box 9.4).

The presence of fraud or duplicity has to be proven beyond any reasonable doubt. Moreover, a manager or supervisor resisting a claim for compensation may have the legs cut out from under them by the actions of a superior, who may decide that the case is not worth fighting, whatever its merits.

## Box 9.4   Customer complaint: example

Consider the following:

You are the manager of a small branch of a national shoe shop chain. You are in the middle of a busy Saturday's trading when a man arrives at the counter. He puts down an expensive pair of shoes. He demands a refund, pointing out a split down the side of one of the shoes. A price tag and bar code is on the bottom of one of them.

You inspect the shoes. During the course of your inspection the following happens:

- You know you have not sold them. You do not keep the particular brand in stock, though you are fairly sure that they are sold elsewhere in the country by your chain.
- You look at the split in the shoes. You are pretty certain that the shoes have been slashed with a knife – this is commonplace in the trade when people demand refunds.
- The man becomes agitated. When you ask him for the receipt, he starts swearing at you. He threatens to complain to your Head Office. Some customers are looking uneasy, others are already leaving the shop.

What do you do? There is no right answer.

- You can refuse point blank, and accept any consequences that there may subsequently be.
- You can refund on the spot before you lose any more trade, and again accept the consequences, especially if it turns out that your company does not, in fact, stock the particular brand.
- You can gain as full information as possible about where and when the man bought the shoes in the hope that he will either give himself away as a fraud, or that he will demonstrate to your satisfaction that he did indeed buy the shoes at one of your other branches.

Whatever you choose, you hope that he will respond in such a way that more customers are not driven from the shop.

## Box 9.5   Public service complaints

Senior managers in frontline public services – health, education and social work – do not normally resist complaints, but rather investigate them fully. Indeed, all health, education and social services departments have specialist teams to do this. This brings a particular problem in that when complaints are made, the specialist teams suddenly have a reason for existence and have something to get stuck into, to justify and demonstrate their prowess and effectiveness. There are other problems also:

- Many complaints are only undertaken because of the propensity to investigate rather than resist; they therefore tend to be treated as legitimate from the start rather than on their own individual merits.
- Complaints that turn out to be trivial are extremely stressful and expensive; complaints that turn out to be false are extremely damaging and destructive to morale when they are given credence. Complaints of professional malpractice against individuals (especially abuse and negligence) are extremely traumatic and destructive when proven to be false.

At the core of all this is a small substantial swathe of serious malpractice that always needs to be investigated and remedied.

Whenever anything is investigated, evidence is required as to what was said, what was not said, what was done or not done, and what was written and not written. The ability to resist a complaint therefore depends on the quality, volume and availability of this evidence.

## Public service complaints

The effective management of complaints in public services is dependent upon the accuracy and completeness of information and record keeping. By and large, all complaints against public services are subject to investigation. Those with any managerial or supervisory responsibility in these services have, therefore, to be able to provide written records, log sheets, diaries, tables and charts in order to be able to demonstrate:

- actions taken and the reasons for these
- who took the actions, where, when, why and under what authority
- what the outcomes of these actions were intended to be, what actually happened, and why there are any discrepancies between the two
- what remedial action, if any, was taken, and why
- what outcome was intended
- what actually happened as the result (see Box 9.5).

Those responsible for the management and supervision of frontline public service activities have, therefore, to ensure that recording systems are kept fully comprehensive and up to date. Any shortfall can then be clearly demonstrated;

and it can also be ascertained much more easily that no shortfall has occurred if this approach is taken.

## Dealing with difficult people

Difficult people fall into the following categories:

- over-mighty subjects and representatives of over-mighty departments
- major customers and suppliers, either from the point of view of prestige, association or financial clout
- powerful personalities, especially those who are strident and unpleasant, and whose unpleasantness is known, believed or perceived to give them influence
- powerful or influential roles, including trade union officials, local and sectoral dignitaries.

This list is then extended to include anyone with whom the individual manager or supervisor feels uncomfortable or threatened.

### Threat reduction

The first move is therefore to reduce or remove the threat. This is achieved initially by:

- concentrating on the issues, not the personality
- allowing someone who is angry to blow themselves out and then questioning them on the issues
- establishing, as quickly as possible, whether there is the likelihood of agreement, and if so, the basis. If not, it is essential to come out of the situation and hand it on to those with greater authority
- where verbal or physical abuse has taken place, a formal complaint should always be made and followed up in writing

---

**EXAMPLE**

A nurse, a man in his early thirties, was in charge of a hospital ward. One day, a hospital surgeon ordered him to come off his ward. This was because the nurse had parked his car in the surgeon's parking space. When the nurse refused, the surgeon hit him.

The nurse complained. He was persuaded to drop his complaint both by his superior and his trade union. Both told him that complaints against surgeons always did more damage to the nurse's career than the surgeon's.

The surgeon was subsequently dismissed from his post for carrying out private work during contracted NHS hours. Once he had left, it became apparent that there had been a total of 27 similar complaints of physical or verbal abuse made against him, and that on each occasion, the hospital manager had persuaded the complainants to withdraw. The inquiry found that the reason was that the Deputy Chief Executive of the particular health care trust said that he 'didn't quite like to tackle the particular surgeon because he could be a bit nasty'.

---

- the moment that the powerful individual makes a threat, withdraw from the situation and hand it on to those with greater authority, making it clear why
- the moment that the powerful individual makes requests that the manager or supervisor cannot deal with, hand them on to those with full authority in these matters.

## Use of language

It takes courage to stand up to powerful, influential persons and threatening behaviour. The first step towards this is using the words, 'What do you want me to do', and then writing down verbatim everything that is said. The second step is to ensure that, wherever possible, there are witnesses present and a note-taker.

---

**EXAMPLE**

The black box carried by every airliner records every word and sound in the cockpit during the course of each flight. It is the flight note-taker and key witness. In the event of an emergency or crash, these recordings give vital evidence as to the causes and circumstances. For example:

'On 13 January 1982, a freezing cold snowing day in Washington DC, Air Florida Flight 90 took off from National Airport but it could not get the lift it needed to keep climbing. Down, down it went until it crashed into a bridge linking the District to the State of Virginia and plunged into the Potomac river. Of the 74 people on board, all but five perished, many floundering and drowning in the icy water while horror stricken bystanders watched helplessly from the river's edge. Experts later concluded that the plane had waited too long after de-icing to take off. A fresh build up of ice on the wings and engine brought the plane down. How could the pilot and co-pilot have made such a blunder? Didn't at least one of them realise it was dangerous to take off under these conditions?

In accordance with airline regulations all conversations that take place in the cockpits of planes are automatically recorded. Listening to the black box recordings in this case, it became clear that the pilot had little experience of flying in icy weather. The co-pilot had a bit more and it became heartbreakingly clear on analysis that he had tried to warn the pilot, but that he had done so indirectly.

The co-pilot repeatedly called attention to the bad weather and to ice building up on other planes.

*Co-pilot:* 'Look how that ice is just hanging on his back, back there, see that? See all those icicles on the back there and everything?
*Captain:* 'Yeah'.
*Co-pilot:* 'Boy, this is a losing battle here on trying to de-ice those things. It gives you a false feeling of security, that's all it does. Let's check these tops again since we've been sitting here a while'.
*Captain:* 'I think we get to go here in a minute'.

---

The co-pilot repeatedly called the pilot's attention to dangerous conditions but did not directly suggest that they abort the take-off. He was expressing his concern indirectly, and the captain did not pick up the hint – with unspeakably tragic results.'

Source: D. Tannen (1994) *Talking from 9 to 5*, Virago.

The third step is to understand what the powerful individual wants from the situation. This is understood by the manager or supervisor from a combination of what is said, the way it is said, facial appearance, and other body language. From this, it becomes clear whether the particular person wants:

- their problem addressed which is legitimate; or
- to let off steam, to rant and rave; or a fight that they cannot possibly lose – neither of which are legitimate (see Box 9.6); or
- a victim, which is against the law. The commonest form of this is to pick a quarrel with a junior member of staff and then either discipline or else bully them as the result of something that they say after the battle has been joined.

## Box 9.6   Where are my socks?

A useful lesson can be learned from a parallel domestic situation that runs as follows.

*Person 1:* 'Where are my socks?'
*Person 2:* a) 'In the drawer' – a clear, straightforward response. If Person 1 actually wants a fight, they have to make further running, e.g., 'Well I couldn't find them'; or 'Which drawer?'
*Person 2:* b) 'Where you left them' – a scuffle is clearly indicated, which may or may not gain life and lead to a fight.
*Person 2:* c) 'How the hell should I know?' – in which the fight is definitely on, and in which both are prepared to get involved.

By understanding the approach, and applying it to work situations, steps can be taken to ensure that if battle is to be joined, the protagonist has to make all the running. And if there are witnesses and/or a note-taker present, this will be clear to all concerned, and in any subsequent investigation.

# Conclusions

There are no blueprints for solving problems. The best approach is to take the principles indicated, and to apply them as necessary to particular situations. This involves the use of judgement, evaluation and analysis, rather than the learning of what must necessarily be an incomplete and imprecise set of techniques.

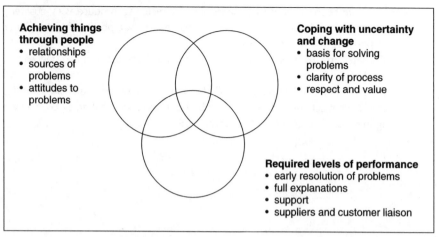

**Achieving things through people**
• relationships
• sources of problems
• attitudes to problems

**Coping with uncertainty and change**
• basis for solving problems
• clarity of process
• respect and value

**Required levels of performance**
• early resolution of problems
• full explanations
• support
• suppliers and customer liaison

*Figure 9.3*   Chapter and model summary.

Moreover, any technique can only be guaranteed when the result is predictable on every single occasion in which it is used. Whether addressing staff problems, operational issues, or difficult people within an organisation, or whether dealing with external customers, clients and suppliers, no technique is ever going to be fully predictable, because the human response cannot be guaranteed. It is much better to understand the full range of human responses, and to be prepared accordingly. That is the thrust of this approach to problem solving. So long as once the problem is identified:

• as much information as possible in the circumstances is gathered
• the means of assessment, analysis and evaluation are capable of scrutiny and examination
• a solution is delivered face to face to the person requiring it, and it is supported in writing.

anything that occurs at a place of work can itself be reviewed and evaluated, whether or not the solution worked in the particular set of circumstances. Development of this approach is certain to give a better set of long-term results than either guessing at answers, or else learning a set of precise responses that are never going to apply to all circumstances.

Using the Model referred to at the start of Chapter 1 (Figure 1.1), the material in this Chapter 15 summarised in Figure 9.3.

QUESTIONS

  1. You have received reports of a fight between two members of your staff. What are you going to do about it, when, where and why? How would your response differ if it was a) a fight between a member of your staff and someone from another department; and b) a fight during working hours between a member of your staff and a member of the public?

2. You have been ordered by your managing director to produce your quarterly figures in one hour's time. You know that this is not possible. What is your response to this request and why?
3. Consider Box 9.4. What would you do in the particular set of circumstances, and why?
4. Consider the Example on page 167. What in your view, were the causes of this crash? What actions and steps should be taken to ensure that an air crash never again occurs in such a set of circumstances?

# ▦ Ṽ **10** Negotiating

## Introduction

Negotiating is the process of undertaking discussions with a view to finding terms of agreement; and arranging and delivering those terms of agreement. All managers and supervisors have to be able to do this on a daily basis. The keys initially are:

- knowing what you want from the situation, and what the other party or parties want
- knowing what you do not want from the situation, and what the other party or parties do not want
- knowing what is acceptable, and unacceptable, to both yourself and the other parties.

Even the most overtly trivial and straightforward situations benefit from a moment's thought along these lines. Everything can then be considered from the point of view of the following:

- the rights and wrongs of the situation – operationally, professionally and morally (see Box 10.1)

### Box 10.1    Masters of the Universe

McKinsey, the international management consultancy practice, always negotiates with its potential clients on the basis that it will, a) drive down the client's costs; b) drive up the client's short-term share value.

Overwhelmingly, the ways in which it recommends that this is achieved is through downsizing, resizing and rightsizing, i.e., making large numbers of staff redundant. Radical restructuring and extensive redundancy programmes are known, believed and perceived to drive up short-term share values for clients.

It is a very short step from this to consultants making assumptions that the client's staff are lazy; unproductive and expensive. The stress and trauma caused by redundancy has already been noted. Moreover, this approach pays little attention to the operational side, even in the short-term – it is simply assumed that people will carry on doing a good and effective job with this threat hanging over them. This attitude is reinforced by the overwhelming tendency of any consultant–client relationship to treat the staff as an operational expense, rather than as an investment. The consultant–client relationship therefore becomes a substitute for real negotiation, and real agreement, rather than a genuine negotiating process. This is because it sticks to a narrow brief targeted at efficiency, rather than a broad brief targeted at effectiveness.

Source:  Channel 4 *Masters of the Universe* (1999).

- the question of setting precedent – implications for future dealings along similar lines
- internal and external pressures – especially pressures from subordinates, superiors and backers
- the need to be seen to be doing something
- the opportunities and consequences of agreeing to something
- the opportunities and consequences of not making an agreement
- what is open to negotiation and what is not.

From this, the context in which the substance and process of what is to be negotiated and agreed becomes apparent.

## Substance

The substance of negotiations is centred around:

- *Orders* – purchase orders, inputs, department, divisional and organisational requirements concerning regular and steady-state activities, and especially addressing the management and resolution of crises and hold-ups on the supply side.
- *Outputs* – distribution and delivery outputs, internal organisation functions, and the management of shortfalls and problems, crises and hold-ups.
- *Inter-departmental issues* – addressing, managing and resolving misunderstandings, gaining cooperation and agreement, the management of organisational political systems (realpolitik).
- *Internal issues* – especially daily and enduring human resource management issues, handling discipline, grievance, disputes and dismissals, resolving personal and professional disputes.
- *Customer and client relations* – especially in the handling and resolving of complaints.
- *Contracting arrangements* – on both supply and output sides, and ensuring that what is agreed can be delivered or implemented.
- *Gathering resources* – especially where this is known, believed or perceived to be a competitive or distributive issue (i.e., one department, division or function gains resources at the expense of others) (see Box 10.2).

## Box 10.2 Competing for resources

This is always wrong. Resources should be allocated on the basis of direction, priority and need.

In all but the smallest of UK organisations, this goes on to some extent. For example:

- A staff training department at one of the large oil companies asked for £100,000 for management training for those wanting to move from field operations into strategic and operational planning. This was refused on the grounds that the money had already been allocated to eight weeks of director's briefing at an exotic location in the Far East.
- A motor manufacturer refused investment in production line upgrading at an established site, preferring to spend the money on starting up a green-field operation in one of the ex-Communist Bloc countries.
- A civil service department response to budget cuts was to send a party of higher executive officers away to a luxury country retreat for a week to propose how the cuts were to be made. Their first recommendation was to remove the office tea and coffee making facilities, requiring people either to bring in their own, or to go out and buy it from a local provider. Their second recommendation was to ration office activities: reduce e-mail quotas, telephone usage, paper and envelopes. This led to calls and requests not being answered and a backlog building up.

In each of these three examples, the proposal was driven through by an over-influential individual requiring resources to demonstrate a triumph. In each of the three cases, the individual concerned was *promoted* away from the chaos that they had caused.

Anything that is agreed has to be capable of sustenance and delivery. A part of the substance therefore concerns:

- authority to make the agreement
- attention to detail
- resources to deliver and implement the agreement
- attention to the ability of organisational systems to make sure it continues to work.

┌─ EXAMPLE ─────────────────────────────────

Delivering and implementing that which was agreed ought to be obvious. However:

A Borough Council agreed to take a large volume of office stationery from a new supplier. It was a major gain for both parties, especially the Borough Council which would show a 20% saving on its office supplies bill. The agreement was duly made and signed. The supplier's terms of agreement and payment for such orders were thirty days in arrears, and monthly after that.

The Borough Council paid all its bills six months in arrears, and at six-monthly intervals after that. When no money arrived, the supplier first requested, and then demanded, payment. Finally, after five months, it wrote and threatened to sue. Lawyers became involved. In the middle of the exchanges, payment for the six month supply was received, having been issued automatically under the Borough Council's automatic payment system.

The case was dropped. It was then resurrected three months later when the same thing happened. Exactly the same process was gone through, with the same results. The matter was finally resolved on the third cycle. It came to light that:

- none of those who made the initial agreement had read the other's terms of business
- none of those involved had the authority to vary those terms of business in order to reach a genuine agreement
- the lawyers involved received fees totalling over £100,000 shared between the two parties. This more than offset any commercial or buying advantage that the headline agreement had produced.

Clearly, this is not so much of an issue in small matters. On larger or substantial issues, it is unlikely that one person is going to be able to address, cover or deliver everything. This means that negotiating teams and groups have to be formed (Chapter 12). Work can then be divided so that the issues present and implicit can all be addressed before, not after, a substantial agreement is reached or signed. Each person involved then carries expertise, authority and influence in their particular aspect. This is illustrated in Figure 10.1, which also shows the process involved.

## Process

The process of negotiating and making sustainable agreements, whatever the circumstances, is based on:

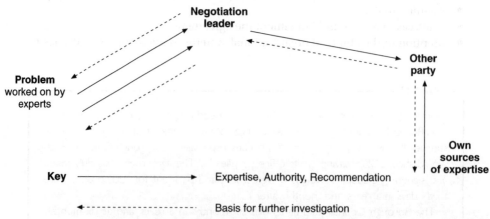

*Figure 10.1* Individual expertise, authority and influence.

- understanding the nature of the relationship required
- understanding the prevailing state of relationships.

There are two extremes of this (see Figure 10.2), which give rise to the need for the presence of and application of interpersonal skills.

## Interpersonal skills

Interpersonal skill is the application of communication to particular situations with particular people who are undertaking specific roles. Interpersonal skills combine the spoken and written word, with specific desired aims and objectives, with the presence of, or lack of, authority, responsibility, accountability, expertise and integrity, and with the specific pressures and drives inherent in the situation. Interpersonal transactions are then undertaken from the points of view shown in Table 10.1.

The stated and actual point of view may, or may not be, the same. The actual point of view, especially duplicity and dishonesty, is always quickly clear to all those involved. When this happens, it becomes very difficult not to treat everything that is not stated or written in precise and measurable terms with suspicion. Above all, phrases such as:

- 'There are no plans at present to . . .'
- 'A commitment in principle to . . .'
- 'We will seek to . . .'
- 'As soon as possible . . .'

are treated with suspicion, if not contempt.

The basis on which negotiations are to proceed forms the foundation of the interpersonal, inter-professional, inter-occupational and inter-organisational relations that are to exist for the duration. Life is much easier and more

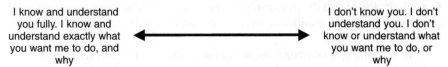

*Figure 10.2*   The prevailing state of relationships: extremes.

*Table 10.1*   Interpersonal transactions

| | |
|---|---|
| Openness and honesty | Duplicity, dishonesty |
| Clarity | Obfuscation |
| Cooperation and willingness | Conflict and unwillingness |
| Understanding | Misunderstanding, refusal to understand |
| Empathy, sympathy | Antipathy |
| Trust | Mistrust |

straightforward if this basis is open and honest, because it means that a great deal of the ritual otherwise involved can be avoided.

## Interpersonal rituals

Where there is a basis of conflict or mistrust, or the knowledge, belief or perception of duplicity or dishonesty, it is usual to engage in a series of rituals by which the boundaries of a particular transaction are established. This can be observed in all walks of life, for example:

- those who are trying to by buy property normally put in an initial offer sufficiently low that it will be rejected by the seller or vendor
- those who are trying to buy 'considered purchases', e.g., a new car, a new washing machine – normally ask if there is any discount for cash or other 'easy terms'
- those who take their car for the first time to a garage to have it serviced are normally greeted with a baffled shake of the head on the part of the mechanic
- those who engage professional, legal, consultancy or building services normally seek to get advanced quotes for the work; while those providing these services normally seek to estimate rather than quote precisely.

All that is actually happening is that a relationship is being formed and developed. While it is plainly not a perfect way of doing things, it is one that is widely used and well understood. It has, therefore, to be made to work in any set of circumstances.

## Extras

Furthermore, in these circumstances everyone likes to know, believe or perceive that they have got something for nothing – something extra – out of the particular situation. There are, therefore, some serious problems to address:

- Anyone clearly and demonstrably not getting something from the situation is likely to harbour resentment which will come to light at some point in the future.
- Anyone gaining at someone else's expense is likely to be resented.
- Any form of agreement that results in a clear dominance–dependency relationship is certain to be resented by the dependent party.

## Pride

Everyone has their pride! Few people in work situations are prepared to endure a public humiliation for the good of their organisation, department, staff, peers or superiors. When someone has clearly come off worst – lost – in a negotiation, they need to be allowed to save face, to take something positive from the situation. Otherwise again, resentment builds up (see Box 10.3).

## Box 10.3　Pride, humiliation and humility

This part of all interpersonal transactions and negotiations has to be fully understood and carefully managed. The two hardest phrases to use in management and supervision are:

- 'I am sorry'
- 'I was wrong.'

This is because individuals who are prepared to acknowledge mistakes, errors and failures are likely to have to account for these under different sets of circumstances away from their precise context. Consider the following example:

A sales executive for a national car rental chain negotiated and agreed a fleet leasing arrangement with a computer company. The sales executive, a man in his late forties, covered all the ground required. His margins accorded with the demands of his superiors. The payment intervals and lease coverage were all agreed and accepted by both parties. Everyone was happy for some time until the man's superior found out as the result of a chance conversation at a professional conference, that the computer company had been quite prepared to pay very much higher for the same package. The sales executive was confronted with this. He admitted an error in not taking a broader view of price. He pointed out that everyone at the time was happy with the deal. However, because he 'admitted his error' his career was frozen for a year. He was made to retrain and re-orientate before being allowed back into the field. He gained a reputation in the company for being a soft touch and a bungler. Eventually, at the age of forty-nine years and nine months, he was forced out altogether. The company quite deliberately ensured that he left before he was eligible for early retirement under the company' non-contributory pension scheme.

## One up and one down

It is usual, at present, for the outcome of negotiations to be delivered as a package, as a whole, rather than on a step-by-step basis.

Negotiations are however conducted on a step-by-step basis. The consequence of this is that, at any given point, one party is likely to be 'one up' on the other – and consequently, the other is 'one down'.

There are behavioural problems if one party goes 'two down' unless they can be certain that they are going to 'catch up' by gaining subsequent concessions or advantages.

There consequently has to be a 'route map' through the process that is known, understood and accepted by all concerned. If this is not apparent, then the parties finding themselves in the 'one down', or worse, position, are likely to begin to doubt any advantage to themselves from the final outcome.

## Box 10.4 Make them wait

At the outset of a potentially confrontational negotiation, it is quite usual for one party to keep the other waiting. Senior managers keep juniors waiting outside their offices, to be summoned at will. Buyers turn up late for appointments with sales people. Trade union officials turn up late for appointments with managers.

The period of waiting causes feelings of uncertainty and anxiety, so that when the negotiating does start, the other party has a perceived advantage.

It is not ethical, but it goes on. Moreover, anyone who finds themselves in the position of having to wait can, by understanding what is being done to them, turn the matter to their own advantage, at least partly. It is usual for the one keeping the other waiting to begin the conversation either by apologising for the lateness or by making some reference to it. The standard response should always be: 'Oh, are we late? I hadn't noticed'.

This is especially important to understand from the point of view of those who find themselves in the dominant position. To press home the advantage in the wrong way, or without understanding this, is likely to ruin the relationship, and often ruins the outcome (see Box 10.4).

## Getting to win:win

This position was identified in Chapter 8 as the most satisfactory for long-term productive and harmonious relations. In this, everyone gets something with which they can be happy. In negotiating, the consequences of the other positions have to be clearly evaluated as:

- *win:lose* – the loser will come back to you with further demands, some legitimate, others not so
- *lose:win* – often leads to the hunt for scapegoats and victims
- *lose:lose* – strikes and disputes (HR); loss of confidence (purchasing and contracted transactions); recourse to litigation (contracted arrangements).

The relationship between short-term advantage and long-term stability have therefore to be clearly evaluated (see Box 10.5).

## Box 10.5 Short-term advantage and long-term stability: public sector pay and rewards

For many years, UK governments imposed pay restraints and restrictions on all the professions working in public services. This was reinforced through careful short-term pressures, on each occasion emphasising the good future of particular sectors.

In reality, each group – especially teachers, doctors, nurses and social workers – has had its position genuinely reinforced only once every four to five years. Over the rest of the period, pay and rewards have been dampened down, and professional and occupational demands raised.

In the short-term, departmental annual budget limits have been met. In the long-term, there are staffing crises in each sector:

- A quarter of all GPs and a half of all secondary school teachers will have left their professions by 2010.
- The shortage of nursing staff is now so acute that UK health authorities have established recruitment drives in China, India, the Philippines, Malaysia, South Africa and South America.
- The shortage of social workers has caused social services departments to have to look to charities and service privatisations in order to manage their client groups; and this has very often taken place in spite of the political persuasions of the particular Councils involved.

## Box 10.6  Triumphs

'The Emperor rode on a horse carved of gold, carried by 200 slaves. Such was his popularity, he was surrounded by nearly a thousand soldiers. Crowds lined the streets waving and chanting his name in case he had forgotten it. Children waved his picture in case he had forgotten what he looked like. Soldiers stood behind them to make sure that they had them the right way up. Every hundred yards or so there was a bright gleaming bronze statue of the Emperor in case the people forgot who he was'.

Source: Terry Pratchett (1990) *Wyrd Sisters* – Fontana.

## The need for triumphs – and victims

It remains true that some organisations, managers and other powerful and influential figures know, believe or perceive that they need:

- A triumph in which their position, or perception of being a great person or shining light, is shored up or reinforced. This is, at best, manipulative, at worst, deceitful and damaging. Above all, it is profligate with organisation resources (see Box 10.6).
- Victims – individuals or groups to be blamed for something that is known, believed or perceived to have gone wrong; and invariably, to distract attention away from the shortcomings of a more powerful or influential figure. At best, this practice is damaging and destructive to morale. In the over-whelming majority of circumstances, it is illegal under employment rights and discrimination legislation, and damages are unlimited against those organisations and their managers that practice this.

Both are therefore to be avoided at all costs. There is a world of difference between celebrating genuine achievements, and self-aggrandisement – especially when the latter also demands victims. The need for triumphs and victims always encapsulates an overwhelming lack of organisational and managerial integrity, and it is always recognised as such by staff.

## Collective bargaining

Collective bargaining is a form of negotiation that used to be the basis on which all staff management and industrial relations were conducted in the UK, and it still remains widespread. Collective bargaining is based on institutionalised mistrust as follows:

- Managers do not trust the staff or their representatives (especially trade unions) and have a core belief that they will work as little as possible for the highest available wages and salaries.
- Staff do not trust their managers or the organisation's owners and have a core belief that they are simply a resource, a factor of production, to be used, exploited and cast aside on a whim.

Inherent in the collective bargaining approach are conflict, and partial and self-interest. The outputs of this form of approach are invariably:

- confrontational and adversarial styles of management
- confrontational and adversarial forms of staff representation
- proliferation of minutely detailed rules and regulations that often contradict each other
- great expense on human resource and industrial relations departments, advisors, functionaries and administration
- proliferation of formalised, ritualised meetings
- the need to reconcile the partial and self-interests present with each other, and with the overall aims and objectives of a particular organisation.

The collective bargaining process works as follows:

- The first offer or claim is always made on the basis that it will be rejected (if for any reason it is accepted straightaway, it generally causes resentment rather than instant satisfaction).
- There then follows a process of counter-offer and counter-claim with each party working its way gradually towards the other.
- The content of the final agreement is usually clearly signalled before it is made, and the basis of what is genuinely acceptable or otherwise to each party is signalled also.
- Serious disputes occur either when one side is determined not to settle, or when there is a genuine misunderstanding, or genuine misreading of the signals.
- Settlements are normally couched in positive terms in relation to all concerned to avoid the use of words such as 'loss', 'loser', 'climb down' and

'defeat', which have negative connotations for anyone associated with them, and which tend to store up resentment for the future, and polarise attitudes for the next round of negotiations.

The following standpoints in the process may also be usefully identified:

- It may be necessary to settle with one group, or part of the workforce, at the expense of others (this is know as the *distributive* effect).
- It may be possible to resolve problems to the satisfaction of all concerned; or it may not be possible to satisfy everyone.
- It may be necessary to take a hard initial stance to try and persuade the other party to revise its expectations.
- It may be necessary to settle quickly with one group, to prevent or dissuade others from joining in the fray.
- It may be necessary to engage in a protracted dispute with one group in order to persuade others to revise their expectations.
- It may be necessary to extend and protract bargaining processes in order to take the heat out of a particular situation.
- It may be necessary to condense and speed up bargaining processes in order to take the heat out of a particular situation.

For this form of negotiation to work, it is clearly essential that everyone involved understands the demands, pressures and constraints in the particular situation. It is also evident that there are strong behavioural pressures that have to be considered.

## Behavioural aspects of collective bargaining

The following key behavioural pressures have to be understood:

- *The distributive effect:* the opportunities and consequences of settling with one group at the expense of others.
- *Integrative drives:* opportunities and constraints of settling everything to the satisfaction of all involved.
- *Influencing attitudes:* in which attitudes are formed, modified and developed by the nature of the orientation that each party has towards the other and towards the matter in hand. This may either be:
  — confrontational, whereby the parties are motivated to defeat the other or win them over to their own point of view
  — individualistic, in which the parties concerned pursue their own self-interests without any regard for the position of others
  — cooperative, whereby each party is concerned about the others as well as its own position
  — collusion, whereby the parties concerned form a coalition in which they pursue a common purpose possibly to the detriment of other groups within the organisation, or else to the detriment of the organisation as a whole.

The following additional behavioural and ritualistic aspects have to be addressed:

- *Use of language:* which may be confrontational or cooperative; whichever is the case, it is necessary to look for signals and cues in order to gauge the likely and possible outcomes of the matter in hand.
- *The formality–informality balance:* especially the need for informal systems of communication between the parties involved in order to better gauge the real positions of those involved. These may not always be apparent in formalised and ritualised negotiation settings.
- *Employee expectations:* for a generation, employees have expected an annual percentage pay rise and improvement in working conditions, devised partly to offset the effects of inflation, and also to reward them for the past year's performance. There has, therefore, grown up the concept of 'a going rate' for annual pay awards. To meet or exceed this leads to feelings of general satisfaction; while to make an offer that is known, believed or perceived to be under the going rate is likely to be detrimental to morale and performance, especially in the short-term. Closely related to this is the concept of 'the going rate' for a particular job – the anticipation that, by joining a particular occupation, a known range of benefits will be forthcoming.

The approach can be used to manage and make progress in any situation where conflict and mistrust are present or inherent (see Figure 10.3).

A very similar process is also used in claims disputes between contractors, clients and subcontractors in the building, civil and other engineering industries where relationships have always been adversarial (in these sectors though, it is usual to engage lawyers rather than organisational representatives to carry out the negotiations). The collective bargaining approach is so cumbersome and expensive however, that everyone concerned has begun to look for alternative ways of doing things in order to speed up the process, make it more advantageous and less destructive to all concerned.

# Consultation, participation and involvement

Developments in negotiation processes in order to make them speedier and therefore more cost effective, have largely been based on changes in management style and attitudes. These have come together with a greater overall openness in communication style and information provision, and a willingness to recognise the staff as a legitimate stakeholder. There is also greater understanding of the fact that staff, managerial and directoral interests are all bound up in the future prosperity and effectiveness of the particular organisation.

Consultation, participation and involvement all reflect the varying degrees in which organisations have moved this way.
- Consultation is usually limited to openness of information and keeping staff informed of progress, strategy, plans and policies.
- Participation and involvement imply a greater cooperative effort, based on a more complete understanding of the situation by all concerned. Some organisations have taken this to greater lengths than others.

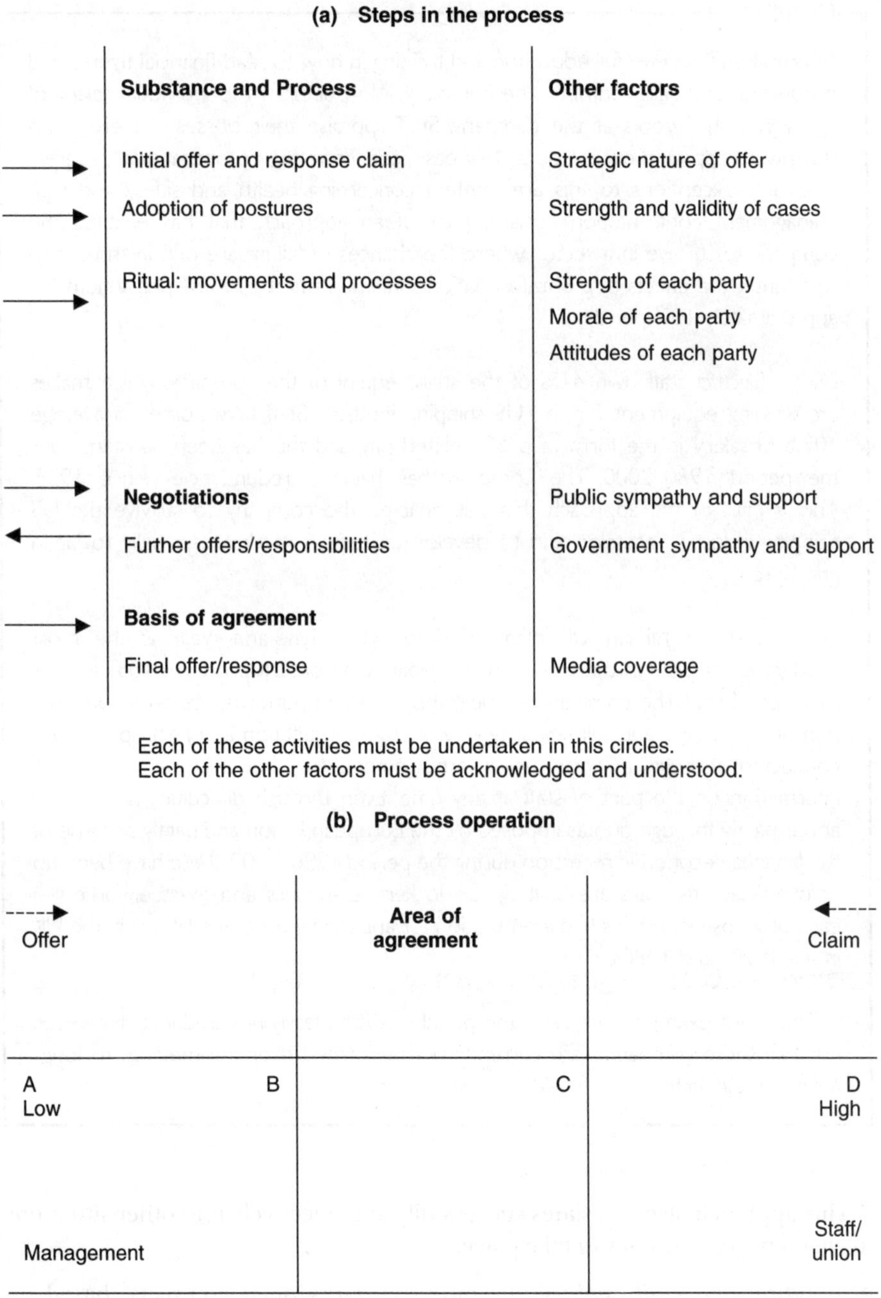

## (a) Steps in the process

| Substance and Process | Other factors |
|---|---|
| **Initial offer and response claim** | Strategic nature of offer |
| Adoption of postures | Strength and validity of cases |
| Ritual: movements and processes | Strength of each party |
| | Morale of each party |
| | Attitudes of each party |
| **Negotiations** | Public sympathy and support |
| Further offers/responsibilities | Government sympathy and support |
| **Basis of agreement** | |
| Final offer/response | Media coverage |

Each of these activities must be undertaken in this circles.
Each of the other factors must be acknowledged and understood.

## (b) Process operation

| Offer | Area of agreement | Claim |
|---|---|---|
| A           B | C | D |
| Low | | High |
| Management | | Staff/ union |

The collective bargaining process: offers between A and B rejected by staff; between C and D instantly accepted by staff; claims between A and B instantly accepted by management; between C and D rejected by management; B–C is basis for negotiated settlement; normal first offer is around A, which leads to instant rejection; normal first claim is around D, but engages the process.

*Figure 10.3*  The collective bargaining process.

*Semco*: all staff receive full education and training in how to read financial figures and production and sales outputs. The company also publishes the individual salary of everyone who works at the company. Staff appraise their bosses – there is no downward appraisal except on a daily basis, concentrating on operational progress (the only exceptions to this are matters concerning health and safety and staff management confrontation). This is part of an approach that has enabled the company to survive in a sector where the chances of failure are one in three, and to counter the effects of a Brazilian national inflation rate of 3000% per annum (or approximately 10% per day).

*Lincoln Electrici* staff own 41% of the share equity of the company which makes arc welding equipment for the US shipping industry. Staff take home on average 102% of salary in the form of profit-related pay, and this has been constant over the period 1980–2000. The company has had no redundancies since 1938. This is part of the approach that has enabled the company to survive the US shipping industry recession and to develop an export market, especially to Japan and Korea.

*Nissan UK*: the Nissan UK plant in Washington, Tyne-and-Wear is the most productive car plant in the world outside Japan and Korea. It produces 105 cars per member of staff. The company has built this quality of performance on a combination of high wages and full flexibility of working. Consultation and participation are conducted through a single union arrangement, together with access to full information on the part of staff at any time. Even through difficulties have come about, partly through quotas imposed by the European Union and partly because of the Japanese economic recession during the period 1996–2000, there have been no enforced lay-offs. Cars are built by ex-dockers, ex-miners and ex-steelworkers – each of whose industries had a reputation for appalling industrial relations in the UK in the 1970s and 1980s.

These are examples only; and the plural of examples is not evidence. However, none of these companies are currently out-performed over the medium to long-term in their sector.

This approach also translates successfully and effectively into other situations in which negotiation has to take place:

- *Building and civil engineering:* moves towards open contracts, based on full participation between contractor and client at the pre-contract stage; moves away from traditional tendering processes based more narrowly on price;

## Box 10.7  Alternative forms of negotiation in the building and civil engineering industries

The traditional tendering process – negotiating and bidding for work on the basis of competitive or non-competitive price tenders – has fallen so far into disrepute that various alternative forms of arrangement have been explored. Some of these are:

- *Public–private partnerships and the private finance initiative:* created and institutionalised by government to try and get contractors to take on a managerial responsibility for the maintenance and operation of the finished facility, rather than being limited simply to building it.
- *Preferred or priority contractor status:* in which particular building and civil engineering companies would be offered first refusal of particular work and projects. This approach has been driven by out-of-town industrial estate, superstore and retail park developments in which the quality of the finished environment has been at least as great a drive as contract price.
- *Partnering:* in which the aim is to secure a long-term and stable relationship between building and civil engineering contractors and public sector clients. This is based on the combination of a long-term umbrella agreement (for which a retainer is normally paid), together with a pre-agreed price schedule and price margins for particular forms of work when they come up (though it should be noted in this particular case that the relationship tends to be dominated by the contractor unless great care is taken at the negotiating stage).
- *Quality, price and deadline assurances:* in which the onus is placed firmly on the contractor to deliver the required building or facility to pre-agreed time scales and quality assurance schedules. This is usually for a higher price than would traditionally have been the case.

exploration of partnering arrangements to ensure the genuine mutual long-term interest, viability and prosperity of all involved (see Box 10.7).

- *Industrial sales and purchasing:* moves towards establishing a long-term mutual interest rather than short-term considerations driven by narrow concerns of cost and price savings and commissions.
- *Operations management:* moves towards ensuring that the staff are much better informed about the broad context of the organisation and the narrow context of their own particular sphere, and the relationship between the two. Part of this is driven by EU Directives on works' councils. These and other EU and UK statutes require all organisations by law to provide full information and to move towards a more participative and open style of management. Above all, they require the elevation of the staff to the same stakeholder status as shareholders and backers (see Box 10.8).

## Box 10.8 Industrial democracy

'Industrial democracy' was the phrase originally used to describe moves towards greater openness, participation and involvement. Indeed, at one point, there was a strong political drive towards 'full industrial democracy'. The phrase has now fallen into disuse. Democracy has the following drawbacks in organisations in general, and in negotiated situations in particular:

- The majority of people may not vote for what is correct in the circumstances.
- The majority of people may vote for their known, believed or perceived narrow self-interest.
- A powerful or influential figure or group may be able to deliver a dominant block vote to manipulate the situation to their own advantage.
- Narrow voting splits (e.g., 51–49) mean that effectively half of those concerned are dissatisfied.
- Where there are more than two points of view expressed, it is possible to get a 40-30-30 split (or the equivalent) and a decision then has to be taken on whether to go ahead with what the 40% voted for, on the grounds that they were the largest group; or whether to reject the matter because the majority voted against it. There are also problems to be addressed concerning the duration of a voted and agreed outcome in an ever-changing world.

There is now a much greater understanding that moves towards full participation and involvement can only be successful if they are based on the presence of full and adequate information, together with the ability to understand and use this effectively. If this is fully developed the need for votes is removed – an informed consensus is certain to emerge.

Sources: H. Phelps-Brown (1976) *The Origins of Trade Union Power*, Fontana; C. Brewster (1998) *Modern Industrial Relations*, Penguin.

## Conclusions

Negotiating and reaching agreements is based on understanding the situation as a whole and, from there, establishing what is required, what is possible and achievable, and recognising the behavioural 'route' (including rituals) that has to be followed if success is to be achieved (see Figure 10.4).

It is then possible to draw up a set of guidelines and principles that underpin all successful and effective negotiations. These should be practised regularly, and should form the basis of any negotiating skills development programme:

- Preparation is everything, and this includes understanding the behavioural and operational pressures of the situation, the point of view that you have to

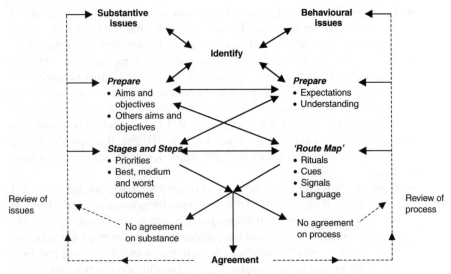

*Figure 10.3* The collective bargaining process.

deliver and defend, and the point of view that the others involved will be bringing.

- Know your opponents – where their priorities lie, what their expectations and aspirations are, and if they are indeed your 'opponents', then understand that this negotiation is being conducted ultimately for the resolution of conflict.
- Be clear about aims and objectives, priorities and deadlines, and be clear about where the absolute boundaries lie – what you are prepared to settle for, and what you are not prepared to settle for.
- Understand where agreement may quickly be reached, and where the points of contention are likely to lie.
- Understand the behavioural aspects and any rituals that you may have to go through in order to gain successful outcomes.
- Confirm every step of the way in writing including: outset, stages, and the final outcome.
- Deliver that which has been promised. Never infer, only to withdraw (see Box 10.9).

## Box 10.9  Peter Bennett-Jones: six rules of negotiation

Peter Bennett-Jones is an agent who represents some of the UK's major entertainment stars, including Rowan Atkinson, Lenny Henry, Harry Enfield and Barry Humphries. In order to maximise the position of his clients, he has to undertake extensive negotiations with large and powerful media, entertainment and sponsorship companies. He sets out his position thus:

- *Be prepared:* he says: 'I go into a negotiation pretty certain about what I want to come out with, and knowing exactly what the other half wants, because successful negotiating is not going to come out of confusion'.
- *Straight and open dealings:* don't play games or bang the table – 'May be if you ask for things in a very polite way, people are slightly bamboozled. But I don't think I am deceptive and I believe bluffing should be kept for poker. I hate aggression – it gets you nowhere. A deal works when both parties think they have got a good deal. I have never walked out of a meeting, although I have got cross a couple of times. If people think they have to scream and shout and get angry, it's gone wrong, it's broken down'.
- *Build up a good relationship:* 'I actually really like all the people I negotiate with on a regular basis. I may not be so keen on the dark forces behind them but I enjoy their company, which is why face to face always beats the phone. Going into the jugular from the word go is a waste of time. Some agents do conduct things like that but the loss of goodwill that such a move involves outweighs the benefit. You can hold anyone to ransom on one occasion, but if next time you want something more complex, it makes life harder'.
- *Detail is all:* 'I am a great believer in pen and paper. Putting down in writing is important to me. But you'll never get an American agent to agree to that. That suggests an attempt to avoid the awkward issues that will come back and bite you later'.
- *It isn't just price that matters:* 'Price is one element of the equation, not the key thing. If you make price the dominant factor, you are likely to slip up elsewhere. Get a long-term commitment on a deal if possible, and remember the importance of piggy-backing other concessions to achieve what you want. That way you can plan properly. Never do anything in a hurry – which is the converse of the way the City works –

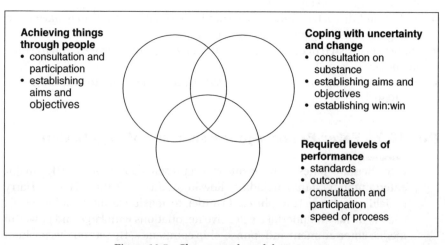

**Achieving things through people**
- consultation and participation
- establishing aims and objectives

**Coping with uncertainty and change**
- consultation on substance
- establishing aims and objectives
- establishing win:win

**Required levels of performance**
- standards
- outcomes
- consultation and participation
- speed of process

*Figure 10.5*  Chapter and model summary.

short-term, turning a buck. Think long-term. People like John Cleese and Ronnie Barker have forty years in them'.

- *If all else fails, be prepared to walk away:* a TV executive who deals with Bennett-Jones confirms that this is a possibility – 'He will walk away. That's very clever. But if he doesn't get what he wants, he just says no'.

Source: 'The Secrets of a Negotiator' – *Management Today* (May 2000).

As stated in the introduction to this chapter, managers and supervisors have to be able to negotiate on a daily basis. Bad or inadequate skills in this area are not only expensive and cost ineffective, they also eat into managerial and supervisory time that is, in any case, at a premium. Understanding of the substance and procedure of negotiations, and the pressures and constraints surrounding the wider situation, is therefore essential.

Using the Model referred to at the start of Chapter 1 (Figure 1.1), the material in this Chapter is summarised in Figure 10.5.

QUESTIONS

1. Identify a dispute with which you are familiar, or with which you have been involved. Why did it arise; and how and why was it resolved to the satisfaction of all concerned (or, if it was not resolved to the satisfaction of all concerned, why)?
2. How would you train your subordinates to be effective negotiators? Justify the steps you have indicated.
3. Identify areas where you know that your staff have shortfalls in the volume and quality of information available to them. What is preventing this information being available? What steps can you, and should you, take to begin to remedy this situation?
4. Identify a negotiation from a non-working situation in which you have been involved (e.g., house purchase, car purchase). What went well and what went badly in the particular situation? How might the situation have been made more successful? What lessons from this, if any, can usefully be applied to working situations?

# ☒ 11 Health and safety

## Introduction

All organisations and their managers are responsible, so far as is reasonable and practicable, to ensure a healthy and safe working environment for their staff and for all those who attend places of work from time to time, including suppliers, subcontractors and other visitors.

There are three strands to address:

- health
- safety
- the environment.

## Health

The clear relationship between health and organisational output and effectiveness was first demonstrated in the UK by the Cadburys in the mid-19th Century (see Box 11.1).

### Box 11.1  Cadburys

The Cadburys owned a chocolate factory. They built a model village for their employees in the countryside outside Birmingham in order to ensure that they had a good quality of life both inside and outside work. They ensured that their staff were fed properly. Education was provided for both adults and children. There was a strong ethical Christian element to all this – the Cadburys were Quakers.

Everything was designed to ensure that, as far as possible, the company had a healthy, happy, contented workforce, prepared to work hard, productively and effectively, for longer periods than would otherwise have been the case.

Creating and maintaining healthy places of work and ensuring the health of the staff, ought to be a clear and unambiguous managerial priority. Yet in the UK at least, health at work is constrained by a combination of legal uncertainty,

## Box 11.2 Affluent workers

The relationship between work and employee health was again made apparent by the 'affluent worker' studies of the 1950s; this has subsequently been developed by the 'inequality and health' study carried out by Richard Wilkinson in the late 1980s in society at large. In summary, the findings are as follows:

- Physically and mentally repetitive work, and mentally undemanding work, leads to decline in mental and physical health.
- Specific workplace tasks cause specific illness, stresses, strains and ultimately, disease and disability.
- Bad or inadequate wage levels reinforce poverty traps and poverty cycles; as well as leading to declining health, it also causes declining work performance.
- Not enough attention is paid in general to the effects of work on physical and mental health.

(Sources: J.H. Goldthorpe et al (1958) *The Affluent Worker*, Cambridge University Press; R. Wilkinson (1992) *Unhealthy Societies*, Routledge.)

homespun wisdom and a lack of willingness to accept responsibility for anything other than the attendance of the employee (see Box 11.2).

The studies outlined in Box 11.2 established the moral and ethical standpoint and drew a direct relationship between staff health and profitability. In the pursuit of a healthy workforce, attention has to be paid to the following:

- quality of working environment (see Chapter 2)
- specific and general issues; including occupational health.

## Quality of working environment

This is an organisational, managerial and supervisory responsibility. Every place of work, whatever the sector involved, should be clean and tidy. Cleanliness prevents the spread of germs, coughs and colds, and more serious diseases, as well as contributing to the avoidance of health issues that may be inherent in the product or service delivery process. Cleanliness of toilet, washing and catering facilities is also essential in the prevention of more serious problems. This is especially a problem where there are large workforces or where large numbers of people are present.

┌─ EXAMPLES ─────────────────────────────────────────────

- *Buckingham Palace:* Buckingham Palace retains a full-time consultant on *sick building syndrome* — the relationship between types of building, the presence of particular germs, and their propensity to spread and cause a health hazard. He is responsible for attending to all aspects of the building — work areas, visitor areas, and the private apartments. He has particular responsibility for staff quarters and those areas visited by the public during summer opening hours.

- *Universities and colleges:* the proliferation of meningitis scares in UK universities and colleges over the past decade has coincided exactly with reductions in expenditure, and consequent declining standards, on cleaning and property maintenance services.

- *Hospitals:* both staff and patients find themselves in a highly contagious and infectious environment! Again, the identification of 'hospital-acquired infections' (HAI) has coincided exactly with reduced expenditure and priority on premises' cleaning and maintenance services. Hospitals are not allowed to use fans to keep staff or patients cool during periods of warm weather because this spreads germs and contributes to increases in HAIs.

More generally, the knowledge that the staff are having to work in dirty and unkempt facilities contributes to loss of morale and therefore output. Any illness, however minor, is then attributed to a lack of cleanliness (whether or not this is actually the case). Any consequent investigations are always expensive, time consuming and damaging to morale.

## Specific and general issues

For most managers and supervisors, the following specific and general issues are apparent.

### Stress

Stress is the term used to describe any occupational, managerial or environmental pressure, constraint or constriction that has a negative effect upon the health and well being of employees. In the workplace, the following main causes of stress can be identified:

- *Organisational change:* changes in technology, working hours and practices; the pressures associated with this including retraining, redeployment, relocation. Closely related to this are changes in organisation ownership, direction and management style.
- *Redundancy:* people continue to base their patterns of life on the perception that they will have a job, not that they will not. The possibility, threat or reality of enforced job loss has therefore to be managed or supervised from the point of view that those concerned have been placed in the position of being unable to fulfil their life and work commitments, as well as from the narrow perspective of being deprived of their livelihood. Severance payments for the great majority of staff do not in any way compensate for the trauma of job loss (see Box 11.3).
- *Responsibility for other people:* the most stressful occupations are those where there is a direct or inherent responsibility for other people, e.g., nursing, air traffic control. This may be called 'emotional labour', and this reflects the amount of energy or effort that those concerned have to put into managing their true feelings in order to be effective in their job (see Box 11.4).

## Box 11.3  Redundancy and stress management

The best organisations are starting to address this through the following.

- *Redundancy and stress counselling:* the provision of trained specialists and experts to help people over the behavioural and psychological side of job loss.
- *Financial advice:* in particular managing changes in cash flow brought upon by the loss of regular income.
- *Outplacement services:* the engagement of recruitment consultants in order to find alternative employment for those being displaced; and the marketing of CVs by the particular organisation to others that might be interested in employing the redundant members of staff.

The best managers and supervisors are those who are prepared to concede that the greatest consequences of stress are work, management and supervisory style-related, and who are consequently prepared to give as much attention as possible to reducing or eliminating factors present in the work situation.

The best organisations and managers are those that are prepared to be straightforward when redundancy or other stressful situations are certain or likely to occur. Especially when job losses are known to be imminent, it is essential that:

- precise information is given to the process and time scale involved
- the precise term is used – i.e., redundancy or job loss – rather than self-comforting euphemisms such as downsizing, rightsizing, outplacement, or even (as used by Kent County Council in 1992) 'enabling you to seek opportunities elsewhere'.

Occupational stress is a recognised medical condition and needs to be treated as such. Any organisation that refuses to acknowledge medical confirmation of the condition of stress is certain to face claims for substantial damages from employment tribunals and/or the courts.

## Box 11.4  Stress, responsibility and emotional labour

It has been estimated that 25% of men's jobs and 50% of women's jobs call for some kind of emotional labour. Emotional labour is asked of people when they have to manage their emotions so as to present a particular face to the customer on behalf of the organisation, for example, the ever-smiling friendly air cabin crew or the coldly business-like debt collector.

As these different sets of feelings are paramount in performing the role of either cabin crew or debt collector, it is practically inevitable that such people will often be alienated from what they really feel about the job and the public they deal with in performing it. But cabin crew who express their true feelings even after many hours in the company of obnoxious passengers would not last long in the organisation. Neither would a debt collector calling on a poor widow with young children who was emotionally moved by her plight to overlook the debt.

'At its extreme the performance of emotional labour for a living can lead to a condition described as burn-out. This condition is found among people in what are called the caring or helping professions – medicine, social work and counselling. The clients of people in these professions are themselves often under stress and will therefore make emotional demands on the professionals they deal with because they are feeling frightened, angry or distressed.

Burn-out has been studied quite widely in the medical professions. Doctors and nurses suffer a high incidence of emotional exhaustion compared to other occupations. Nurses may also suffer from reduced personal accomplishment and doctors may be prone to depersonalise their patients and treat them in what seems to be a cold and unfeeling manner. The medical professions also have much higher rates of suicide, alcoholism, drug abuse and depression than other professions'.

(Source: D. Statt (1994) *Psychology and the World of Work* – Macmillan.)

- *Underload:* people become bored or disaffected with work when there is either not enough for them to do, or else what they do does not use anything but a tiny part of their full capability. Many jobs also do not carry sufficient responsibility, human or emotional commitment to render them worthwhile or valuable to the jobholder. In these circumstances, it is essential to consider work enhancement and enlargement, and staff training programmes that address each of the four aspects of personal, professional, occupational and organisational development.
- *Hours of work and work patterns:* both length of working week, and also patterns of work, cause stress if not managed properly. For example, cultures of long working hours, institutionalised overtime, and being on call for work at short notice, are mentally and physically draining, and also disrupt the relationship between work and the rest of life. Irregular attendance and shift working patterns disrupt sleep and social life patterns with the consequence that those who have to follow them being susceptible to health problems.
- *Management and supervisory style:* stress is always higher where the management or supervisory style is dishonest or lacking integrity. Nobody knows where they stand or what is true. This is inherent in situations where bullying, victimisation, harassment and blame cultures exist; where there is racial or gender prejudice; and in any situation where there is a proliferation of disciplinary and grievance cases.

## Occupational health

All organisations, managers and supervisors have statutory responsibilities for the health of their staff. Many organisations have their own occupational health schemes. These take the form either of subscribing to, or registering with, a local GP practice, or else to have a form of occupational health insurance. This is because organisations are increasingly having to assume responsibility for the good health of their staff. Good occupational health schemes are particularly strong and valuable in the early diagnosis of job specific illnesses and injuries. They also provide a valuable general source of medical knowledge by which the organisation may assess the overall state of its workforce's health.

The management of occupational health covers the following areas.

### Illness and injury

This includes especially:

- occupation-related illnesses – silicosis (mines and quarries); some cancers (e.g., those related to chemical, defence and nuclear work); hospital acquired illnesses (those working in clinics and hospitals); allergic reactions (those working in food, chemical and cosmetic production
- occupational-related injuries – especially related to back injuries (e.g., lifting, manual labour; also prevalent in nursing and social care); fixed position work (e.g., driving long distances, driving forklift trucks, attending production and information workstations and telephone services stations); computer work (including Repetitive Strain Injuries (RSI) brought about by constant keyboard usage, and eye strain brought on by staring at the screen) (see Box 11.5).

## Box 11.5  Injury, illness and regulation

There are rules and regulations in place to ensure minimum and absolute standards of workplace practice. Both the EU and UK government have legislated extensively in the area so that there are, for example, regulations that cover the following:

- Health hazards, especially the Convention on Substances Hazardous to Health (COSHH), requiring anything with a toxic or allergenic content to be issued only under supervision.
- Repetitive Strain Injuries and other physical injuries, which all organisations are expected to be aware of.
- Health promotion at workplaces – attending to cleanliness; and also promoting the healthiest possible working environment in the circumstances.
- Specific regulations for dealing with unhealthy circumstances – especially extremes of heat, cold, wet, dry and dust.
- Nurses on site: in specific sectors; it is usual for food, chemical and cosmetics manufacturers to employ a full-time nurse.

- First-aiders: all organisations with more than 17 employees in the UK are required to have a qualified first-aider. There are specific regulations limiting the keeping and issuing of some drugs to staff qualified and trained to do so.

## General issues

Particular responsibility is required in the management of:

- smoking – in which organisations should make clear the stance to be adopted; and that if they wish to exclude smoking from their premises, they should consult with staff and offer counselling and support to those who have to change their behaviour
- alcohol and drugs usage – in which it is normal to support those with addiction problems, at least initially; and to offer counselling, rehabilitation and reference to medical authorities wherever possible
- HIV/AIDS – in which there is a balance to be struck between ensuring that those who suffer from the virus are treated with respect and dignity, and the legitimate concerns and fears of other staff members, supplier, customer and client groups.

## Production management

All steps necessary to secure the health of those working in a situation are required in the following circumstances:

- allergies – from food ingredients, chemicals and primary substances
- passenger and freight transport – where there are working hours regulations designed to prevent fatigue, stress and protection from fumes
- chemicals, oils, nuclear and other fuels industries – to prevent health- and life-threatening contamination and diseases
- air transport – to address and minimise the effects of working in pressurised confined spaces for long periods of time
- food manufacture, processing and production – to ensure that machinery, ingredients and handling are all carried out without contaminating the final product

---

**EXAMPLE**

In April 2000, a royal visit was arranged to a cheese factory on the outskirts of Melbourne, Australia. The Duke of Edinburgh visited the factory with a small entourage.

Upon entering the factory, the royal party was asked to put on protective overalls, gloves, boots and hairnets. With the exception of the Duke of Edinburgh, the entire party agreed to do this.

The visit went ahead as planned and the Duke duly went into the areas where cheese was being manufactured, without the protective clothing.

Because of the contravention of regulations, the entire day's production had to be thrown away and the plant thoroughly cleaned from top to bottom.

---

- protective clothing and use of barrier creams – what is required is normally governed by a combination of statutory regulations, and acceptance and understanding of what constitutes best practice. Extremes of heat, cold, noise and dirt must be protected against; the management of actual or potential allergic and adverse reactions is also required whatever the sector or nature of operations.

# Safety

Workplace safety is a joint responsibility shared by organisations, managers, supervisors and staff. All visitors and subcontractors also have statutory duties to comply with safety regulations and rules when on site, and there are consequences when this does not happen. All places of work in the UK are required to conform to:

- the Health and Safety at Work Act 1974
- the restraints of other legislation, e.g., the Offices, Shops and Railway Premises Act 1963, the Mines and Quarries Act 1852 & 1997
- EU Directives on working hours, access and egress, emergency evacuations and the management and handling of toxic and dangerous substances.

With very few exceptions, all organisations are subject to inspection by the Health and Safety Executive, a statutory body which may enter any premises at any time. In addition, the Health and Safety Executive investigate any occasion when there is a serious accident or incident that causes any member of staff to be off work for more than two full days.

All organisations must attend to the following.

## Emergency procedures

By law, it must be possible to evacuate all premises within twenty minutes of the alarm being raised. Clear directions and signposts must be in place. All staff must receive emergency and evacuation training. It is also required by law that a meeting place away from the premises is established and understood by all so that a roll call can be taken. All organisations must have written emergency procedures that are subject to inspection by the Health and Safety Executive at any time. Regular training and drills must be undertaken.

## Creating a safe environment

All organisations must have in place their own regulations, available for inspection by the Health and Safety Executive at any time. They must also be aware of the likelihood and potential for accidents and emergencies. All accidents are caused by one or more of the following:

- *Unsafe acts:* which occur as the result of negligence, ignorance, wilfulness or sabotage.

- *Unsafe conditions:* e.g., slippery floors and stairs, trailing wires, lack of attention to cleanliness.
- *Unsafe behaviour:* e.g., fooling around, lack of attention to procedures, procedures not being followed.
- *Unsafe attitudes:* in which an insufficient priority is given, either by the organisation or its managers and supervisors, to safety overall. This is invariably to be found at the centre of all major disasters.

---

**EXAMPLE**

*Zeebrugge:* in 1987, the car ferry *Herald of Free Enterprise* capsized outside Zeebrugge harbour. The ship had set sail with its bow doors open, and seawater had consequently rushed in. 196 people died. It became clear during the inquiry that the practice of setting sail before the doors were closed was required by senior management at the ferry's operators Townsend Thoreson. The senior management response was given in a statement to the media thus: 'We are opposed to a witch-hunt for directors. Everyone is howling for blood.'

*Paddington:* in 1998, two trains collided outside Paddington station. One of the trains was owned by Thames Trains, the other by Great Western Trains. Neither train was fitted with the Automatic Train Protection System (ATPS) which would automatically have stopped both trains once it became clear that they were going to collide. The public inquiry into the crash was told that Thames Trains decided that the £5 million bill to install the ATPS safety system was too high; £5 million was the exact amount paid out in dividends to shareholders during the previous year.

*Redcar:* in 1997, an employee at the British Steel plant at Redcar was driving a locomotive through one of the water cooling towers. This was normal practice. The locomotive was insulated against heat and steam; and there was an escape route from the locomotive in cases of emergencies. On this occasion however, the door flew open; and when the employee tried to escape, he found that the emergency exit from the locomotive had been welded shut. Despite wearing protective clothing, he suffered 70% scald burns to his body. The company denied liability, stating that: 'The driver should have known the state of his cab.' After it became clear that the blocking of the emergency exit and the lack of attention to proper procedures were against criminal law, the company settled on terms dictated by the employee. The company continues to deny that anything at all wrong occurred. In a statement to the media, the company said: 'Our safety record is as good as that of anyone in the EU and better than most of the rest of the world.'

---

- *Insufficient training in health and safety procedures, practices and attitudes:* the outward sign of which is the fact that health and safety are not covered in induction courses, that health and safety training and emergency drills are skimped or cut altogether, health and safety committees meet infrequently and have no teeth, those who try and bring health and safety issues to the fore are treated as pariahs or victimised for their actions.

- *Demands of shareholders' representatives and senior managers:* for short-term profitability, which spending on safety and training would cut into.
- *Ignorance or passive neglect:* of either the broader safety demands and pressures of the situation, or of particular safety issues present.
- *Conspiracy or active negligence:* the outward form of which is, for example, the removal of machine guards to speed up production and output processes, ordering staff to use equipment without following safety procedures.

It is essential therefore to set standards, insist on training and involve everyone.

## Setting standards

The drive to set standards ought to be a full and informed concern for the safety of everyone at the workplace. If this is not present, then the drive ought to be the direct relationship between high standards of safety and long-term effective and profitable performance. It is only possible if:

- full attention is paid to requirements at induction time
- all statutory and operational rules and regulations are reinforced
- any problems that are raised are dealt with quickly
- any changes in machinery, equipment or operational practice is reinforced by job safety training (see Box 11.6).

## Box 11.6 'We will safety ourselves out of business'

This line is spoken by one of the characters in the film *Intensive Care*, a safety film made for the glass industry. The point being made is that too much attention to, and the consequent expenditure on, safety is detrimental to organisational profits.

As we have seen this may be the case in the short-term, especially when having to present an annual account to shareholders for their approval.

By any other yardstick, this is ridiculous. Using the examples from page 198:

- Over the period 1987–1992 people preferred to travel with ferry operators other than Townsend Thoresen. In some cases, people were prepared to wait days to travel with a rival. This was at a time when cross-Channel traffic was growing at the rate of approximately 20% per annum (it was also well before the Channel Tunnel was opened).
- Both Thames Trains and Great Western Trains have had to expend vast sums of money on employing lawyers to defend their positions. They have had to spend great amounts of managerial, supervisory and technological resources on managing the aftermath of the crash, rather than more productive efforts.
- In 1998, productivity at the British Steel plant at Redcar fell to its lowest level since before privatisation; and the company also recorded the highest levels of staff absence, sickness and turnover for nine years. In January 2000, the company was taken over by a Dutch multinational and was renamed *Corus*.

- *Full attention:* this consists of ensuring that emergency procedures and specific hazards are dealt with at the outset. Full training is given on all machinery and equipment. Procedures are walked through and then incorporated into ways of working. Many organisations require new employees to sign papers to the effect that they have received and understood their safety training.
- *Reinforcement:* this refers to what is rewarded and punished. In terms of safety, it is no use trying to insist on high standards of safety if people are to be rewarded for breaking them; nor is it any use trying to discipline staff for breaches if these are subsequently overturned.

Rewards and sanctions have to accord with positive safety demands. If not, all that happens is a proliferation of disciplinary and grievance cases. More generally, a culture of bullying grows up against those who wish to work in as much safety as is reasonable and practicable.

Standards set by first line managers and supervisors must be reinforced by those in senior positions. Where this does not occur, it contributes heavily to major disasters (see above). More generally, it leaves the individual manager or supervisor extremely vulnerable when things do go wrong because they can expect little support from their superiors. So it is absolutely essential to set, maintain and reinforce standards within individual domains.

---

**EXAMPLE**

Bank Underground Station in London has been the subject of six redevelopment schemes over the past twenty years. During one of these, a site manager put up the following notice:

*'No-one will be allowed on site unless they are wearing and carrying the correct safety clothing and equipment. Anyone found on site not wearing the correct clothing or using the correct equipment will be escorted off site'.*

This was opposed by each of the three recognised trade unions involved on the grounds that it was 'unreasonable and punitive'. These unions only withdrew their opposition following bad press coverage of their attitudes after ten men were injured in an underground rock fall.

The notice was also opposed by those at the corporate headquarters of the main contractors on the grounds that it was too strident and that 'no work would be done'. They too were forced to withdraw their opposition after the story was leaked to the Institution of Civil Engineering and was printed in *New Civil Engineer* magazine.

---

## Problem solving

The source of safety problems is a combination of unsafe attitudes and unsafe behaviour. If these are correct and reinforced, problems are kept to a minimum. A key part of problem solving is to ensure that people are:

- fully trained and equipped for the work they are to carry out
- fully aware of all actual and potential hazards
- support systems are in place if things do go wrong.

The human conditions in which safety problems arise are thus kept to a minimum. Therefore, when something does have to be dealt with, the real issues – equipment malfunction, combinations of outside circumstances – are easy to spot and deal with, and resolve for the future.

All problems should be assessed by individual managers and supervisors whether or not the Health and Safety Executive, and any other statutory body, is involved (see also Chapter 9). Investigations are required, together with witness and expert statements. Equipment malfunctions should always be taken up with the manufacturer or supplier. Explosions and leaks should always be traced to source. Accidents and crashes should always be looked at from the point of view of the circumstances of all those involved. The reasons why these events occur can then be proven, deduced or inferred once how and when they occurred has been established.

The priority then becomes remedial action. Whatever is required must be implemented. Not to do so stirs up trouble for the future and may be negligent. Punishments are always much heavier the second time an accident occurs under the same set of circumstances because it means that no lessons have been learned or improvements made. Managers and supervisors who regularly have safety problems in their departments and areas are certain eventually to face statutory investigation as well as that of their superiors. Moreover again, working in an accident or injury-prone department or location is very damaging to both morale and confidence of all staff.

# The environment

In the management of health and safety, the environment is considered from the point of view of creating a healthy and safe working environment; and also in terms of:

- managing and developing that environment
- environmental health and safety management
- using safety committees.

## Managing and developing a safe environment

Responsibility does not end with creating and maintaining the conditions previously indicated. It is a key part of managerial and supervisory duty to take an active part in looking out for new hazards and removing them or limiting their effects. New regulations must be implemented. New equipment must always address the broader health and safety issues as well as narrow operational issues of output effectiveness and efficiency. Changes in premises, design or usage must always be accompanied by upgrading or restating emergency procedures. Attention is always required when there are changes in components in manufacturing, ingredients in food and chemicals, and packaging usage on both the supply and output sides. While serious accidents or incidents have to be reported, a log must be kept of all breaches of health and safety, however minor.

This also goes a long way towards maintaining and developing a high and enduring quality of working life, and an environment that everyone will respect and take pride in. This contributes greatly to enhancement of morale. It reduces the number of non-work related problems that have to be addressed. It reflects the extent to which the overall well-being of everyone concerned is being considered. And it helps to place a general mark of value, respect and concern for all those who have to work in the particular area.

## Environmental health and safety management

Environmental health and safety management concerns:

- waste and effluent production and disposal
- fumes and exhaust
- access and egress from premises, and from departments within premises.

All industrial, commercial, public service and internet activities cause waste. The problems are how best to dispose of it, legal constraints, and costs and charges.

### Disposal

Because of its toxic or poisonous content, by law some waste requires specific disposal, often using named contractors. More generally, arrangements have to be made for tackling whatever volume of waste and effluent is generated.

On the face of it, this is straightforward. However, it remains true that many organisations are not helped by the attitudes of some of the specialist waste disposal companies who insist on particular volumes being accumulated before they will turn out; or particular storage arrangements being made, often at great expense. This area of activity is not bounded by straightforward regulation.

It is true, however, that waste or effluent leakages are expensive and damaging to the environment. When they do occur, it is normally because:

- the organisation and/or its staff have been negligent or criminal
- storage facilities were inadequate, or under-maintained or supervised
- there was insufficient understanding of, or attention to, the facilities required for the purpose.

Investigations normally start by addressing these points in turn. Prevention, therefore, requires a realistic and informed assessment of the standards required, and of what can and may go wrong. Organisations, managers and supervisors then have to arrive at a view of their legal responsibilities and their moral responsibilities.

### Legal responsibilities

As stated above, these may or may not be clear. They normally require knowledge of, and adherence to, specific regulations and statistics. Managers and supervisors must understand these – they will be called to account for anything that does go wrong, and especially have to explain why any breaches of regulations did occur. Where the law is less precise, it is best to establish the highest possible levels of performance.

## Moral responsibilities

These require arriving at a view based on a combination of long-term viability of activities and ordinary common decency – 'what is right'. If waste and effluent are treated in a cavalier manner, the organisation is certain to be caught and so both tests fail, for this is not sustainable in the long-term, nor is it decent. Knowledge, belief or perception that waste is being disposed of in this way leads to an overall lack of value, commitment and respect – and it is also extremely expensive.

---

**EXAMPLE**

In March 2000, the Japanese government refused to accept a consignment of processed uranium. This had been exported by British Energy as part of a commercial contract to supply radioactive material for the power generation and defence industries.

The Japanese had found out that safety checks at the company's reprocessing plant at Sellafield had been skimped, falsified or simply not carried out. When a full investigation was launched within the company, these findings were confirmed.

Meanwhile, the company was having a problem with one of its power stations. The Dungeness power station, on the Kent coast was found to have failed to give adequate publicity to radioactive and carbon dioxide leaks that had occurred on its premises. When it was confronted with this, the company admitted that the leaks had indeed taken place. When it was asked why it had not publicised them before, the response was 'Nobody asked'. This was in spite of the fact that the company has a legal responsibility to notify the public at large, and the nuclear inspectorate, when such leaks do occur.

The company failed the legal test on both grounds. It also failed the moral test – as well as being wrong, the secrecy surrounding both events was broken. The position was therefore not sustainable in the long-term. There is also a shareholder interest in this. Between May 1999–April 2000, the company's share value fell by 76%.

---

## Using safety committees

All organisations are required by law to consult with their staff on all health and safety issues, and to constitute safety meetings. Trade unions and staff representatives are entitled to information on all matters that are known, believed or perceived to affect organisational workplace or personal safety. All organisations with twenty or more staff are required by law to constitute a formal safety committee. This is obliged to meet regularly. It must include management and workforce representatives, including representation from all recognised trade unions. Safety committees may be consultative, advisory or executive. Whichever is chosen, there are statutory requirements for complete openness of information and specific attention to known, believed, perceived or potential hazards.

The key therefore is access to, and use of, information. There is no test of commercial or operational confidentiality. In public service bodies and government departments, Crown immunity from prosecution has largely been removed on safety issues. Safety committees must specifically address:

- real and potential hazards
- accidents and emergencies, including fire, spillages and leaks
- infestations
- product and service issues
- staff management issues
- staff safety training, including emergency procedures.

Health and safety at work may not be the subject of negotiation or collective bargaining (Chapter 10). Results and outcomes of consultations and discussions must always be publicised in writing and made available to all staff. There is also a statutory duty to disclose information if it can be proved or demonstrated that there is a real or potential hazard to the surrounding environment or region.

---
EXAMPLE

Because of the effects of the BSE crisis in the UK in the mid-1990s, a country incinerator was requested to increase its capacity from 1,200 to 6,000 tonnes of rubbish per week. It agreed to do this. Within a week, the local MP, County Councillors and the Environmental Health Department were flooded with complaints. These concerned:

- noise and traffic pollution caused by the five-fold increase in deliveries to the site
- smell caused by the burning of beef cattle waste products
- pollution caused by the great increase in the operation of the incinerator
- infestation – because the incinerator was not able to operate at the speed with which deliveries were being made, the cattle waste was having to be stored and this led to a plague of rats and flies.

The local residents sued and received substantial compensation. This was because both the company, and the government departments who requested the work, had failed to consult adequately on the new nature of operations, or to inform the surrounding locality of the full consequences.

---

# Conclusions

The keys to being an effective manager of workplace health and safety are:

- Taking positive steps to promote a healthy and safe environment
- Understanding real corporate attitudes to health and safety.

The two are not always easy to reconcile (see the Example on page 203).

It is also certain in the medium term, that statutory duties and the management of health and safety will be made more stringent. The institutions

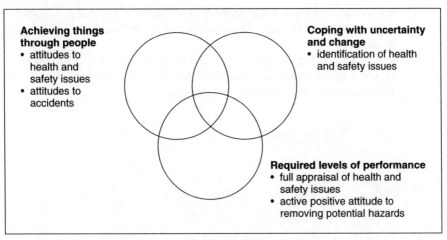

**Achieving things through people**
- attitudes to health and safety issues
- attitudes to accidents

**Coping with uncertainty and change**
- identification of health and safety issues

**Required levels of performance**
- full appraisal of health and safety issues
- active positive attitude to removing potential hazards

*Figure 11.1*   Chapter and model summary.

of the EU place a high priority on workplace health and safety and the management of the environment. While clearly it has taken a long time to get real action and improvements in this part of the quality of working life, it is certain that the emphasis is towards tighter regulation and control. This is to be carried out in four ways:

- specific attacks on specific activities, especially staff training and the handling and movement of all goods
- strengthening in the medium to long term of powers of inspection
- raising the profile of health and safety as a feature of the broader management of the environment
- consultations and reductions in pollution control and the effects of toxic substances with a view to both incremental and specific legislation in the long term.

It is also clear that both legal and moral approaches to health and safety at work require ever-greater positive and proactive attention to the rights of the individual to work in an environment that is as free as possible from real and potential hazards. Managers and supervisors must therefore have a full understanding of all of the health and safety constraints in their own situation if they are to be truly effective in this part of their work.

Using the Model referred to at the start of Chapter 1 (Figure 1.1), the material in this Chapter is summarised in Figure 11.1.

QUESTIONS

1. Conduct a hazard spotting exercise in your own department. Draw up an action plan to address the items that you have discovered.
2. What potential causes of stress are there in your working situation? How should these be resolved?

3. Identify and quantify, as far as possible, all of the costs involved in one of the disasters discussed on page 198, or else a disaster with which you yourself are familiar.
4. What actions would you take, and why, in your department in order to minimise the effects of: a flu epidemic; an infestation of cockroaches. How, when and where would you measure these efforts for success or failure?

# ■ ᴍ **12** Working with groups

## Introduction

Groups and teams are gatherings of people drawn together or organised and united by common purposes and objectives. These common purposes must be understood by all. Ideally also, these are the overriding concerns – where problems and conflicts do occur within groups, members subsume their private interests to those of the group.

Effective teams and groups lead to:

- creativity
- harmony
- improved job and work satisfaction
- increased energy
- increased motivation, commitment and identity
- progress, development and enhancement
- flexibility, dynamism and responsiveness.

Teams and groups tackle tasks that are too large for one person. They bring a collective approach to bear on given issues. They generate and reinforce confidence and direction.

Teams and groups may also generate elitism. This is sometimes known as 'group think', a form of conformity more influential than that of the organisation as a whole (see Box 12.1).

## Box 12.1   Group think

All groups may develop 'group think'. This is especially a problem with high performance groups or those selected on the basis of excellence, high status, or advanced technical knowledge. In these cases, it is often only a short step for members 'knowing that they are always clever and excellent', to believing that 'they are always right'.

In extreme circumstances, this may develop into a bunker mentality. This is where a group becomes so divorced from reality that it develops its own view of the world and this becomes the basis for its investigations, activities, operations and decision-making processes, regardless of the true nature of the wider environment. It is a phrase derived from the bunker used by Hitler and the other leaders of the Nazis in the last days of World

War II. Rather than come to terms with the reality of their impending defeat, they created their own version of the world within their operations room or bunker.

Another form of this is the canteen culture. In this, groups of workers set their own norms and standards based on what is important to them, rather than what is important to the organisation. They become self-regulating, self-motivating and self-disciplining. In extreme cases, this gives rise to bullying, harassment, victimisation and ostracism, and if it is not identified early and dealt with swiftly, it can become very difficult to weed out.

# Types of groups

It is usual to distinguish the following types of groups:

- *Formal groups:* constituted and directed for a purpose, to solve problems, develop products, conduct projects, run production lines; these will have formal and organised agendas, constitution, composition and results.
- *Informal groups:* in which staff organise themselves in ways important or necessary to themselves, for example for the purpose of professional development, information generation, awareness, improved inter-departmental or inter-functional communication, self-regulation, and work improvement.
- *Purpose groups:* these are formed either on a compulsory, coercive or voluntary basis for specific purposes. Some are distinguishable from others in that they are often not formally constituted and are expected to meet in their own time (e.g., quality circles, work improvement groups). Others include lobbies and vested interest groups in support of particular initiatives, and think-tanks involved in the generation of creative flows of ideas as part of the wider development processes within organisations.
- *Psychological groups:* viewed from the standpoint that membership is dependent upon people interacting with each other, being aware of each other, and perceiving themselves to belong.

From this, an initial general set of group characteristics may begin to be identified.

## Group characteristics

The major characteristics that must be in place are:

- the ability of each member to communicate with every other member of the group
- a collective identity based on a combination of the circumstances, environment and work of the group

- shared aims and objectives
- roles and responsibilities
- structure and order
- Nnrms and rules.

The presence of each of these characteristics ensures that both work and behaviour can be regulated and ordered to best advantage whatever the circumstances, task, or matter in hand. It also acts as the basis for creating effective groups for other matters – controlling work, project work, problem-solving, creative activities, brainstorming and information gathering, and the investigation and resolution of conflicts, grievances and disputes.

## Work groups and the individual

Teams and groups serve organisational purposes. They provide a useful and effective means of dividing and allocating tasks. Within organisations, individuals have a high propensity to work in this way. Belonging to work groups is a means of satisfying social and affiliation needs, as well as being the basis for developing an effective and rewarding pattern of work.

Membership of work groups also give individuals:

- distinctive work roles with which they can be comfortable and happy
- distinctive work roles and associations that satisfy feelings of self-esteem
- the establishment of a self-summary and self-concept that can be presented to others in the work group, and also to the world at large
- the opportunity to contribute to productive, positive, profitable and effective activities
- the ability to fulfil personal aims and ambitions (these normally have to be harmonised and entwined with those of the particular groups or organisation)
- the ability to identify with a collection of individuals; and above all, the ability to take pride in this identification.

Managers and supervisors with responsibility for creating effective work groups have to recognise the extent and prevalence of each of these elements within the members of their teams and groups and, where necessary, take steps to ensure that these are satisfied.

## Conformity

In all group situations, there is normally a strong pressure placed on individuals to conform. Indeed, in many cases, individuals must conform or be expelled or rejected. If they choose not to conform they may be ostracised.

Conformity is therefore a very powerful pressure. It affects both the nature and the effectiveness of the performance of the group. Conformity may also lead to group think, canteen culture and bunker mentality (see Box 12.1).

# The creation of effective groups

It is usual to identify four key elements to the creation of effective groups:

- *Forming:* the coming together of the individuals concerned; beginning to learn about each other; assessment of group purpose; assessment of individual personalities, strengths and capabilities; introduction to the tasks, aims and objectives; initial social and personal interaction.
- *Storming:* the first creative burst of the group; energising the activities; gaining initial markers about capabilities and capacities; mutual appraisal and assessment of expertise and process.

Effective forming and storming depends on early output and success in results terms, as well as mutuality of interest in human and professional terms. Failure to deliver early and positive results normally leads to members wondering about the integrity or viability of a particular group.

It is also true that initial conflicts tend to become apparent at this stage. Opportunities and diversions may also become apparent. Conflicts between group and personal agenda, aims and objectives also start to emerge.

- *Norming:* the establishment of norms and rules; behavioural boundaries; codes of conduct; forms and standards of discipline; the identification of acceptable and unacceptable conduct, performance, attitudes, values and activities.
- *Performing:* the addressing of matters in hand; tackling the task to be carried out; getting results; assessing performance; developing individuals and activities (see Figure 12.1).

## Other factors in the creation and maintenance of effective work groups

The following are also factors in the group creation, maintenance and development process.

### Adjourning

This is where a group is shut down, either because it has no task in hand at the particular point in time or because it is failing to carry out its task effectively and therefore its processes and operation need appraisal and modification.

### Rejuvenation

This stems from a combination of realising that the group is under-performing or under-achieving, or that its present expertise, knowledge and qualities can only take it so far.

Successful rejuvenation normally comes about as the result of:

- general acceptance on the part of everyone concerned that it is necessary to rejuvenate

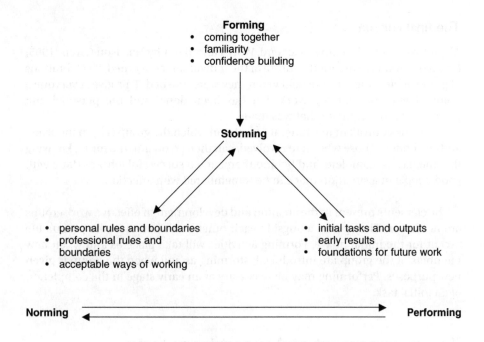

Figure 12.1 The creation of effective groups.

- identity between members, together with a strong desire to succeed
- universal acceptance that the present state of affairs is not adequate
- clear understanding of the required future direction.

Once these points are understood, adequate and effective attention to the need for new expertise, skills, knowledge and qualities can then be paid.

It may also become apparent that group processes are ineffective, or that rules and regulations, and behavioural norms, need modification.

## Reprocessing

This involves going through a version of the initial cohesion process as follows:

- re-forming
- re-storming
- re-norming; with a view to
- re-performing.

This is most likely to be effective where the need for the group and its work is strong, but where insufficient attention has been paid to group processes.

### The final curtain

All groups eventually come to an end. Work carried out by Harrison Owen (1985) found that it was better for the future of the individuals concerned, if celebrations of group achievements were held when they were finished. This gives everyone a point of reference for the work that has been done, and the personal and professional commitment that was made.

This is the equivalent to a funeral or wake, in which the group is both mourned and celebrated. Those who were involved, can then go on into the future knowing that the past is 'complete' and behind them, and a successful job was done with good people in a situation that can be remembered with affection.

The elements present in the creation and development of effective work groups are not linear. They go on alongside each other at all points in the group's life except for the initial phase. Forming activities will take place as and when new members of the group are introduced; storming as and when the group is given new purposes. Performing may be necessary at an early stage in the completion of an initial task.

## Key management and supervisory tasks

For groups to be effective, a variety of attributes must be present and a range of activities carried out. The different roles and functions that must be addressed consist of:

- group administration
- attention to detail
- creativity and ideas
- leadership and direction
- polishing and completion of tasks
- team, group and task maintenance
- team, group and individual discipline.

If some, but not all, of these qualities are present, the team will malfunction. If members are all creative, the group will generate a lot of ideas but complete very little; conversely, if there is no creativity, the group may nevertheless be very strong in its own processes and identity.

Group size must be relevant to the matter in hand. Any pronouncement on ideal size must be seen in this context. Size is governed by the range and complexities of tasks to be carried out; the nature of the technology; and the broader environment of activities. Within that context, any group of less than five may suffer from a restricted range of qualities and capabilities; while any group of more than ten may create administrative problems, subgroups, and cliques. Difficulties also arise with large groups in ensuring that all members contribute and are involved; or in the case of committee and meeting type groups, that they can, indeed, all get together at the same time (see Figure 12.2).

(a)    **Simple**

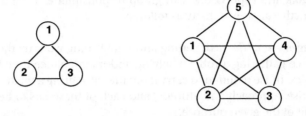

–    Size and work location form no physical or psychological barriers

(b)    **Complex**

(i)    *Linear (e.g. production line)*

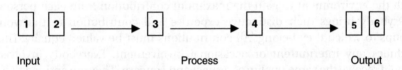

Input                          Process                          Output

*Notes:*
–    Close relationships formed between 1 and 2, and 5 and 6, only
–    Isolation of (1+2), (5+6), 3 and 4 enhanced by length of line, noise, invisibility barriers

(ii)    *Subgroups*

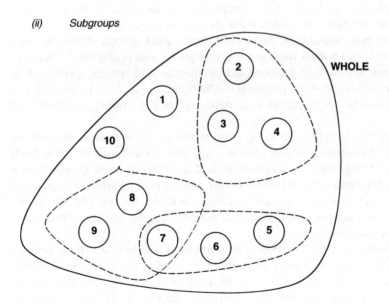

*Notes:*
–    isolation of 1 and 10
–    divided loyalties of 7
–    propensity for barriers and cliques

*Figure 12.2*    Factors and constraints in the size of groups.

Managers and supervisors with group responsibilities have then to attend to ten distinctive areas of activity as follows:

- *Management of the task:* setting and establishing work methods, time scales, resource gathering, problem solving and maintenance functions. If a task is complex, those required to carry it out may also bring a mixture of experience, expertise, approach and attitude, and each of these has to be harmonised in pursuit of the given purpose.

  Management of the task also includes reference to the nature of technology used and required, and the degrees of expertise that it commands. This also affects the physical layout of the work and environment. Both have effects on the interaction of group members.
- *Management of the process:* the use of interpersonal skills and the interaction with the environment to gain the maximum contribution from each person. Everybody brings their distinctive expertise and contribution to the work groups to which they belong. All contributions must be valued equally. This includes any intermittent or occasional involvement. Everybody involved should receive the same quality of respect and concern. They are entitled to be treated fairly and equally, whatever the nature of their contribution or expertise.

  Distinctive and highly prized expertise has also to be harmonised and integrated with the overall purpose. When individuals or subgroups who have this distinctive or highly prized expertise try to use this for their own advantage, this has to be addressed early and 'nipped in the bud'.
- *Managing communications:* between different work groups, disciplines and professions, and within work groups, disciplines and professions. This is to ensure that inter-group relations are productive and not competitive. It is necessary to identify early potential conflicts and to nip these in the bud. It is also essential to ensure that all information is freely and openly available, and shared.
- *Managing the individual:* making constructive use of individual differences; ensuring that individual contributions are both valued and of value. Each individual brings their own aspirations and ambitions to work groups. Group memberships enhance and retard career paths, personal ambitions, pay and rewards, and personal and professional development. People are drawn towards those groups held in high and positive esteem, and away from those where the converse is true.
- *Management style:* the creation and adoption of a style that is both positive and dynamic, and also suitable to the management needs of the situation. Whatever the style felt necessary or adopted, the keys to its effectiveness are integrity (see Chapter 2) and leadership (see Chapter 13). The prime purpose of the adoption of a particular management style is to ensure that people are capable and willing to carry out the tasks to the best of their ability in the situation.
- *Maintenance management:* ensuring that administration and support services are suitable to the needs of the group; and ensuring that, where administrative problems are identified, they are remedied early.

- *Common aims and objectives:* which should be understood, valued and adopted by all group members. These have to be the overriding common purpose for being in the situation. Where this is not the case, group members have to be persuaded to adopt the common aims and objectives; or else remove themselves from the situation.
- *Shared values:* standards of behaviour, attitude, quality and performance that all members of the group must be able to agree to and in which they have confidence and belief.
- *Group and team spirit:* a combination of the shared values, together with the ethics and ethos of the group or team concerned; and the extent of a positive identity and loyalty that members have to each other, to the tasks in hand, and to overall objectives. It is a summary of the strength of respect and identity held by members for each other and for the group to which they belong. It is underlined and developed through other factors including pride, esteem, value and respect. If these factors are not present, then a genuine and enduring group and team spirit cannot be generated. Group and spirit must always be positive. This, in turn, gives all those concerned a positive, rather than coercive, reason for belonging to the group. In reality, everybody needs to take a sense of pride in the work that they carry out and in the situation in which it takes place.
- *Managing conflict:* the potential for conflicts within all groups must be assessed openly and honestly. The usual causes are:
  — the nature and mix of personalities involved
  — the nature and mix of expertise and talent present
  — a divergence of objectives between group members and individual agendas, and the objectives of the group
  — the means and methods of communication, consultation and participation are not adequate
  — the levels of confidence, trust, respect and regard are not adequate
  — the working environment is not adequate or suitable
  — the form of management style adopted is wrong or inappropriate, or else lacking in integrity;
  — the group has no chance in succeeding in the tasks that it has been set – this is usually due to factors beyond its control, especially lack of resources, unavailability of expertise, or lack of value placed on the group's                                                                outputs
  by the organisation at large. Each of these elements arises through neglect and indifference on the part of the organisation concerned. Those with managerial and supervisory responsibility must be aware of the potential for conflict, and, wherever possible, to have at their disposal the means for its resolution.

# Group behaviour

Figure 12.3 illustrates the forms of group behaviour normally identified.

| Internalisation | Compliance | Acceptance | Regimentation | Alienation |
|---|---|---|---|---|
| – shared positive values | – acceptable values | – combination of self and group interest | – overriding single interest (usually economic) | – single interests (overwhelmingly economic) |
| – commitment | | | | |

**CONFORMITY** ⟵————————————————⟶ **ALIENATION**

| | | | |
|---|---|---|---|
| – high degree of motivation | | | – high turnover of members |
| – possible blind obedience | – disputes are minimal | – low quality of working life | – canteen cultures |
| | – rejection of eccentrics | | |

*Figure 12.3* The group behaviour spectrum.

# Conformity

Conformity is the outward manifestation of behavioural, professional, organisational and operational activities. It ensures a series and set of standards and outputs. It gives the organisation and its groups their own distinctive identity and consistency. Measures of conformity are plainly essential in certain circumstances.

The universal use of organisational colour schemes, logos, slogans and staff uniforms gives a strong distinctive and positive identity. Organisational procedures and processes are devised to ensure that staff are treated with fairness and equity. The styles of management and supervision are designed to reinforce this. Codes of practice – especially concerning discipline and grievance – underline this.

Attention also has to be paid to standards of behaviour, address, attitude and performance. Groups and organisations establish norms, customs, modes of dress, modes of behaviour, attendance patterns and work manners.

# Regimentation

Regimentation is the coercive approach to conformity. It is imposed by the organisation. It consists of absolute requirements to adhere to codes of practice, conduct, dress and address.

This is most useful in dangerous and other extreme conditions where sets and series of behaviour can be devised in order to control the danger as far as possible, and to provide step-by-step approaches if, and when, emergencies do arise. It is used in more general organisational terms in military forces. It is also used as a pattern of discipline in emergency services – police, fire, medical, coastguard and lifeboat.

The regimentation approach to conformity also exists in traditionally structured organisations – those designed along strictly hierarchical lines where there are well-defined orders of progression from one position to the next, where promotion and advancement are based on loyalty and longevity of service, and where there are highly structured jobs, tasks and practices.

## Internalisation

This is the receptive approach to conformity. Those working in the particular group adopt its attitudes, values and beliefs as their own. The interests of the organisation, the groups, and the staff, coincide exactly.

For internalisation to exist and be fully productive and positive, there is an overwhelming responsibility on the organisation to ensure that what people internalise is fully wholesome. This also applies to group managers and supervisors. The attitudes, values and beliefs in question must be positive, beneficial, ethical and have a universal long-term interest.

If the attitudes, values and beliefs in question are negative or corrupted, they may still be internalised. The whole process then becomes both subjective and self-serving. This becomes the basis for the creation of canteen cultures and bunker mentalities – and therefore the basis on which people are bullied, victimised and harassed.

## Compliance and acceptance

Compliance and acceptance recognise the validity of the organisation's claim upon the talents and expertise of its staff for the duration of the period of employment. While at work, individuals accept the discipline, priorities and ordering of the organisation. By accepting a job within the organisation, individuals accept strictures and rules and regulations that may be legitimately devised and enforced.

Compliance and acceptance may also be negative and divisive, especially between ranks in organisational hierarchies. For example, where the organisation goes to no trouble to provide anything other than a wage-work bargain for some members of its staff (above all, those at the lower end of hierarchies, or at the frontline of operations and services), it is unreasonable for those in managerial positions to expect any positive identity. This problem is exacerbated if the organisation is known, believed or perceived to take better care of those in more senior positions.

## Eccentricity

Eccentric behaviour is neither condoned nor encouraged, nor is it rejected. Most organisations are normally prepared to accommodate eccentricity for its own purposes, especially where particular individuals have rare or special talents and skills. Forms of eccentric behaviour may also be encouraged and nurtured by organisations as part of their own creative processes. Research and development departments, for example, require creative and imaginative individuals; and this also applies to some forms of direct selling, and individual production work.

The main managerial and supervisory problem concerns the extent to which eccentric behaviour is to be accommodated. Eccentricity may be dysfunctional to the rest of the organisation – it may cause resentment among those in mainstream and steady-state departments and functions who believe or perceive that they are being forced to adhere to a set of norms and rules that are seen not to apply to the eccentric.

## Alienation

Alienation is where individuals and groups work within organisations without interest or identity. Alienation is destructive to individual and group motivation, morale, health and output; and people who find themselves in alienated organisational and working situations normally move on if they possibly can. Those with managerial responsibilities in these situations need to recognise the great propensity for strikes, disputes, grievances and other unacceptable forms of individual and group behaviour where alienation is apparent (see Box 12.2).

## Box 12.2   Alienation

Alienation always exists where individuals and groups are faced with:

- *Powerlessness:* the inability to influence work conditions, work volume, work quality, speed and direction.
- *Meaninglessness:* the inability to recognise any individual contribution made to the total output of work.
- *Isolation:* which may either be physical or psychological. Physical factors arise from work organisation requiring that people are located in ways that allow for little human interaction. The psychological factors are influenced by the physical. These include psychological distance from supervisors, management and colleagues.
- *Low feelings of self-esteem and self-worth:* arising from the lack of value placed on staff by the organisation and its managers and supervisors.
- *Loss of identity with the organisation and its work:* the inability to say with pride, 'I work for organisation X'.
- *Lack of real or perceived returns:* other than financial on the time, skill and effort put into the work.
- *Lack of prospects:* including change or advancement for the future.
- *Feelings of being stuck or trapped:* in a particular situation purely for economic gain.
- *General rejection:* based on adversarial and dishonest managerial and supervisory style.
- *Poor working conditions:* including quality of working life and environment.
- *Lack of equality:* especially where the organisation is known, believed or perceived to differentiate between different types and grades of staff to the benefit of some and detriment of others.

Alienation is the major fundamental cause of conflict and disputes at places of work. It is potentially present in all work situations. Those who manage work groups need to be aware of it in their own particular situation. They can then take steps to ensure that it is eliminated if possible, or its effects kept to a minimum at least.

# Group constraints

The main group constraints of which managers and supervisors must be aware are:

- *Poor performance:* in which deadlines are missed, output is substandard and customer complaints increase.
- *Group decline:* in which members decline or reject responsibility for their actions, or else in which performance and output declines.
- *Increase in lobbying:* including increasing the number of subgroups and elites; individuals claiming rewards and bonuses for team efforts. This also leads to a culture of blame – one subgroup seeks to blame other subgroups for shortcomings.
- *Grievances:* becoming involved in grievances with other group members.
- *Personal clashes:* increases in numbers of personality and personal clashes; over-spill of professional and expert argument into personal relationships.
- *Increases in levels of grievances, absenteeism, accidents:* moves to leave the group and increases in labour turnover.
- *Lack of interest:* in results, activities, plans and proposals for the group.
- *General attitude and demeanour:* in terms of lack of pride and joy in the work and identity with the group.
- *Favouritism:* which always arises as the result of bad leadership, management and supervision.
- *Dominance and weakness:* where one weak member is holding back the potential of the rest; or where the group is dominated by one or two powerful individuals.
- *Rejection:* when individuals are rejected by the rest of the group. Rejection occurs in two main ways – where an individual is rejected because of an error that he or she has made, and where new members are ostracised and given no chance to settle in and become effective.
- *Physical layout:* of premises, department or division.
- *Technology:* the nature of the technology that is required to be used.
- *Extreme operating conditions:* that exist because of the required outputs – especially noise, silence, heat, cold, wet, dry, dirt and cleanliness.
- *Extreme operating conditions:* that exist in spite of the required outputs (see Box 12.3).
- *Location of activities:* is a particular constraint when:
  — the location that everyone is required to attend is away from where people live, meaning that they have to commute
  — people within the group work at different locations at different times
  — some people within the group work in a central location while others do not (see Box 12.4).
- *Nature of work:* this becomes a constraint when some people are known, believed or perceived to have to do the bad or dirty jobs, or that some get all of the opportunities going while others do not.

## Box 12.3 Extreme conditions and their effect on groups

As stated in Chapter 2, there is no problem with having in place and having to manage extreme conditions where there are operational drives. For example:

- ice cream has to be made and stored in conditions of extreme cold
- cooked and processed food is normally produced under conditions of extreme heat
- building sites, mining and quarrying, take place in conditions of extreme dirt
- the production of sterile medical equipment takes place in conditions of extreme cleanliness
- the oil industry works in all of these extreme conditions in different parts of the world and has to adjust both the attitudes and expectations of the staff, and also the technology.

Examples of unacceptable extreme conditions are:

- Forrest Mars, the founder of the Mars chocolate company, arrived in the office of one of his manufacturing managers. He had just been up to one of the production areas and had found the temperature there to be 33°C. Mr Mars asked the production manager why this was so. The production manager replied blandly that the cooling system was broken but it was out of his control. Mr Mars summoned a maintenance crew and had the production manager's desk moved into the production area where the temperature was 33°C. The production manager had the cooling system fixed the following day.
- A very famous architecture school in central London prides itself on its creativity. The students who graduate from the school go on to be some of the best architects in the world. The school resembled a combination of art establishment, studio, building establishment, and gallery. The Health and Safety Inspectorate took a different view of this. A prohibition notice was placed on the school, requiring it to clean itself up in thirty days. The 'creative' environment had in fact long since become subsumed by total self-indulgence.

## Box 12.4 Locations of work: 'the grass is always greener'

There is great potential for inter-group problems where work is carried out by clearly identifiable groups from a variety of locations. Parts of the group process are only effective if full attention is paid to ensuring that everyone knows why they are required to work in particular ways from the different locations. This is also a key managerial and supervisory skill – ensuring that everyone is drawn together regularly in order to maintain cohesion and identity. Problems that regularly occur are:

- *From the point of view of those at the central location:* they perceive those in the field, on the move, or at home to have an easy life – self-accountability, lack of supervision and discipline, work when they feel like it, work if they feel like it, have high expensive perks and benefits, can do the shopping in work time.
- *Those working away from the central location:* believe or perceive that those at the central location have a peaceful, sheltered working day – do nothing that services clients or customers, gain the advantages of familiarity, visibility and knowledge inherent in being present, and therefore visible, at head office, get treated favourably when the time for appraisals and performance reviews and pay rises come around, and have the first shot at promotions and other opportunities.

Each of these points of view may be founded in fact or in fantasy. It is important to recognise:

- If people believe it, it has currency all of its own. It does not actually matter whether any or all of it is true. It always causes real problems that have to be addressed on their own merits from the protagonist's point of view.
- If any of it is actually true, it has to be tackled and remedied. This form of divisiveness is extremely destructive to team and group morale and performance.
- If none of it is true, this needs to be stated, demonstrated and reinforced so that the myth is dispersed.

- *Nature of rewards:* especially where rewards are distributive not integrative (see Chapter 5). Genuine teamwork is rewarded evenly, differentials are expressed in salary not bonus terms.
- *Value:* placed on individual contributions within the team or group. From a human and ethical point of view, this must always be on the basis of equality. Nobody should be employed or present if their own particular contribution holds no value.

---

EXAMPLES

*NASA:* an example that is regularly quoted concerns a conversation between President Lyndon B. Johnson of the USA, and a man who worked as a cleaner on the Apollo rocket launch pads. When President Johnson asked the cleaner whether he enjoyed his cleaning job, the cleaner replied, 'Oh no Sir. I am not just a cleaner. I am helping to put a man on the moon.'

*Semco:* place a value on individual contributions by giving 23% of retained profits over to the staff. It is allocated on an equal basis to the groups. Each group is then responsible for deciding how their particular part of the bonus is to be divided up.

*Todd Morden Ltd:* conversely, this company (not its real name), that sells industrial heating, lighting and water pumps in the north of England, has consistently taken the view that the company exists purely for the purpose of its owners. Its sales staff regularly exceed targets; each time this happens the company revises the bonus thresholds in terms disadvantageous to the sales staff. The consequence is that it finds it extremely difficult to attract, retain or motivate sales staff for any length of time and continues in existence only because of the extremely high mark up on a product that more or less sells itself.

The key skill is to recognise the extent and prevalence of each of these constraints. Where necessary and possible, steps have to be taken to ensure that their effects are eliminated, or else minimised. Where this is not possible – especially where the manager or supervisor has no authority or influence to act in the matter of these constraints – then the effects on the morale and output of the group must always be recognised.

## Problem areas with groups

Having identified constraints, it is now essential to pin down those specific areas where problems can, and do, arise.

Problems arise, above all, where the balance of attention to the group and to the task is wrong. If a task is over-emphasised, effectiveness is nevertheless reduced because those involved become demotivated, pressurised, stressed and alienated. Over-attention to the group itself leads to a reduction in importance of the task, and therefore inevitably, to reductions in output and quality.

Other problem areas include:

- aims and objectives not being set and established clearly and accurately
- lack of common or mutual interest, especially where it is clear that some members are present in the group against their will
- conflict between the individual agenda and purposes of members, and of those of the group
- lack of recognition of the influence of constraints, especially related to resources and technology, and the impact that these have on overall group effectiveness
- lack of clarity and consistency of direction, especially where what is expected of the group is constantly being changed, and where these changes lead to many tasks being half completed, or not completed at all
- lack of group identity or inappropriate group identity. Where there is no identity at all, a void exists in which members pursue their own agenda rather than the group's purposes
- lack of recognition: especially involving attention to the ways in which the work of the group is received. It is a real problem where the organisation style sets great store on the recognition of achievement, and where, for whatever reason, some groups receive this but others do not.

# Group development and performance

The creation and formation of effective teams and groups is not an end in itself. To remain effective, cohesion, capabilities and potential must be maintained and developed. This takes the following forms:

- infusions of talent from outside, bringing in people with distinctive qualities and expertise
- infusions of new skills, knowledge and qualities from within through training and development, and targeted work and project work that has the purpose of bringing out the required expertise
- attention to the relationship between group processes, task and achievement: this usually involves using good teams to carry out difficult and demanding tasks, or using difficult and demanding tasks to build good and effective teams.
- attention to team roles, both to build on strengths and also to eliminate weaknesses (see Figure 12.4). This is likely to involve reassessing what the requirements and priorities are, assessing the strengths and weaknesses of each individual, and leading to reallocation, rotation and translation of roles and infusions of new talent and expertise.

| Type | Symbol | Typical features | Positive qualities |
|------|--------|------------------|--------------------|
| Company Worker | CW | Conservative, dutiful, practicable | Organising ability, practical commonsense, hard-working |
| Chairman | CH | Calm, self-confident, controlled | A capacity for treating and welcoming all potential contributors on their merits and without prejudice A strong sense of objectives |
| Shaper | SH | Highly strung, outgoing, dynamic | Drive and readiness to challenge inertia, ineffectiveness, complacency or self-deception |
| Plant | PL | Individualistic, serious-minded, unorthodox | Genius, imagination, intellect, knowledge |
| Resource Investigator | RI | Extroverted, enthusiastic, curious, communicative | A capacity for contacting people and exploring anything new An ability to respond to challenge |
| Monitor-Evaluator | ME | Sober, unemotional, prudent | Judgement, discretion, hard-headedness |
| Team Worker | TW | Social orientated, rather mild, sensitive | An ability to respond to people and to situations, and to promote team spirit |
| Completer-Finisher | CF | Painstaking, orderly, conscientious, anxious | A capacity to follow-through Perfection |

Source: R.M. Belbin (1986).

*Figure 12.4* Archetype team members.

- recognising the concept of group lifecycle, especially recognising points at which infusions and re-energising may need to be made
- recognition – group development activities have their greatest effect when everyone is involved and where real problems and issues are addressed. When results are achieved, everyone feels a sense of success. Everyone is known and seen to have made a full contribution. Invariably, it is also culturally necessary for external recognition to be accorded. As stated above, problems occur when the group members know themselves that they have succeeded, but where wider recognition is not forthcoming.

Team and group development and enhancement has the general purpose of increasing the potential for achievement and output. It augments existing levels of creativity, dynamism and performance. As this takes place, the group develops its own commitment, identity, involvement, ownership and participation along the way.

## High performing teams and groups

Managers and supervisors need to be aware of the characteristics of high performing teams and groups. They can identify the extent and prevalence to which these exist within their own spheres of influence, and can take remedial action where required. These characteristics are:

- high levels of autonomy, the ability to self manage and self organise
- positive self regulation and self discipline, coupled with early identification of the negative aspects of this – bullying, victimisation and harassment
- fair and unambiguous performance targets capable of being achieved
- full responsibility for all aspects of production and output, quality assurance, customer relations, and customer complaints
- job titles and work do not include reference to status differentials or trappings
- team-based reward systems are available and payable to everyone who contributed
- full flexibility of work, multi-skilling and interchangeability between tasks and roles. Group roles are assigned to people's behavioural strengths and they are also assigned as a mark of individual and group development
- continuous development of skills, knowledge, qualities, capabilities and expertise; continuous attention to performance, quality and output; continuous attention to production, quality, volume, value and time; continuous attention to high levels of service and satisfaction
- simple, clear and supported policies and procedures covering rules and regulations, staff management, discipline, grievance and disputes
- continuous monitoring and review to ensure that the intended focus and direction is maintained and pursued.

## Conclusions

The creation of effective work groups increases the burdens placed on managers and supervisors in terms of the attention required to behavioural as well as

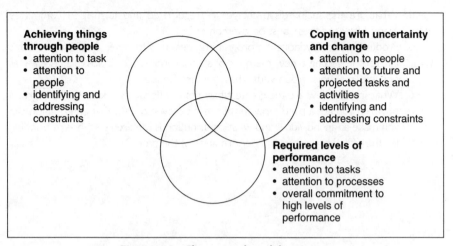

**Achieving things through people**
- attention to task
- attention to people
- identifying and addressing constraints

**Coping with uncertainty and change**
- attention to people
- attention to future and projected tasks and activities
- identifying and addressing constraints

**Required levels of performance**
- attention to tasks
- attention to processes
- overall commitment to high levels of performance

*Figure 12.5*   Chapter and model summary.

operational factors. Successful groups come about as the result of a combination of the effectiveness of each element. There is, therefore, a certain amount of groundwork that managers and supervisors have to carry out if effective team and group working is to be achieved. Some of this requires reference to points made in other chapters:

- quality of working life; reward structures (Chapter 2)
- style and approach of leadership (Chapter 13)
- adoption of effective communications between organisation and group, and within group (Chapter 3)
- presentation and interaction arrangements (Chapter 4).

These are then reinforced through the style of management that is in daily use – positive or negative, present or remote.

Other critical elements and factors that must be present are clarity, conformity, harmony, achievement, spirit and pride. This reflects the twin themes of attention to the group itself, and attention to the quality, value and effectiveness of the output that were identified at the start of the chapter.

Using the Model referred to at the start of Chapter 1 (Figure 1.1), the material in this Chapter is summarised in Figure 12.5.

QUESTIONS

1. Identify the main roles and functions of team and group leaders.
2. Identify the main reasons why subgroups and canteen cultures arise. What steps should managers and supervisors take to ensure that they are identified and dealt with early?
3. Produce an outline training and development programme to ensure that every member of a work group with which you are familiar can carry out at least three of the Belbin archetype team member roles.

4. What are the major disadvantages of regularised and formalised committee work? How can these best be overcome?
5. Produce a two-day induction programme designed to cover all of the problems inherent in getting a new member of staff as productive as possible, as early as possible in a work group with which you are familiar.
6. What, in your view, are the greatest barriers to effective work in the work group of which you are a part? How might these be overcome? What contribution can you make as an individual; and what contribution is required by those responsible for the effective running and performance of the group?

# M 13 Leadership

## Introduction

As organisations move away from the use of administrative systems and hierarchies, and towards the empowerment of individuals and groups, so they expect more of managers and supervisors in terms of accepting and wielding authority and influence. In other words, they expect more of the 'leadership function' of managers and supervisors. This is born out by some standard definitions:

- 'A leader is someone who exercises influence over other people.' (Huczynski and Buchanan, 1993).
- 'Leadership is the lifting of people's vision to a higher sight, the raising of their performance to a higher standard, the building of their personality beyond its normal limitations.' (P.F. Drucker, 1986).
- 'Leadership is creating a vision to which others can aspire, and energising them to work towards this vision.' (Anita Roddick, 1993).
- 'There is a need in all organisations for individual linking pins who will bind groups together, and represent their groups elsewhere in the organisation. Leadership concerns leaders themselves, subordinates and the task in hand.' (Handy, 1993).

Each of the key points indicated – exercising influence, raising of performance, energising, and binding together – are required of all managers and supervisors, whatever their status, seniority, field of activity, or length of service.

Leadership is a key part of management, and as a consequence, there have been a great many studies of leaders, directors and managers from all walks of life and all parts of history. By studying such a range, it is possible to infer and draw conclusions as to what was the basis for their success or otherwise, and what were the reasons and causes of this. These approaches have normally fallen under one or more of the following headings:

- traits and characteristics
- leadership styles
- leadership in its environment, or the contingency approach.

# Traits and characteristics

Attempts to identify the traits and characteristics present in successful leaders are largely inconclusive in that none identify all the attributes present in all successful situations.

However, the following are found to be applicable in most situations:

- *Inspiration:* the ability to interest people in the proposed venture or direction.
- *Communication:* the ability to communicate with all people involved, and using language that those on the receiving end will be able to understand and respond to.
- *Decision making:* the ability to take the right decisions in given situations, to take responsibility and be accountable for them, and to understand the consequences of particular courses of action.
- *Commitment:* to matters in hand, the people involved, and the organisation's interests.
- *Concern for staff:* respecting, trusting and committing oneself to them, and above all, treating them on the basis of equality and confidence.
- *Quality:* a personal, as well as professional, commitment to ensure that everything is done to the highest possible quality in the circumstances.
- *Sets of values:* with which others will identify and to which they will commit themselves.
- *Personal and professional integrity:* reflected in the managerial approach (and this is required whether an authoritarian, participative or democratic style is adopted.
- *Positive attitudes:* held by the leader and transmitted to staff and others involved.
- *Mutuality and dependency:* which is essential if integrity and trust are to be established (see Box 13.1).

## Box 13.1   Traits and characteristics: the Rosemary Stewart studies

Rosemary Stewart (1967) summarised studies of leadership carried out in the 1950s in the USA. These studies had the twin purpose of establishing the traits and characteristics required of successful military officers; and those required of business leaders.

The following list was produced.

- Judgement
- Integrity
- Human and interpersonal skills
- Dependability
- Fairness
- Dedication
- Cooperation
- Initiative
- Foresight
- Drive
- Decisiveness
- Emotional stability
- Ambition
- Objectivity

The problem found with this approach was that it was very difficult to pin down these qualities and to measure the true extent of their prevalence in individuals. For full effectiveness, it was necessary to observe their presence, or to infer it, over a period of time.

Subsequently, such a list was found to take little account of the negative attributes that may be present, especially stubbornness, vanity, self-centredness, arrogance and conceit. In a subsequent study (1999) of the wars of the 20th Century, even more extreme characteristics were found to have existed in those responsible for their inception and direction – these characteristics included delusions of infallibility and immortality, vain gloriousness, and using the military situation for personal ends.

Sources:  Rosemary Stewart (1990) *An Anatomy of Leadership*, Harper & Row; Channel 4, *Great Military Blunders*.

## Leadership styles

Leadership styles are normally classified on an authoritarian–democratic continuum, in which it is assumed that authoritarianism and a democratic approach are opposite ends of the same spectrum. Whichever is adopted, any leadership or management style must be supported by mutual trust, respect and confidence between manager and subordinates, or between leader and follower. If these qualities are not present, then no style is effective. There must also be a clarity of purpose and direction, and an overall commitment to purpose. Participation can only genuinely exist if this clarity is present, and an authoritarian approach will be truly effective only if everyone is clear about what is required, and why this style of leadership or management has been adopted (see Table 13.1 and Figure 13.1).

It should be clear that whatever the style adopted, it brings obligations and commitments as a result. Whichever style is adopted must also include the following elements:

- *Two-way communication:* authoritarianism especially is both diluted and corrupted when it becomes apparent or perceived that bottom-up communication is not possible as a result of the management style. This always reduces the effect of an authoritarian approach. Whichever style is adopted, two-way communication leads to problems being identified early, and steps being taken before they become dramas and crises. It also enables understanding and support to be generated for specific activities.
- *Satisfaction:* must be present in the work. However relaxed the style of leadership and management, people will still become demotivated and disenchanted if there is no intrinsic merit or achievement in the work itself.
- *Attitude:* must also be positive. It is quite possible to have a negative and destructive attitude present in participative situations; similarly, many authoritarian situations are successful because there is also a very positive attitude.

A full understanding by all involved of each other's point of view and each other's hopes, aims and aspirations must be present. This is a problem in authoritarian situations; on the other hand, there is no reason why this cannot be achieved, provided that openness of communication and mutuality of trust and interest can be maintained. Similarly, in participative situations, discussion of real issues may be avoided.

The presence of barriers, especially psychological barriers, must be understood and addressed. Again in participative situations, these may be apparent but not tackled; and again, the positive approach to authoritarianism may result in a good authoritarian leader identifying and breaking these down.

Priorities must be clear and established, understood and agreed to by all. This tends to become tainted at the authoritarian extreme, where it is very easy for the

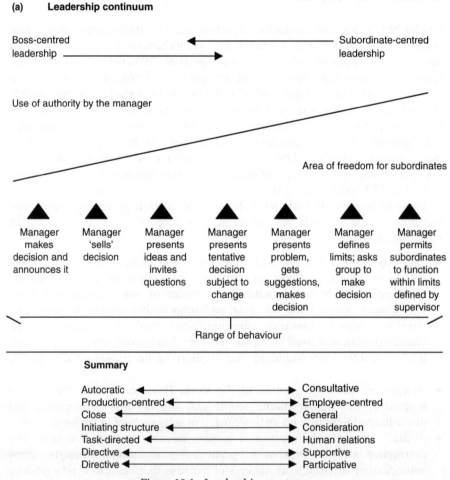

(a)    **Leadership continuum**

Boss-centred leadership

Subordinate-centred leadership

Use of authority by the manager

Area of freedom for subordinates

| Manager makes decision and announces it | Manager 'sells' decision | Manager presents ideas and invites questions | Manager presents tentative decision subject to change | Manager presents problem, gets suggestions, makes decision | Manager defines limits; asks group to make decision | Manager permits subordinates to function within limits defined by supervisor |

Range of behaviour

**Summary**

Autocratic ←——————→ Consultative
Production-centred ←——————→ Employee-centred
Close ←——————→ General
Initiating structure ←——————→ Consideration
Task-directed ←——————→ Human relations
Directive ←——————→ Supportive
Directive ←——————→ Participative

*Figure 13.1*   Leadership spectrum.

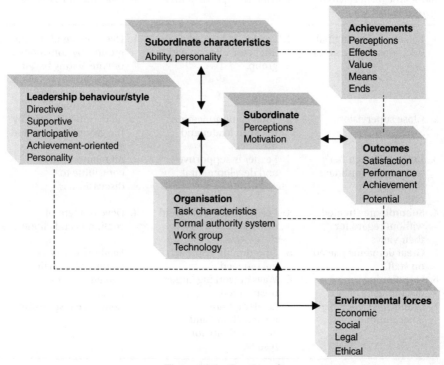

*Figure 13.1*   Continued.

person with authority to impose personal priorities and superimpose those required by the organisation or operations, and at the participative extreme, where those imposed by the group tend to override organisational or operational priorities.

## Leadership in its environment, or contingency approaches

The contingency approach to leadership takes the view that, while traits and styles are present, they require adaptation to the pressures of the working environment. This requires acknowledging the pressures that exist between the organisation and its environment and the pressures that exist within the working environment. Elements that can and cannot be controlled must be identified, separated and recognised.

This approach was first adopted by John Adair who studied leadership in its environment from the point of view of:

Table 13.1   Leadership and management styles

| Autocratic (benevolent or tyrannical) | Consultative/participative | Democratic/participative |
|---|---|---|
| 1. Leader makes all final decisions for the group. | 1. Leader makes decisions after consultation with group. | 1. Decisions made by the group – by consultation or vote. Voting based on the principles of one person, one vote; majority rules. |
| 2. Close supervision. | 2. Total communication between leader and members. | 2. All members bound by the group decision and support it. |
| 3. Individual member's interests subordinate to those of the organisation. | 3. Leader is supportive and developmental. | 3. All members may contribute to discussion. |
| 4. Subordinates treated without regard for their views. | 4. Leader is accessible and discursive. | 4. Development of coalitions and cliques. |
| 5. Great demands placed on staff. | 5. Questioning approach encouraged. | 5. Leadership role is assumed by Chair. |
| 6. Questioning discouraged. | 6. Ways of working largely unspecified. | 6. Agreed ways of working. |
| 7. Conformist/coercive environment. | 7. Leader retains responsibility and accountability for results. | 7. Collective responsibity |

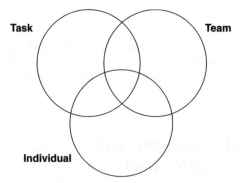

Task          Team

Individual

*Figure 13.2*   Adair model of leadership.

- achieving the task
- building and developing the team
- concern for the individual (see Figure 13.2).

Adair (1968, 1998) stated that, having identified the pressures, strengths and weaknesses of the particular situation, these factors always required attention in

| Table 13.2 | Key leadership functions | |
|---|---|---|
| Direction | Planning | Decision making |
| Communication | Appraisal | Creativity |
| Coordination | Control | Resourcefulness |
| Assessment | Development | Flexibility |
| | | Adaptability |

every set of circumstances. As the result, the key leadership functions required are as shown in Table 13.2.

From this, the view was developed that characteristics, traits and qualities could be identified and developed; and that once these were developed, they could then be applied to any situation. The part that could *not* be trained or developed in this way was situational knowledge and understanding; this became the responsibility of organisations and managers in particular situations. A key part of the contingency approach is therefore that leadership skill requires modification and adaptation in all situations if authority and influence, as well as direction and purpose, are to be truly effective.

It is therefore worth summarising briefly these sources of authority and influence.

## Sources of authority and influence

Authority and influence may be wielded legitimately or illegitimately. Their sources are:

- *Physical:* the power exerted by individuals because of their bodily shape, size and strength in relation to others. Large multinational and multi-location organisations also exert their own equivalent of physical power and influence.
- *Tradition:* whereby the ability to command and influence derives from accepted customs and norms, e.g., the hereditary principle whereby office or position is handed down from parent to child, or where a manager grooms a successor in order to succeed them when they move on.
- *Divine right and the natural order:* each have been used in the past to reinforce the position and influence of those in power; each is used most insidiously at present, for example, when a powerful or well known personality uses phrases such as, 'Do you know who I am?'
- *Expertise:* held by individuals and groups, it is a resource to be used positively and legitimately when required; it can also be used illegitimately to block or corrupt progress.
- *Charisma:* this is the effect of one personality on others, the ability to exert influence based on force of a personality. Again, this may be positive or negative.
- *Resource command:* this is the ability to influence others – again, positively or negatively – based on the ability to command resources.

- *Reward:* the ability to influence behaviour and activities by holding out and offering rewards for compliance and acceptance.
- *Punishment:* the ability to threaten, punish and penalise those in a particular situation as the result of carrying out particular activities.
- *Coercion:* the ability to bribe, bully or threaten people into doing things that they would not otherwise do.
- *Conformity:* where organisations and managers set distinctive norms, attitudes, values and behaviour standards which those who wish to be a part of a situation are required to accept.
- *Legal/rational:* the wielding of influence and authority according to a prescribed, pre-set, and understood and accepted set of rules and norms; this is the overwhelming mode of authority and influence used in the majority of organisations. It is a key feature of organisation design; though it is clear that other forms of influence become present once the organisation has been designed and is operating.

## Are leaders born or made?

With the exception of the major religious leaders of the world – Jesus Christ, Mohammed, the Buddha and Zarathustra – leaders are made, not born. It is quite true that some people have more highly apparent skills and qualities of leadership than others; nevertheless, they become good and effective leaders only by working on these and, where necessary, presenting them to best advantage. As examples:

- *Julius Caesar:* was able to exert his authority for over twenty years because, as a political leader he never took rewards – especially illegitimate rewards – that were available to him in his position within the Roman Senate. And as a military leader, he never asked his men to do anything that he himself was not prepared to do (if they walked, so did he; if they went without food, so did he). He also walked with them in triumphal processions at the end of his campaigns.
- *William the Conqueror:* was able to put together a force to invade England in 1065–1066 because he was able to persuade others with influence in northern France (Normandy) of the rightness and merits of his case (the throne of England had been promised to him, and then usurped by Harold the Saxon). This relied on his powers of persuasion, which he had to develop.
- *Adolf Hitler:* was manufactured by the presentation and propaganda techniques of Josef Goebbels and Leni Riefenstal so that the people – his followers – had an image and aspirations with which to associate him. He and his party then reinforced this by gaining the active support of the army, civil service and heavy industry; and the creation of new modern industries, especially cars, civil engineering and armaments, with which to provide a bankrupt country with work.
- *Richard Branson:* has built the reputation and brand of Virgin on product and service excellence, quality and value. He has reinforced this through a series of

high profile activities – the fastest sea crossing of the Atlantic, attempts to circumnavigate the world in a balloon, media coverage of him serving drinks to customers on his airline, dressing up in bridal gear to launch the Virgin Bride part of the group. In practice, he never goes into any line of business without a full business and investment appraisal, costing and projections with which he is entirely satisfied, and by hiring top experts from existing players elsewhere in the particular sector.

In each case, traits, styles and the relationship with the environment are apparent and exhibited. In order to be able to do this to best advantage, each has to be identified, learned, developed and improved, in the same way as any expert in any other field. Also, as with other expertise, some parts come more easily than others. However, they each have to be tackled. For example:

- *Determination:* Caesar only managed to cross the Channel to England at the fourth attempt; Richard Branson had three attempts at the Blue Riband crossing of the Atlantic; and four at the non-stop balloon flight (at which he remained unsuccessful).
- *Commitment:* William the Conqueror burnt his boats (hence the expression) on the south coast of England before setting off to do battle at Hastings; Branson committed himself to a five-year plan at Virgin Rail and refused to be put off by difficulties that became apparent in the first two years.
- *Adversity and setbacks:* Hitler was unable to accept or cope with these; and this applies to many political leaders. Indeed, many political leaders find themselves unable to admit to any mistakes in any circumstances. This always calls into question their overall determination, commitment and above all, integrity.

## Lessons for managers

Staff expect all of these qualities in their own particular situations and environments from their manager or supervisor. These skills and qualities therefore require developing in the particular context of a given situation and, as stated above, this must be allied to operational and environmental knowledge and understanding.

### Charisma and identity

All people at work give their manager or supervisor an identity, either positive or negative. It is, therefore, the manager's responsibility to ensure that this is positive, mutually acceptable and productive. Aspiring managers have therefore to ask themselves:

- What is the nature of the identity that I wish to have?
- How do I get it?
- How do I develop it from there?
- How do I know I have got it right?
- How do I ensure that this is acceptable to everyone?

There is a personal and professional responsibility in doing this. Many adversarial, bullying, and downright unpleasant, managers have quite consciously adopted this approach, normally for one or more of the following reasons:

- It is the only approach that they know, and they have never been taught otherwise.
- They see themselves as strident, determined or larger than life (rather than as a bully).
- They adopt it in the always mistaken belief that it never did them any harm when they were on the receiving end (the fact that they adopt it proves that it did harm).
- It is a demonstrably successful approach within their organisational occupation (i.e., bullies are known, believed or perceived to make progress up career ladders). Where this is the case, it is very hard to prevent those with ambitions from consciously adopting this approach.

It therefore becomes clear that the choice is consciously made and that skills, qualities, attitudes and behaviour are then learned, developed and refined.

## Perceptual gap

It is however, always important to recognise the difference between:

- the way managers see and perceive themselves
- the way staff actually see and perceive the manager
- the way managers think the staff see them (see Box 13.2).

The greater the overall integrity of the relationship, the more easily misperceptions become apparent and can be remedied. Whichever leadership

## Box 13.2  The perceptual gap

Research carried out by Charles Handy at the London Business School centred on a group of managers and supervisors who prided themselves on their open, approachable and supportive style of management. They had become self-congratulatory to the point of complacency, and held themselves up as a model for others within their organisation to follow.

When a survey was carried out on their own staff to try and ascertain whether this was the case, a very different result was achieved. Staff who worked for these managers viewed them as oppressive and adversarial. These same managers who had scored themselves highly on openness, honesty and participation had been scored very low on each of these qualities by their staff.

Source:  C.B. Handy (1984) *Understanding Organisations*, Penguin.

approach is adopted and engaged, the integrity of the relationship with the staff must never be compromised; and if this is (or is likely) to happen, the style and traits adopted must be changed.

## Social leadership and role models

Everyone's perceptions of what a leader should be like is influenced by the media, and the known, believed or perceived adoption and identification of major public individuals as 'role models'. It is important to recognise:

- the power of the media, especially television, in producing these influences
- the influence that powerful figures have over their own presentation
- the use of colour, dress, backdrops to reinforce the desired presentation (see also Chapter 3).

It is further important to recognise that:

- people in leadership positions within organisations do not have the same advantages and so they have to make their own
- people within organisations nevertheless have expectations of leaders/ managers and these have either to be met, or else some other qualities substituted that more than meet previous expectations
- people in managerial positions do not have the perceived charisma of such public figures as Richard Branson, Madonna or David Beckham; yet because they are expected by their staff to have it, it is essential to reinforce positive identity.

Just as with public figures and the media, identity is reinforced positively and negatively by each activity undertaken, e.g., the handling of problems, weekly meetings, scheduling and prioritising of work. This is in addition to reinforcement through general interactions (see Box 13.3).

### Box 13.3   'I'm sorry'

Good leaders and good managers share praise with their staff and accept the blame themselves when things go wrong. This goes with the job (see Chapters 1 and 2).

Externally, managers must never blame their staff for mistakes even if they were the fault of the staff. If a mistake is made, managers must acknowledge their responsibility and accountability. Any inquest can then be conducted within the department, and the reasons why things went wrong can be established without apportioning blame or seeking victims.

The only departure from this is where a member of the department has deliberately destroyed or sabotaged a particular task. This is then dealt with as a disciplinary matter (Chapter 10).

## Knowing your limitations

The best leaders recognise the things that they can do and the things that they cannot do. (The worst never acknowledge those things that they cannot do, but rather give the impression that they can do everything.). It is essential therefore to commit to the following:

- acknowledging when answers to questions and problems are not known, and at the same time making a commitment to find the answers out quickly
- allowing people who do have greater expertise to take the lead and give advice – and evaluating their expertise (see Box 13.4).

## Box 13.4   Promoting tradespeople

It used to be the tradition that the best tradesperson or expert was promoted into the leadership or management position. This is fundamentally flawed – organisations that do this are losing their best tradespeople to positions that they may not be able to carry out. The fact that they are good at their trade does not make them automatically good at management because a complete set of skills and qualities has to be learned.

A very high profile current example of this is the football industry. This industry is riddled with ex-great players who have subsequently turned out to be poor managers. Indeed, many of the best managers in the football industry have come from much more lowly parts of the reputational hierarchy; and they have subsequently taken steps to ensure that they have been trained so that they can be expert in this part of the industry.

It is absolutely true, however, that any manager must learn the boundaries, pressures and commitments involved in the particular jobs and tasks for which they are responsible. For example, the project manager in charge of the Twickenham rugby union stadium development over the period 1993–1997 had never been to a rugby ground or match before he was put in charge of this project. Once he was appointed, however, he took an active personal and professional interest; and is now a regular follower and watcher of the game. This enthusiasm he developed as the result of being appointed to the particular leadership position.

## Remoteness

With the best will and commitment in the world, organisational and operational pressures can, and do, cause managers to become remote from their operations from time to time. This is especially a problem for senior managers and directors in expanding and diversifying organisations.

Problems arise when:

- remoteness causes psychological distance and, in the worst cases, alienation (e.g., in the banking and civil engineering industries)
- remoteness causes serious industrial relations problems brought on by misunderstandings and conflict; and these are generated, in turn, by frontline managers and supervisors working in isolation (often either under-trained or untrained) from their own superiors (e.g., car production in the UK, with the notable exception of the Japanese companies)
- remoteness causes bullying, victimisation and harassment to become endemic (e.g., the police service, the education service, the National Health Service)
- remoteness causes a general complacency about the effectiveness of operations

As the result, Adriano was able to reposition, not the activities themselves, but the context in which they were carried out. A unified system of billing was worked out that guaranteed that the price on the shelves would always match those on the checkouts.

A 'crewing' arrangement was worked out so that groups of people took responsibility for particular shelf lines, and how they filled these was a matter for their own self-determination.

As the result, productivity on the nightshift shelf-filling activities went up; and customer complaints and stress levels on the tills went down.

Source: *Back to the Floor*, BBC2, 'Sainsbury's Supermarkets' (2000).

Problems are addressed by:

- prioritising activities that ensure that managers spend at least some time with their staff
- understanding the generally detrimental effects that lack of quality contact has on overall performance
- continually reflecting on questions such as: 'When did I last meet with my staff?', 'How long for?', 'What were the effects?', 'What did they want from me that I did and didn't deliver?'
- walking the job wherever possible to reinforce the integrity, visibility and identity of the relationship (see Chapter 2), and understanding that if this does not, or cannot, happen, the staff will inevitably begin to call into question the integrity of the relationship (and this happens even if managers know and believe themselves to be acting within the highest possible standards).

# Rewards

Leaders give rewards to their followers. This dates back through history – victorious generals allowed their soldiers to loot, Kings rewarded their supporters with Dukedoms or Earldoms, over which they were allowed to hold absolute sway and rule them as they saw fit.

By the same token, organisation followers expect rewards. In managerial terms, these are based on:

- understanding what is, and what is not, available to them in the situation at the outset
- expecting the rewards promised or indicated, provided that the results are forthcoming
- expecting that organisations and their managers will keep their word on this
- expecting that they will be looked upon positively provided that they do their job well and in the ways required (see Chapter 5).

The loyalty and commitment of followers and staff is compromised when one or more of these are not delivered. Managers therefore commit themselves to delivery once a promise or inference is made. Moreover, if rewards promised are not delivered due to circumstances beyond the individual manager's control, then problems are certain to occur anyway, and the manager needs to recognise this and be prepared for it.

## Toxic rewards

Problems also arise when rewards are given for something other than operational and functional performance, especially when they are given to known, believed or perceived favourites. These problems are as follows:

- Receivers of the favours treat the giver with contempt because they know fully the basis on which the rewards have been given.
- Those who do not receive the favours treat both givers and receivers with contempt.
- Those who wish to gain the favours and rewards set about jumping through the necessary hoops rather than concentrating on operational requirements.
- Those who do not wish to remain in such a situation concentrate their efforts on getting out, rather than on the matters in hand.
- Those who do remain in the situation, will tend to exploit it as far as possible for their own self-serving ends.

---

**EXAMPLE**

In 1992, eight members of a corporate human resource management function of a large County Council came up with a proposal for making 'merit pay' awards. These awards could be of anything up to 20% of basic salary. They would be given at the discretion of the Council's Chief Officers to staff, in their opinion, who 'had enhanced the corporate and staff HR performance in ways above, and beyond, normal expectations'. The proposal was approved by the team's Chief Officer and by the Council's Chief Executive. It went to the Council's Personnel Committee which also approved it, and it was implemented in 1993.

It was killed stone dead the following year when one member of the Personnel Committee, a Conservative, noticed that, of the eleven awards made, eight had been awarded to those who devised the scheme in the first place.

---

## Distributive and integrative rewards

It is usual to distinguish these as follows:

- distributive is where one group or individual is rewarded at the expense of others
- integrative is where everyone is rewarded.

### Distributive

In general, a distributive approach to rewards is unwholesome and divisive. This should only be contemplated where there is a genuine and publicly supportable case that a group or individual has made an exceptional contribution outside the normal remit of activities; or to bring the lower paid up to more equitable levels of reward (see Box 13.5).

## Box 13.5 Distributive rewards

The counter view is presented by overtly high trade, income and profit frontline generators, for example, IT specialists, stockbrokers, foreign exchange traders, and industrial and commercial goods sales people. These groups assert that, because they are the ones who actually generate the work and income, they should be rewarded accordingly. This is a spurious argument. Differentials should be expressed in the salary ranges, not the bonuses.

If the organisation is well run, everyone should be in a job that contributes to the frontline performance. Thus, for example, the quality of performance of sales people is dependent upon the efforts with which their diaries and schedules are managed, the speed at which back office and support functions translate orders gained into deliveries, the speed at which deliveries are made, and the quality of after-sales service. Seen in this way, the salesperson – or specialist stockbroker and trader – is simply the visible tip of a fully integrated whole.

### Integrative

This is overtly much more equitable and, so long as everything else is right, works the best. The normal basis is that additional rewards are distributed as an equal percentage of salary. Thus, for example, if 10% of salary bonus is awarded across the board, the percentage is the same for everyone. The amounts clearly vary though – someone on a salary of £10,000 per annum would receive a 10% bonus of £1,000; someone on a salary of £30,000 per annum would receive a 10% bonus of £3,000; and so on. Any problems can then be related to salary rather than bonus levels.

# Establishing culture, values and attitudes

A key part of the leadership function of managers is the establishment of required and acceptable ways of doing things, standards of attitudes, behaviour and performance, and personal and professional conduct. These standards are established and agreed by:

- stating clearly what they are and why they are required
- stating clearly how they are to be reinforced
- stating clearly – and applying – the sanctions that are to be imposed when these standards are not met.

Problems initially arise when:

- standards are not clear
- standards are not enforced, or enforced equitably.

In the latter case especially, as the EU and UK both tighten individual rights at places of work, the onus is placed on organisations and their managers to demonstrate that they have, at all times, acted with fairness and reasonableness when enforcing standards. Organisations are normally now required to explain in great detail why someone is treated differently to others in overtly similar sets of circumstances.

## Ethics

Interrelated with this is the requirement to establish and reinforce what is normally 'right' in the situation. The greater the fundamental basis of integrity (see Chapter 2), the more straightforward this is to establish. They key issues here for managers in their leadership role are:

- establishing standards of ordinary common decency as the basis of supplier, staff and customer management
- establishing an operational basis of effectiveness designed to ensure, as far as possible, the long-term viability, profitability and security of their own domain
- identifying and stamping out unwholesome or dishonest practices, e.g., fiddling production and output figures, blaming suppliers for product shortfalls, or quality assurance problems
- identifying and stamping out abhorrent and unacceptable behaviour – bullying, victimisation, discrimination, harassment, vandalism, violence and theft (see Box 13.6).

## Box 13.6  Absence of standards

The absence of standards is always clearly indicated in disasters and serious disputes. The case of the *Herald of Free Enterprise*, operated by Townsend Thoresen, illustrates this (see also p. 198).

This car ferry, operating on a crossing between Dover and Zeebrugge, capsized on 6 March 1987 with the loss of 192 lives. The reason why the ship capsized was because the bow doors were left open. The inquiry into the disaster found:

- no evidence at all of ordinary common decency in staff or operations management; after the disaster the company immediately sought to blame a single junior member of staff for the tragedy
- the practice of closing the bow doors as the ship set sail was ordered by company directors on the basis of short-term expediency and tiny cost advantage, rather than long-term viability, security and integrity
- clearly stated safety standards (see Chapter 11) were not enforced; self-evident through the bow doors having been left open on the occasion of the tragedy. The company also was found to have sailed so short-handed as to have been unable to have effectively fought a fire should it have occurred or to have been able to evacuate the ship via the lifeboats should this have been necessary.

The inquiry concluded that the operation was riddled with 'the disease of sloppiness'. The inquiry went on to assert that the overwhelming reason for this was that the ship's crew behaved as it did because it was required to do so by the company leadership. This was reinforced by evidence given by junior and middle managers, as well as the ship's crew, which clearly stated that the crew on board at the time of the tragedy had behaved in ways both acceptable and required by the company before the tragedy occurred.

## Conclusions

It is clearly apparent that the leadership aspects of the management and supervisory task are both complex and also critically important to overall success. It is also apparent that each of the skills and qualities indicated can be learned and enhanced, and a commitment made that they will be used and deployed when required.

Leadership is a very practical part of the management task. It is essential that it is learned, developed and applied if the rest of the tasks and skills required are to be carried out effectively.

More generally, all leaders – managers or otherwise – have to have authority, influence and followers. For managers and supervisors, this is quite straightforward – each is given as the result of the appointment to the managerial or supervisory position. Measures of authority are given and received upon appointment, influence is wielded through the style and approach adopted, and the staff are the followers. From whichever point of view this part of managerial and supervisory practice is studied, therefore, it is essential to understand the full content of the leadership part of the position, and to be able to identify, practice and develop those skills and qualities indicated in this chapter.

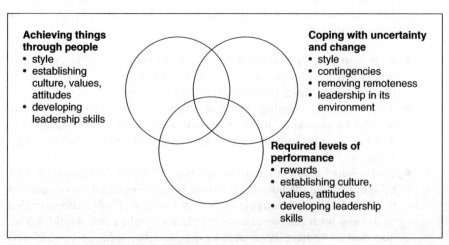

*Figure 13.3* Chapter and model summary.

Using the Model referred to at the start of Chapter 1 (Figure 1.1), the material in this chapter is summarised in Figure 13.3.

QUESTIONS

1. What are the key attributes of your manager or supervisor (or college or university tutor) in their leadership role? To what extent is their effectiveness limited by the constraints in which they find themselves; and to what extent is their effectiveness limited or enhanced by the qualities that they exhibit?

2. To what extent may the last three UK Prime Ministers be considered successful? Identify the criteria and means by which they are judged, and state whether or not you think these are valid and reliable.

3. Devise a leadership training programme for junior managers and supervisors with aspirations to become more senior; and to become more effective in their current positions. This should be of 3–6 months duration. It should indicate aims and objectives, content, learning methods and the means by which success/failure would be judged and evaluated.

4. What is the role of organisational leadership in a crisis or disaster?

5. What are the best ways of securing a positive identity and visibility within your own organisation? To what extent does the organisation's ways of working limit and enhance these? How might these factors be overcome?

6. Devise a programme of self-development for yourself, with the purpose of enhancing your own leadership skills and qualities. What are to be the criteria for success? How, when, where and by whom should this be measured for success or failure?

# ■ ˇ 14 Conclusion

## Introduction

In the first chapter of this book, it was stated that the basic skills required of all managers and supervisors were:

- the ability to get things done through people
- the ability to cope with change and uncertainty
- the ability to identify, establish and develop required and desired levels of performance.

Each subsequent chapter has then sought to illustrate the ways in which these are combined, in more or less universal sets of circumstances that apply to all managers and supervisors, whatever their sector or location. These are sometimes referred to as *subordinate* or *transferable* skills.

None of these skills are an end in themselves – they are all capable of development, improvement and refinement. Increasingly, managers and supervisors are required, both by membership of any professional or managerial association, and also by EU and UK legislation, to undertake continuous professional development and updating in order that what they carry out in organisations reflects current levels of expertise and best practice.

## The professionalisation of management and supervision

There is a clear drive towards the professionalisation of management. This is based on attention to expertise, knowledge and qualifications, and the relationship between these and the value added to organisations by expert managers and supervisors, and the levels of skill required.

The classical professions – medicine, law, the priesthood and the army – are identified through having the following properties.

- *Distinctive expertise:* not available elsewhere in society or its individual members.
- *Distinctive body of knowledge and skill:* required by all those who aspire to practice in the profession, and which is formally taught.

- *Entry barriers:* in the form of examinations, time serving and learning from experts.
- *Formal qualifications:* given as the result of acquiring and proving the body of knowledge and clearing the entry barriers through formal examination.
- *Distinctive morality:* e.g., for medicine, the commitment to keep people a live as long as possible; for law, a commitment to represent the client's best interests; for the priesthood, a commitment to godliness and to serve the congregation's best interests; for the army, to fight within stated rules of war.
- *High status and value:* professions make a distinctive and positive contribution to both their organisations, and to individual members of the society.
- *Self-regulating and self-disciplining:* professions set their own rules, codes of conduct, standards of performance and qualifications; and they establish their own bodies for dealing with problems, complaints and allegations of malpractice.
- *Unlimited reward levels:* according to preferred levels of charges and the demands of society, and the willingness of customers and clients to pay.
- *Self-discipline:* commitment to personal standards of behaviour in the pursuit of professional excellence.
- *Continuous development:* of knowledge and skills; a commitment to keep abreast of all developments and initiatives in the field.
- *Governance:* by institutions established by the profession itself.

In absolute terms, management falls short in many areas. Formal qualifications are not a prerequisite to practice, though they are highly desirable and increasingly sought after. Discipline and regulation of managers is overwhelmingly a matter for organisations and management institutions. Management institutions and professional bodies act as focal points for debate, and they also have a lobbying function; they do not however, act as regulators.

Nevertheless, this gives a clear indication of the development and direction – the professionalisation – of the principles and practice of management. Many of the skills required above all, the ability to analyse, evaluate, come to an informed opinion and support it – are clearly equivalent to those of medicine and the law. Moreover, effective development and improvement can only be undertaken once there is an enduring personal commitment (see Box 14.1).

## Box 14.1 The professionalisation of management: Artisan Group Ltd

'I believe in as hard a line as possible being taken by the management on the staff, a harder line being taken by the owners on the management, and the hardest line of all being taken by the owners on themselves. Creating this environment is very difficult and so a strong approach must be taken in every area. The working atmosphere must be tightly controlled and be all-pervasive or else it will not work.

The vital ground rules must be ascertained (no more, no less) and then they must be stuck to absolutely rigidly. The Japanese conformity approach should be made to look weak when it comes to the ground rules. On the other hand, once these rules are adhered to, as much flexibility as possible should be allowed. In this way, individuality is achieved through conformity. As long as the important things are taken care of, people can do what they want and express themselves freely through their jobs. I don't care how they do something as long as the end product is good. Mavericks who can work within the guidelines are welcome and a great source of creativity and inspiration.

It may be possible to summarise the ground rules into simply one thing. You must keep to your agreements. This encourages the development of a person's integrity, their ability to make choices, and their sense of responsibility. It then gives us the opportunity to ask them to agree to what we really want – i.e., be at work at 8.00 am. If they agree to this, we will hold them to it precisely. Two minutes past 8.00 is not 8.00 and provided we can maintain enough front (and maintain this level of integrity ourselves) then we will pull them up on it.

Reasons are not relevant (e.g., the bus was late). It then becomes a matter of personal power which we want to foster in the staff. It is possible to act as if you are responsible for everything that happens in your life, whether this is true or not. Doing this eventually means it will end up as being true in your reality. It is possible to look ahead and manipulate the environment. If you expect traffic, then you can leave earlier. If the staff were paid £100,000 just for turning up on time, they would be there. This principle can be applied to everything we want and although it may seem strange, in the long-term it will benefit the individual as much as us'.

Source: David Scott (1993) Artisan Group Ltd., Business Plan.

There are three final general points that should be made:

- fashions and fads in management
- knowing your limitations
- references to old, new and future sectors of activity.

## Fashions and fads

Fashionable and faddish approaches to management have been an enduring managerial problem, at least since the end of World War II. For a long period of time, there was substantial received wisdom that being a good senior or executive manager was only possible if the person had previously undertaken military officer training. This view was only truly destroyed when the Royal Military College for officer training at Sandhurst decided that it would introduce management training as an *additional* feature of its overall programme. And there still remains an enduring prejudice, especially among shareholders' representatives that the best managers are men.

## Recent fads and the rise of management consultants

The problem has been compounded more recently through faddish approaches to management, very often sold at great expense to struggling companies by firms of management consultants. These faddish approaches are based overwhelmingly on the false premise that the complexities of management indicated in this and many other books, and also in the reality of business and public service experience, can be made simple somehow.

There is clearly a place for management consultants, just as there is for consultant, in the medical sector. However, few organisations ever get a second opinion from another firm of management consultants (yet this is commonplace in medical practice) in order either to confirm the view of the first, or to present alternative diagnoses from which the company (the patient) can then draw their own conclusions.

The management consultancy approach, unfortunately, has all too often taken to persuading companies to buy what the consultancy practice has to sell rather than attempt a serious remedy or improvement in performance. The high levels of charges made by the major consulting firms also make it psychologically and behaviourally very difficult to reject their advice.

The end result has been that those approaches – total quality management, business process re-engineering, benchmarking, empowerment – have done little except enhance short and medium-term shareholder value. They have done nothing, above all, to ensure long-term corporate success; nor do any of these approaches genuinely concern themselves with staff, supplier or customer interests. Above all, none of them show how the new restructured organisation is going to recover its costs/investment in restructuring from the sale of real products and services to real customers; or in public services, how this is going to result in more clients receiving better services more quickly.

All too frequently these simply become additional pressures and constraints within which managers and supervisors have to work. These pressures only recede when there is demonstrably sufficient quality of management available to ensure that shareholders' representatives do not turn elsewhere for a quick fix even when this is so demonstrably wrong.

## Knowing when and where to go for help

Clearly, not everyone can do everything or know everything! It is therefore necessary to be able to know when and where to turn for help, advice and guidance, and for expert and executive contributions, when necessary. Indeed, one of the things that sets many successful people apart from their peers is the fact that they are prepared to concentrate on their own strengths, and hire the necessary expertise to carry out the parts that they themselves do not know. There is also no harm in checking things with others in any case.

---

**EXAMPLE**

A junior doctor on duty at a hospital had a decision to make. A patient had been admitted with a condition that he recognised and he knew the right drugs to prescribe. But these drugs were recommended for a number of conditions and in different dosages. The junior doctor was not sure what dose was right for this condition. So he had to make a quick decision – would he interrupt the supervising registrar during a meeting to check which was correct, or would he guess at the answer?

What was the problem? The welfare, and maybe even the life, of the patient was at stake. However, something else also had to be considered – the reputation, and maybe even the career, of the junior doctor. If he interrupted the registrar to ask about the dosage, he was making a public statement that he did not know the answer, as well as making himself unpopular.

The junior doctor decided to guess – and his guess turned out to be correct, and there were no negative effects. However, problems like this are commonplace; and they tend to be compounded by organisational, social, peer and superior pressures requiring everyone to give the impression that they know what they are talking about all of the time.

Source: Tannen (1999) *Talking from 9 to 5*, Virago.

---

## Old and new sectors

All of these skills and qualities apply to all sectors equally, though their emphasis clearly varies. For example:

- a great deal of behind the scenes work in dot.com and telecom companies in the *new* industries is mundane and repetitive, and so the problems of motivation, morale and satisfaction apply to these in exactly the same way as to traditional factory production or retail activity.
- The satisfaction inherent in work such as nursing, teaching and flying airliners is enhanced or destroyed by the quality, skill and expertise of management and supervision that is there to support those who actually carry it out.
- The fundamentals of visibility, integrity, respect and value can be applied equally to deep mining, shipbuilding, retail and internet companies. There is nothing to prevent managers and supervisors at all levels being visible and having access to their staff in these or any other sectors.

## Finally . . .

The range of skills, qualities and expertise indicated and discussed are essential in order to create, maintain and develop a working environment where high and effective levels of performance can be generated. To do this takes a great range of skill, as we have seen. And in a business and public service environment where ever-greater attention is being paid to the contribution that managers and supervisors actually make, it is essential that this range of skills is present, and capable of being developed and applied in any situation with which the individual is faced. Moreover, the commitment to professionalisation makes it certain that these skills are known to be required, to be demonstrably present, and capable of development and improvement, in future managerial and supervisory appointments.

# ▼ Bibliography

Adair, J. (1968) *Action Centred Leadership.* Wiley.
Adair, J. (1998) *Leadership in Action.* Penguin.
Ash, M.K. (1985) *On People Management.* MacDonald.
Belbin, R.M. (1986) *High Performing Teams.* Wiley.
Cartwright, R. (1994) *In Charge: Managing Yourself.* Blackwell.
Cartwright, R. (2000) *Mastering the Business Environment.* Palgrave.
Drucker, P.F. (1986) *The Practice of Management.* Heinemann.
Drucker, P.F. (1988) *The Effective Executive.* Fontana.
Drucker, P.F. (1999) *Management Challenges for the 21$^{st}$ Century.* HarperCollins.
Goodworth, C.T. (1990) *Recruitment as Selection.* Gower.
Handy, C.B. (1990) *Understanding Organisations.* Penguin.
Handy, C.B. (1993) *The Empty Raincoat.* Penguin.
Herzberg, F. (1960) *Work and Motivation.* Wiley.
Huczynski, A. and Buchanan, D. (1993) *Organizational Behaviour.* Practice Ltd.
Kent State University (1997) *Developments in the Understanding of Workforce Motivation.* Ohio.
Lessem, R.S. (1987) *Intrapreneurship.* Wildwood.
Maslow, A.H. (1960) *Motivation.* Wiley.
Morita, A. (1987) *The Sony Story.* Fontana.
Owen, H. (1985) *The Spirit of Organisation.* Wildwood.
Packard, V. (1960) *The Hidden Persuaders.* Penguin.
Peters, T. and Waterman, R. (1982) *In Search of Excellence.* Harper & Row.
Roddick, A. (1993) *Body and Soul: The Body Shop Story.* Ebery.
Semler, R. (1992) *Maverick.* Free Press.

## Books by Richard Pettinger

*Introduction to Management* (Macmillan – now Palgrave, 1994)
*Preparing and Handling Industrial Tribunal Cases* (Pitman, 1995)
*Introduction to Organisational Behaviour* (Macmillan, 1996)
*Introduction to Corporate Strategy* (Macmillan – now Palgrave, 1996)
*The Management of Discipline and Grievances* (NCVCCO, 1996)
*Introduction to Management* (2nd edition) (Macmillan – now Palgrave, 1996)
*Measuring Business and Managerial Performance* (STC Ltd, 1996)
*Human Resource Management of Public Services* (PhD Thesis, 1997)
*Marketing Construction* (Macmillan – now Palgrave, 1998)
*Managing the Flexible Workforce* (Cassell, 1998)
*The European Social Charter: A Manager's Guide* (Kogan Page, 1998)
*Mastering Basic Management* (Macmillan – now Palgrave, 1999)
*Effective Employee Relations* (Kogan Page, 1999)

*Investment Appraisal: The Business Case* (Macmillan – now Palgrave, 2000)
*Mastering Organisational Behaviour* (Macmillan – now Palgrave, 2000)
*The Future of Industrial Relations* (Cassell, 2000)
*Mastering the Skills of Management* (Macmillan – now Palgrave, 2000)

# ▌ ▼ Index